Teaming Up

Teaming Up

Making the Transition to a Self-Directed, Team-Based Organization

Darrel Ray

Howard Bronstein

McGraw-Hill, Inc.

New York   San Francisco   Washington, D.C.   Auckland   Bogotá
Caracas   Lisbon   London   Madrid   Mexico City   Milan
Montreal   New Delhi   San Juan   Singapore
Sydney   Tokyo   Toronto

Library of Congress Cataloging-in-Publication Data

Ray, Darrel.
    Teaming up : making the transition to a self-directed, team-based
organization / Darrel Ray, Howard Bronstein.
        p.   cm.
    Includes bibliographical references and index.
    ISBN 0-07-051646-4
    1. Self-directed work groups.   I. Bronstein, Howard F., date.
II. Title.
HD66.R3917   1995
685.4'02—dc20   94-33604
                                                                      CIP

Copyright © 1995 by Darrel Ray and Howard Bronstein. All rights
reserved. Printed in the United States of America. Except as permitted
under the United States Copyright Act of 1976, no part of this publication may be reproduced or distributed in any form or by any means, or
stored in a data base or retrieval system, without the prior written permission of the publisher.

    4 5 6 7 8 9 0   DOC/DOC   9 0 9 8

ISBN 0-07-051646-4

*The sponsoring editor for this book was James H. Bessent, Jr., the editing
supervisor was Stephen M. Smith, and the production supervisor was Pamela
A. Pelton. It was set in Palatino by McGraw-Hill's Professional Book Group
composition unit.*

Printed and bound by R. R. Donnelley & Sons Company.

 This book is printed on recycled, acid-free paper containing a
minimum of 50% recycled de-inked fiber.

Contents

Part 2   Designing for Self-Direction

Foreword

Most employees *manage*: a house with financial obligations; rearing and parenting children; founding, managing, and maintaining any number of social, religious, and activity-centered groups, institutions, and organizations. The fact that they do not do this *on the job* is more a statement of management assumptions than the motivation of workers. What we do at work was once an extention of what we do at home. With modern work organization there is complete separation of these two spheres. They need not be separated completely. People can still gain emotional gratification from their work, and the people they work with, just as they do from their family and neighbors. Integration of people into meaningful work groups completes the emotional cycle for many people and gives them the security and gratification that is necessary to obtain high productivity.

A basic assumption woven into this book is that *the art of managing is in empowering individuals and groups to do what they already do for themselves in their private lives.* We have built this book on real examples of the astounding productivity and efficiency gains yielded by the self-directed work teams structure. Some of the gains and improvements would be hard to believe if not described by the people and organizations that experienced these breakthrough benefits.

The success of work teams may be the result of several issues that organizations now face. Market forces may be squeezing employers so hard that the need for profound change in the way the workplace is managed is seen. Perhaps reformed regulations, altered laws, or challenging labor negotiations show the weaknesses of traditional management structures. In each organization that embraces self-management, someone steps up and says, "We must change." You will learn about several such people and their organizations in reading this book.

But the traditional, century-old system of managing employees, in which the daily evidence of waste and inefficiency is ignored, is still the norm. Organizational leaders are tempted to blame workers for problems. People will be laid off or transferred and managers reorganized to gain more control over failing enterprises. At times, contemporary organizations appear remarkably like the Soviet Union under Brezhnev rule. The worse things get, the tighter the controls—and the less is actually spoken about the true condition of the company.

The empowerment embraced in this book is in many ways an organizational *Glasnost*. Opening up corporate life to *all* so that workers can fully participate is, for most people, a wholly new way to work. But you will see just how well this new way to work works!

This is not the first book to suggest solutions to management morass. But the tendency has always been to seek out simple techniques to cure the ill instantly. It started with participative management in the 1970s, then quality circles and the One Minute Manager in the 1980s, and on to continuous improvement and total quality management in the 1990s. The diseases management faces—low productivity, declining morale, low company loyalty, poor quality—are largely self-inflicted and will not be cured by simple techniques. Rather, the following pages present a new management *technology*.

Like any technology, the whole is greater than the sum of its parts. For example, the invention of the steam engine was the impetus for developing railroad technology. The steam engine was simply a technique for moving rail stock. That technique has long since disappeared in favor of highly efficient and powerful diesel electric engines. As you read this book, you will see that the new management technology makes permanent and penetrating change possible. This is not so much a how-to book as it is about a technology which is rapidly developing and still growing. Some of the techniques described in this book may come or go over time, like the steam engine, but this emerging technology of human resource management will likely live longer than railroad technology.

Implementing self-directed teams requires the concurrent development of the human resource infrastructure which will support team behavior. Compensation, recognition systems, performance appraisal, new employee indoctrination, training systems, union-management relations, equipment acquisition, customer research, marketing, purchasing, accounting, and many more will all be dramatically affected by the new technology. As you explore the ideas in this book, the traditional way that we have lived and worked for a hundred years will become apparent for what it is—an outdated system designed to support an entirely different type of work behavior.

The old human resource technology was designed to control individuals (not groups), to manage people closely, and to ensure compliance with the centrally planned corporate economy. To simply designate teams and not change the old mindset is a formula for disaster. Where the new management technology has been put in place, teams have thrived. When the technology is not adopted, the team concept dies rapidly.

This lack of supporting human resource technology is the primary reason teams have had great difficulty getting a foothold in bureaucratic organizations such as large corporations, agencies, and government. These organizations have centrally administered reward and recognition systems and centrally planned economies, which are not easily changed at the local or team level. Unless the entire organization, from the top all the way down, moves to change its human resource technology, it is unlikely teams will add any great long-term value.

This book is about changing the patterns of communication in organizations. It is about teaching employees and managers how to take control of their own culture and destiny. It is about *Glasnost* in the workplace—treating teams and people like full partners in the business of doing business.

Darrel Ray, Ed.D.

Preface

This book's vision of self-directed work teams is presented in the same order that the transition to teams should be undertaken: *preparing*, *designing*, and *doing*. Darrel Ray has been the guiding force in literally hundreds of self-directed work teams in scores of organizations. Manufacturing and service companies, government and social service agencies, and *Fortune* 500 as well as small and moderate-size corporations in all sections of the country have provided Darrel opportunities to teach, and learn, about self-directed, team-based organizations. His experience—and that of the thousands of people he has worked with—is integrated into the fabric of this book.

The work he has done over the course of his career is the basis for all the concepts, skills, and techniques discussed in this book. Any exceptions to this rule will be noted at the time. Often, names, companies, positions, and other identifying data have been omitted in order to maintain client confidentiality. The intention is to share the vision of how an organization embraces and enacts a self-managed team management structure. Darrel's is surely not the only approach, but it is the only one presented in this book!

From the day we first discussed putting his life's work into this book, our mutual respect and interest in each other made for easy collaboration. We agreed that I would take his raw text, flush out research and interview possibilities, and build each chapter from there.

I knew about teams as "the marketing guy." I had read some of the articles about Darrel's work, had seen snippets of it in action, and was able to discuss it in general. But now I am a zealot. When an idea is given voice through strangers who are willing to share their enthusiasm, excitement, and yes, joy in their work, it can become profound.

In researching this book, I heard real stories of the transition to and the difficulties and rewards of self-directed work teams from the people who live in this structure. They showed me a practical way to unleash the vast potential of people in companies, organizations, offices, and workplaces *everywhere*. Workers want the opportunity to contribute to their organizations in ways not traditionally required, or even requested. There is no other structure for organizations which has the power of self-directed work teams.

Listen to the voices of this book. These are people who took time away from their teamwork to talk. According to these clarion voices, the program described in this book has brought a better quality of work life and increased productivity. For these folks, and their organizations, the transition to true teams has given them what *they* describe as the best work experience imaginable. Yes, there are challenges, and happiness will not be ubiquitous. But this system makes empowered employees and more effective organizations—and that is according to those who have experienced it.

The most expressive statement of the case for self-managed teams came from an interview with three people at Leader National Insurance. They sat by a speakerphone answering questions from a stranger about their life at work. They were open and honest, and explained that they liked things with teams more than without. Of everyone I talked to in the course of preparing this book, Kari Keys, in that conversation, best made the link between the practical and the potential, the most dramatic connection between the life of business and business of life. She said, "A year ago I would have said 'no way' to the team positions. Now I have a whole new outlook. This program with Darrel has helped me in my work life and personal life. I have learned more about me and how things can be if you just allow yourself."

Thank you, Kari, and all the other people who taught me an astonishing lesson: self-directed work teams *allow* everyone.

Darrel's proprietary program information and techniques are combined in this book with the best of current human resources theory. As a teacher, writer, management consultant, and president of ODT, Inc., I am experienced in making "expert information" available and useful to a wide array of clients. Together, we intend to make the reader a key client, to provide the reader with a comprehensive overview of all the information required to prepare, design, and do *Teaming Up: Making the Transition to a Self-Directed, Team-Based Organization*.

Howard Bronstein

Acknowledgments

Sir Isaac Newton once said, "If I have seen further, it is by standing on the shoulders of giants." Consultants rarely acknowledge how much they owe to their clients. There are many companies discussed in these pages, and there are many more from whom I have learned. I owe a debt of gratitude to those managers and CEOs who gave me the opportunities to observe and test methods of developing teams and empowering employees. When owners, CEOs, and managers truly believe that people are most important, they can make miracles happen with teams.

I owe a good deal to Barbara Wiley, friend and colleague, who first exposed me to teams and true employee empowerment when she was a team leader at the Gaines Dog Food plant in Topeka.

Thank you to many others who have been supportive in this project and provided valuable information and access: Pete Worth, vice president at Leader National Insurance; John Seymour, HR manager, and Joe Forlenza, vice president, at Standard Motor Products; Ernest Lewis, chairperson, UAW, Standard Motor Products, whose patience and wisdom have shown how important union leadership can be to the team concept; Tony Leonardi of Sara Lee Direct (formerly VP at Wolferman's, Inc.); Jack Padavano, vice president and general manager at Wolferman's, Inc.; Gary Henrie, director of South Central Counseling, a friend and colleague who has proven beyond a doubt that self-directed teams can and do work, even in mental health; Dr. Margaret Sears of Bell Atlantic, whose review of this book and feedback on the system have been invaluable; Janie Payne, pioneer of teams at Bell Atlantic; Cheryl Highwarden, my colleague, whose encouragement and feedback helped me refine many parts of the process; Dan Dana, whose friendship and counsel have been invaluable over the years; Fran, whose support and encouragement kept me writing; and my children Adrienne and Aaron, who can't quite figure out what I do, but think it is interesting anyway!

D.R.

First and most, I thank Dr. Darrel Ray, who believed in adding my voice to his work. I echo Darrel's thanks of those mentioned above, and also thank the people mentioned throughout the book, both those identified by name and those who chose anonymity. The key to this book was involving the people who have lived *Teaming Up*. For his technical guidance, for covering our office for me while I worked on this book, and for being my mentor and friend, I thank Bob Abramms. For her assistance, her support, and being the best partner I could have in this life, I thank my wife, Ellen E. Baer.

H.B.

Teaming Up

Introduction

The Fable

Once upon a time there was a CEO who became totally overwhelmed by the task of keeping his company competitive. Although he considered himself intelligent, well-informed, and competent, his job seemed more daunting each day. In his darker, more depressed moments, he worried about the very survival of his large company and the jobs of hundreds of employees, himself included.

But he thought, "This is part of my job, the reason I am the highest paid member of the firm. In fact, this is why it's so lonely at the top."

Now this executive, as often happens in fables, had "come up from the mailroom," and his rise to the executive suite had been a long, but steady, climb through the organization. His ambition had led him to greater responsibilities, increased rank, swelling stature, and of course, an escalating salary.

Along the way he invested some of his hard-earned money in real estate. He was landlord to about fifty middle-income tenants. He paid little attention to the people who lived in his buildings. The real estate was strictly investment and cash flow. The details were managed by a professional real estate company and its fee was a small price for hassle-free money. (Remember, this is a fable!)

One day our CEO got served with court papers by a tenant. It concerned something or other he thought the real estate manager had long since handled. The CEO turned it over to his attorney; the CEO was too busy running and worrying about his company. But, the local ordinances required the owner of record to answer the court summons.

So, off he went to court. On his way, he momentarily stopped worrying about competing in the global marketplace and wondered about the tenant who was hauling him into court. The court papers said something about tenants having been promised new appliances and that used ones had been substituted, despite a written addendum to the lease. Details, details. He was used to having others handle all that.

He went to court and lost. The judge ruled that the tenant had, in fact, proved that our CEO must provide the promised appliances. The tenant, without using a lawyer, had prepared a good and convincing case. She used the lease, letters, receipts, cost projections, and a sworn statement from a rental agent.

So our CEO fired the real estate manager and hired one who promised to keep promises. This little annoyance taken care of, he went back to running his company. He did his job, worrying about global competition and managing the directors, who manage the managers and supervisors, who manage the people who do the company's work.

A few weeks later he received a note from The Tenant, thanking him for his gracious response to the court orders. In the letter The Tenant mentioned that she was an employee of the CEO's corporation. "Surely The Tenant must be a manager in my company," thought the CEO. But he could not picture The Tenant in a company context. He recalled how in court The Tenant had mapped out exactly the difference in cost to run the used, less-efficient appliances compared to the new ones that had been promised. The promises made to The Tenant were documented and the CEO could only acquiesce to this well-executed deployment of facts, figures, and information.

"Clearly, this is the kind of person I need to help me manage and worry about this organization," said the CEO. He checked and found that The Tenant was a trusted, loyal employee, whose job was at the very bottom of the organizational chart. There were ten tiers of managers, directors, and supervisors between this CEO in his executive office and The Tenant's spot "on the front lines."

"Hmmmm," said the CEO, barely aware he had uttered any sound at all. He returned to his work and worry. But some time later the CEO found himself thinking about that very competent case against him, built up by an employee whose responsibility was to work, while others managed the work done by herself and her coworkers on the front lines. "Hmmmm," said the CEO. "Perhaps that tenant should be promoted to management."

Whack! A thought hit our CEO so sharply he felt it. "That tenant could be her own manager!" His head was flooded with new thoughts about his employees. He began to see them as tenants, and landlords, and homeowners, and managers of their family finances, and people who run churches, synagogues, and mosques, responsible parents who raise children and plan for their future, compassionate individuals who care for elderly or sick family members, consumers who make purchases small and large, people who pursue hobbies, and interests, and activities from acrobatics to zymurgy!

His head was spinning. "Maybe," he thought, "maybe there are other competent workers like The Tenant. Are there are other workers who really could be their own managers?"

Others had already answered his question: "*Yes*, most employees can manage their own work lives. And live happily ever after."

The moral:

> The traditional, paternalistic, and controlling management structure most organizations maintain with their employees can be successfully supplanted by self-directed work teams. Such a culture change yields incredible increases in efficiency, productivity, happiness, and the bottom line.

How significant a change does an organization want to consider? How ready is a company to take the concept behind the phrase "human resources" to a new and stunning level? How willing are employees to embrace empowerment? How prepared is anyone to become a member of a self-directed work team? (Read this book to mold an informed answer.)

Perhaps the moral of the above fable is quite a stretch! After all, life is never as simple as a fable. But the truth in a fable can be transferred to real life.

The Mission and Plan

The mission of this book is to provide a comprehensive overview of the self-directed work team implementation: what it really is, how to know if and when any organization is ready to consider this structure and style of managing, how it can be accomplished, how it cannot be accomplished, and who can help make it happen. This book will provide the skills required to live this dynamic and effective change.

An underlying assumption of this book is that most American management maintains an overly simplistic view of "human resources." Although there have been vast improvements in every kind of technology and "hardware," there have been only piecemeal advances in how people are managed.

American organizations are predominantly manipulated by autocratic and centrally controlled management structures. The traditional paternalistic systems inhibit self-management and confuse accountability. Organizations suffer from bureaucratic duels within that diminish and devalue whatever is produced. Fundamental change is necessary and difficult. Autocratic central control cannot survive self-directed work teams. The converse is also true; self-directed work teams will flounder, fail, and fade if subjected to central controls.

From the structure of the book to every point herein, this book takes the position that self-directed team-based management is the only reasonable way to administer organizations. This belief also compels a warning: the culture change to self-directed work teams is neither easy nor quick. Just reading this book will not empower you to implement this change.

This book *will* show the benefits of "teaming up," how to make the change, and how to maintain teams as a management structure. It presents a complete picture of how self-directed work teams can bring productivity, efficiency, profits, and happiness to your organization. But behaviors large and small must change throughout the organization. This change is a process, a journey. This book presents the map.

The journey to a true-team approach is comprised of many techniques, activities, and concepts. A Van Gogh painting is far more than the sum of its brushstrokes. The force of a classic painting comes from its total vision. Just so with the drama and power of the journey to a self-directed team-based organization. Each section "traveled," each chapter "traversed" is an integral part of the entire itinerary.

PART 1

Preparing for Self-Directed Work Teams

1
Why Self-Directed Teams!

Why Teams!

Should the title of this chapter contain a question mark? Many might think so. But it is omitted with thought and purpose. The expected question: "Why self-directed teams?" We are up front with our answer: *There is no stronger frame for an organization's structure than self-managed teams.* The exclamation point is inserted, the question mark eschewed, to emphasize the book's key position.

Throughout this book we will unabashedly declare our support for this concept. But we hold our position after more than a decade of work. Thus, readers are encouraged to ask that "Why?" question. As with any other concept making its way into the culture, people ask "Why?" even before they have a clear definition of self-directed team organization and what it would mean to them and their work. Before defining the fundamental terms, some startling facts to put "Why?" in a context:

- A data-entry unit of a credit card company instituted a structure of 12 self-managed teams. Once the teams were in place, the unit as a whole in a four-month period reduced customer response time from one hour to less than ten minutes. At the same time, customers were getting answers more than *six times* faster, and error rates plummeted from 3.5 percent to less than one-half of one percent.

- In a service department, the change to 22 self-managed teams brought the following results in eight months: productivity up 80% and quality measures up 120%.

- A glass-manufacturing company had four plants in the United States. It opened a fifth plant using self-managed teams from the first day of operation. By any measure, new plants, like new businesses, need a certain lead time between investment and profit. This fifth glass plant surpassed the others in profitability within five months, a strikingly quick result by most any standard.

- A specialty baking company was looking for ways to remain viable when a corporate purchase rendered it a small division of a business giant. After a chaotic year, they found self-managed teams mean that profits are up, manufacturing waste is down, safety has been improved, as has employee retention. A major segment of their business is mail-order catalog sales direct to consumers, and the winter holiday season accounts for 60 to 70% of the annual profit and sales. In the first year of the self-managed process, there was a complete turnaround in the ability to meet the demands of the holiday season. Holiday packages shipped at a 100% "on-time" level, instead of the approximately 60% "on-time" of the previous year— the last as a traditional manufacturing plant.

Put a more human face on the effects of making these kinds of strides in organizational output and increased effectiveness. In other words, it's swell to have things run more profitably, but what has happened to the people when organizations make basic structural changes?

What would people in your organization say if asked to comment on how effectively their work gets done? Here is a sample of employee comments from companies, after implementation of a change to self-directed work teams:

> It's improved pretty tremendously, because our business has grown. We are able to process our business much faster. We're able to take a lot more phone calls, and we feel like we've done a good job there. That is the area that the teams are most responsible for, and certainly are the people who deserve a lot of the credit.

> It's nice to see the paperwork, now you understand it. We know how we can get in and what we need to do at the beginning of the day and it's up to us to make that decision, it gives us responsibility.

> As far as managers, there's no one around. We just pretty much make our own decisions, as a team, in our department.

> In the past where you would start a new job, you had a manager— he'd come in and show you what to do. And then they pretty much just leave you to get it done. But in this concept [self-directed

teams], the team is responsible for training and they are always there, they're working right beside you, so I was able to learn the job faster and become productive a lot sooner for the company. It made me feel more at home.

Had a case just the other day where one team member went out of the way to do process on a whole operation—and then brought it in before the team. And it was just a magnificent amount of work done. I'd never seen anything like that—and it brought the team to understanding the process, and we immediately that day went through the process, eliminated steps we didn't need to do, and had productivity improvements this very same day.

There is a push, a new drive, that we didn't have before. To get the work out. To make sure it is correct, on time, and every criterion that we need to have, to make a good business.

These quotes are from real people who have experienced a change to self-directed teams in the companies and organizations which employ them. They may appear even more self-serving when it is revealed they were taken from interviews done when preparing a videotape on author Darrel Ray's work. Yes, in a format like this, statements that support the book's premise will be chosen. Rest assured, in future chapters the challenges, even problems and negative consequences, of adopting this vision will be explored. Now, with the above caveats out of the way, reconsider those quotes. These were things said by real people about the real work they do in the real places they work. These are the comments of people willing to be seen on film saying things about how their work is accomplished. What would the people in most organizations say about their work, their peers, their management?

The CEO in the Introduction's fable learned that someone from the "front lines" of his company, a "first-level employee" could manage her own work life. The CEO was used to a work society arranged with him at the top, and his top management responsible to him, and the middle managers responsible to them, and the supervisors reporting results and receiving direction from the managers, and the people on the front lines doing what everybody aforementioned figured their work to be! Jack Padovano, the general manager at Wolferman's, Inc., a specialty bakery, is quite direct in his description of the traditional organizational structure, at his company and in most contemporary workplaces. "Especially in manufacturing, it has been ruled as a dictatorship," says Padovano. Some may find this description a bit harsh, but it is more or less accurate for a great deal of contemporary organizational structure, although some may believe their organization to be run by (or may themselves happen to be) a kind and caring "dictator," sensitive to the needs of employees.

So what happens to companies when they abandon the old-style structure? How can anything be accomplished without managers and supervisors *In Charge?* Can what has always been done and known be replaced by another way? Ask "Why?" Why would an organization want to embrace this dramatic change? The simple answer to that question is because the new way is a better system that makes people more satisfied with the work they do, while that work is done more efficiently and effectively. Padovano and his organization have gone through the transition. His response to the "Why?" question: "Self-directed work teams are a tool to beat your competition and return more to stockholders through process improvements."

Group and Team Taxonomy

Team is one of those easy little words people use all the time, thus causing an expansion of its definition. How many managers say "My group is a real team" or "I believe in the team concept and that is how I run my organization?" Any grouping of people is not necessarily a team, nor is every team self-directed. Metaphors could be built from sports teams and symphonies, examples could be found of coaches and conductors who cover the gamut of styles from autocratic and dictatorial to democratic and self-directed. More goes into the development of a team environment than most managers dream. To set the record straight, the difference between a team and the more common *work group* will be clarified. The approach is to examine the continuum of group structures, moving from the traditional *leader-focused work group* to our vision of *self-led team*. (Because *team* is a widely used, often abused term, it is often not understood that *self-directed team* is a redundant expression. The premise here is that a *true team* must be self-directed. Unless noted, when we say "team" we are always referring to a self-directed true team.) With these distinctions clear, it will be possible to make an informed decision as to where on this continuum any organization fits, and whether it is time to adjust the organization's vision. Figure 1-1 summarizes characteristics of the five types that make up our "taxonomy" of groups.

Type I: Leader Centered/Leader Focused

The traditional work group is highly leader-dependent. It has a manager who is responsible for goal setting, decision making, making job

Group Type	I	II	III	IV	V
Production					
Assigns and schedules work hours	M	M	M (S)	M (S)	G
Assigns daily duties	M	M	M	S	G
May stop production for quality or safety problems	M	M (S)	G	M (S)	G
Keeps and charts daily records of production	M	M	G	G	G
Quality					
Measures quality and productivity	M	M	G	S	G
Charts and gives feedback on quality	M	M	G (S)	G	G
Sets quality goals	M	M	S	M (S)	G (S)
Goal setting/problem solving					
Sets monthly, quarterly & annual performance goals	M	M	G (M)	M (G)	G
Identifies problems/implements corrective action plans	M	M	G (S)	G	G
Determines critical success factors and monitors progress	M	M	G (S)	G (S)	G
Personnel Activities					
Hires new employees	M	M	M	M (S)	G (S)
Participates in appraisal process	M	M	S	M (S)	S (G)
Provides coaching and feedback	M	M	S	M	G (S)
Minor Discipline	M	M	M (S)	S	G
Major Discipline	M	M	M	M	S (M*)
Handles interpersonal issues and conflicts	M	M	M	M	G (S)
Assigns and approves overtime	M	M	M (S)	M (S)	G (S)
Recognizes employees	M	M	M (S)	G	G
Training					
Supervises training of new employees	M	M	G (S)	N/A	G
Identifies skills required for the task	M	M	G (S)	M	G (S)
Trains employees in new skills	S	S	S	S	G (S)
Planning and coordination					
Coordinates production with other groups	M	M	G (S)	G	G
Plans daily/weekly production	M	M	M (S)	G	G
Communicates and briefs other management levels	M	M	M (S)	S	G
Budgeting					
Develops department budget	M	M	M (S)	M	S
Monitors costs, waste, shrinkage against budget	M	M	M (S)	M (S)	G (S)
Responsible for safety					
Monitors safety and workplace hazards	M	M	G	N/A	G
Provides safety training	M	M	G (S)	N/A	G
Functional aspects of groups					
Work is segmented or functional	Yes	Yes	?	Yes/?	No
Easily affected by local management changes	Yes	Yes	Yes	Yes	No
Work is designed around customer requirements	No	No	Yes	Yes	Yes
Line worker involved in policy development	No	No	?/Yes	Yes	Yes

KEY

M= Management is primarily responsible
S= Management and the group share this function
G= Group is generally responsible for this
( )= Indicates in some companies or circumstances
* In Union Shops this may be a sole function of management

Figure 1-1 Characteristics of the five types of work groups.

assignments, performance appraisals, and, in many places, hiring and firing. The work is generally segmented into many different parts, and no one person really sees the entire process or finished product, except the manager. She is often a person who was promoted because of job performance, not necessarily because of the ability to manage a group of people effectively. She is often good at the work and knows more than most others about that work. She may even continue to do some parts of the production process.

She may involve the work group in decisions, ask them to do other things that a team might do, but she is still in charge, and if she leaves, the next manager can supervise in any manner he or she pleases. The group has only the authority the manager gives it. They are not seen as an entity which has a core identity independent of the manager. Decisions and assignments all go through the manager to some degree, and, more often than not, the manager can choose that degree. The group serves in an advisory capacity only, and then only at the behest of the manager. Regardless of how much she wants to think of her group as a team which works together, the inescapable fact remains—she is responsible.

This fact reveals the true nature of the work group. If the method of work is so dependent upon a single person, there is little hope of the group becoming a true team.

Type II: Leader Centered/Function Focused

These groups have historically functioned well in professional settings like advertising, engineering, law, and architecture. These groups have an appointed or assigned leader who coordinates and assigns work, does performance appraisals, and makes many of the major decisions, and who is himself a specialist. As an engineer, he may head an engineering group, but within that group there may be specialists in stress analysis, design, and architecture. He leads the team but does not exercise the day-to-day direction a more traditional manager (like one represented in Type I) would over a group, largely because he is not as knowledgeable about their fields.

This type of manager can be totally autocratic, as the traditional top-down model usually suggests, or he can be involving and open. Because of the creative and/or knowledge-based nature of the work, his style may not be quite as powerful an influence over the group as the traditional manager's. Nevertheless, if he left, the next manager or project leader could manage the group in a wholly different style. Once again, the work group is subject to whims or management style of a single individual. The cohesiveness of the group is dependent upon this one manager's skills and styles.

Type III: Leader Centered/Integrated-Task Focused

In this type of group, individuals are encouraged by management to make many of the on-line decisions and are often completely cross-trained to do the work of others in the group should the need arise. Management may set goals, apportion resources, and do performance appraisals. Much more employee involvement is encouraged than in the first two group types. There are group incentives and the group may attain a high degree of cohesiveness, especially when compared to group Types I and II. Japanese companies are often seen as having been highly successful with this method of management. Many North American companies have tried to emulate this system, using the concept of *total quality management*—often with limited success. This system depends upon large amounts of training in quality tools and problem solving. It is a much more sophisticated structure than that of Types I or II. The major limitation is that it does not fundamentally redesign the human infrastructure. It is largely skills- and process-centered, without giving sufficient attention to the human systems needed to support employee empowerment.

This Type III system works well when the organization shows high commitment to quality processes in every aspect of the business. This is accompanied by an environment where there is a well-engineered assembly line work process, a homogeneous work force who share similar personal and cultural goals, and labor-management relations which are carefully cultivated at every level. This system generally requires the same number of managers as the previous two types, but they can carry greater responsibility and accountability than traditional managers.

Type IV: Self-Led/Time and Task Focused

The fourth group is often found in project or task force environments. It is a group with a clearly defined charge or purpose, and is time-limited. Group members may have clearly defined functions, but boundaries become blurred as goal-directedness and time pressure dictate much of the group's experience.

The group may have a formal leader, but the necessarily high degree of team member cooperation and coordination often leaves the leader on the sidelines. No one person can possibly be involved in all the activity of the team.

This is the first level of true team, according to our imposed "self-directed" definition. The group has an identity independent of the leader, and its own set of agreed-upon norms and goals. Participants are often volunteers or hand-picked by management. The Type IV group most closely resembles the much-touted sports-model metaphor, in which highly skilled players commit to play together for the season to win a championship; when the season is over, the team may disband or change a great deal before the next season. Clear goals and well-understood time constraints tend to bring about cohesiveness in the Type IV group. But there are no procedures in place that encourage and reinforce team behavior after the project is finished.

Some companies in highly knowledge-based industries like oil exploration, engineering, and advertising enthusiastically make use of the Type IV group. These companies are continually configuring and reconfiguring groups to tackle different projects.

In bureaucratic organizations, the rules of the bureaucracy are often suspended for the Type IV group, so the team can get its defining task accomplished. It is taken out of the normal performance appraisal cycle, given access to special resources, and given accolades and rewards once the project is completed. There are often incentives for the group to perform on time and within budget. When the project is finished team members go back to the "same old system." This is often the same system which prevents such positive results from happening routinely.

Type V: Self-Led/Task Focused

Self-led work groups have common, group-determined goals, make most of the decisions about how to achieve the goal, and require little, if any, formal leadership in getting the work done. These groups are permanent, remaining together for years with only routine membership changes. They provide most of their own leadership, and managers function as outside resources. The group is responsible for a whole piece of work and is expected to measure its own performance, correct problems, and report on results directly to management.

The larger system encourages and rewards these team behaviors independent of the manager. Rewards are focused more on the group than the individual, and performance appraisals are done with major input from the team as well as internal and/or external customers. Management provides only major sanctions such as punitive discipline and the broadest outline of resource availability, leaving all other aspects of team functioning up to the team. In these groups members have high levels of training in one another's jobs and often are expected to rotate tasks according to the workload. Even when functional titles are maintained, the boundaries become fuzzy as members learn more and more about one another's specialties and cross over the boundaries to help.

Teams are much rarer than most managers realize. Teams require a fundamental system which supports their existence. This support system is often not in place, even when a "team concept" is desired and attempted.

In a team environment people *are not* managed, controlled, or supervised. They *are* led by their mutual vision of the organization's purpose and its goals. The foundation of a team environment is the organizationwide system which supports the teams. To know if a team environment exists, ask the question "Is there a system in place which rewards and reinforces team goal setting and decision making with minimal management contact?" In a true team environment, the manager no longer serves in a "snoopervisory" capacity.

What type of work group is right for an organization? Before commencing the transition to an organization based on self-directed teams, that question must be examined. To answer it is to explore what kind of work design will be most efficient. Teams in a self-directed model do not work everywhere. There are applications and environments where this model may even be detrimental. Traditional work designs may be quite appropriate in some situations, while a project team approach is best in other situations. Consider the guidelines outlined below to help decide what type of work group is right for the organization.

Type I work groups function well when the work is highly routine and unchanging in a low-wage, low-skill environment. When production techniques and technologies include a predominance of simple manufacturing processes and the worker has very little opportunity to add value or improve the process, Type I groups are often most effective. However, the need for central coordination along with the low skill level of the workers makes this a very slow and unresponsive type of group. When there are rapidly changing market conditions, this type of work design may be a liability to the organization.

Type II groups work well when knowledge, creativity, and central control are valued. The leader of the group provides control through job assignments, performance appraisal, and mentoring for junior members. In some organizations, a group of managers provide performance appraisals to group members. Managers become a valued resource within the organization and the choice of leader can often play a significant role in the failure or success of the particular group he or she leads. A senior group leader who has seen the process many times can provide valuable guidance for the group and provide a superior product. Some senior project leaders become legendary, and assignments to their groups are highly sought after by junior partners. In the absence of highly skilled senior leader types, or an unskilled, abrasive senior partner in the group with minimal leadership skills, the results can be disastrous. Much of the success of the group depends upon the skills of the leader rather than the creative ability of the group.

Type III groups succeed in a tightly engineered, assembly line atmosphere where individuals are empowered through quality circles or other involvement and problem-solving methods to improve the process and ensure high quality. Many North American companies have spent vast amounts of time and money attempting this method, often with very disappointing results. The reasons for this will be explored in Chapter 2.

Type IV groups work well when there is a critical planning task to be done in a finite period of time, for example, planning a new plant or redesigning an established product to reposition it in the marketplace. By definition, Type IV groups are groups with a limited life span. The leader tends to behave more like a coach. She may even change or disappear during the life of the project, yet the team continues to function, often achieving surprising results in an unusually short period of time. Some companies have institutionalized this method of group work very successfully, as in advertising and engineering.

Persons who work in these types of groups report over and over again that a real esprit de corps develops. Many managers have experienced this type of team over the course of their careers and recognize the power of this approach. Once they have this experience, they see it as powerful tool to be reproduced in every work group. Management attempts to reproduce it generally fail, because the larger organizational system does not support this type of behavior. Top management tends to use this type of group because the normal organizational structure cannot, or will not, allow enough creativity or rapid enough development. Group members are often handpicked and given exceptional authority and resources to accomplish their task. In other words, Type IV groups are often formed to break the rules for the greater good of the organization—but are expected to go back to following those same stifling rules when the project is finished.

Type V groups, the true teams, have been known to work well in some very unlikely environments. There is no chart or matrix that can match the work that needs to be done by a particular organization with the most appropriate management structure. This book is primarily about self-directed work teams, Type V groups, and will closely survey this type.

Type V—The True Team

All services which have traditionally been provided in an assembly fashion can be converted to teams quite profitably. When a series of processes can be integrated, such as insurance applications and claims, the Type V group works well. Other examples of work easily adapted to teams are manufacturing applications where a whole process can be designed for cells of 6 to 10 persons. Services in which there are complex procedures involved, as in credit card processing, also adapt well to true teams. In most cases, teams work well when integration of skills or knowledge is required to get the product to market or developed. Good examples of this are teams of marketing, engineering, and purchasing specialists; or oil and gas exploration with geologists, geophysicists, geochemists, engineers, and technicians all working together on the same team. Teams are also a natural response to continuous-process manufacturing situations like glass, chemicals, and food processing. Here, the team's ability to shift work rapidly from one part of the operation to another makes for much greater efficiencies.

The Type V group is known for its ability to respond rapidly to customer requirements and changing market conditions while being able to reduce turnaround time dramatically. Other books are available that document the increasing rate of change of the modern marketplace. Ask behemoths like General Motors and IBM how important the ability to respond in the marketplace is. To maintain a system of Type V groups requires a deep commitment to develop employees over long periods of time and must include sophisticated training processes in developing and maintaining these groups.

Where are teams least likely to succeed? In poor political climates and in places where the work is not conducive to teamwork, the Type V group is an inappropriate structure. *Political climate* means the methods of control and organization practiced by top management. Highly traditional, hierarchical organizations are poor ground in which to sow the seeds of teams regardless of the type of work. For reasons to be discussed in Chap. 2, much work needs to be done in these types of environments before teams can be considered. These organizations include large government agencies, monopoly utilities, and organizations where there will be regular major changes in leadership (elected offices, for example). Exceptions to these might be found where there is an exceptionally visionary leader, or external political or competitive pressures create the opportunity for rapid, permanent change.

The top management in small- to medium-sized family-owned businesses seems to have a great deal of trouble letting go of enough control to allow teams to function properly. Of course, there are some spectacular exceptions. The key is the family's ability to allow others some degree of control over their own work destiny.

There are some instances in which the actual types of work do not lend themselves easily to teams. One clear example would be over-the-road truck drivers. They are not sufficiently interdependent to create a team. It is less clear, however, about the structure for some others whose work is also transporting goods, such as direct store delivery drivers. Driver route sharing and team goal setting have been shown to be possible and successful within a single city or small geographical area. In general, work which spreads individuals over large geographical areas is less amenable to the team approach. Nationwide sales organizations are another example of difficult team structures, although such structures are feasible under the right circumstances. So, too, when the work is low wage and low skill with little opportunity for improvement, teams may not add value directly to the product or the processes. (That is not to eliminate the role of a team structure in enhancing morale and perhaps offering employees the opportunity to participate in accomplishing these tasks, no matter how "low" the level is perceived by some to be.)

Are Teams Appropriate for Your Organization?

Each of the five types of work groups we've described may have a place in the work world. There may even be a place for several different kinds of groups within the same organization. Type I groups are the most common and are greatly overused, most often without consideration of their value with respect to the goals of the organization and type of work. Type II groups have also been overused. Organizations with strong central controls and hierarchical relationships have a tendency to use Type II groups where a less structured Type IV or V might yield better results.

Type III groups, while very successful in Japan, have not done as well in the United States for several reasons. American management often does not have the patience, focus, or time to make these groups reality. The approach is not appropriate for much of the service sector, where direct contact with the customer requires fast response time and good judgment on the part of individuals. This requires that management find the fine balance between control and employee empowerment which comes with a strong relationship between company and employee. Our American heritage of belief in the sanctity of the individual, and all the laws and customs which underscore this belief, make teamwork for the good of the organization alone too often untenable in North America. Finally, it appears that the homogeneous culture of the Japanese makes large-group consensus around core corporate values much easier to obtain than in the diverse American culture with its many competing values and traditions.

Type IV groups are valuable but of limited usefulness, especially in day-to-day production and service providing. These time-focused groups are usually a key part of any quality process or special project which uses Type III groups. Type III groups are often taken off-line and put into Type IV groups to solve certain production or quality problems. But these are limited solutions to specific problems. When the challenges that face an organization send managers and executives off to find solutions and "fixes," that is what they find. When the problem is "solved," the solution is put aside, perhaps until the next challenge sends them scurrying.

Type V groups have been used least, so far, even though they have proven their value over many years and across many industries. The need for fundamental change in key organizational systems has left American managers reluctant to begin the long and involved process of converting to teams. With unrelenting pressure from the market and constantly changing customer requirements, Type V groups are becoming much more common. New and start-up organizations or industries, especially those where great competitive pressure is anticipated and customer responsiveness is essential, become natural breeding grounds for this true team structure.

The ability of self-led groups to deal effectively with challenges and changes, where team members share group goals and cooperate to serve the customer and the work day is filled with the activities necessary for the team to accomplish its work—this is the environment more and more organizations are turning to for their success, as well as their survival.

Those who believe strongly in the efficacy of organizations which have made the transition to a structure based on self-directed teams are encouraged to keep reading. Those less sure where on the group continuum their organization is—or should be—are encouraged to take the time to use the above taxonomy of groups. Identify the predominant types of groups in your organization. Are these the types of groups which will keep the organization competitive in the future?

This book will detail a successful structure where Type V true teams are spawned, supported, and sustained.

2
The Concept of Self-Management

Definition of Self-Directed Teams

The explosion of technology is today accepted as commonplace. In all aspects of life, equipment, techniques, and concepts that are increasing speed, efficiency, and production capacity proliferate. From the steam engine to magnetic levitation, from the telegraph to the cellular telephone, from the mechanical adding machine to virtual reality (and all the mainframe and personal computers it took to get there), from the first assembly line to self-directed teams...But wait. Which one of those phrases does not belong in that list?

The truth is that only a small percentage of organizations have adopted any type of organizational structure that could be considered an improvement in efficiency and productivity. *Most modern organizations are using the hard technology of the next century with the human resource technology of the last century.* There may be other forward-looking systems of human resource management, although the focus here is only on self-directed teams. What is clear is that a change to any such system is going to be a *big* change. How does an organization make any dramatic change in the way it functions? How does an organization decide even to contemplate a new structure like true teams?

The answer to that question begins with the definition: A *self-directed work team* is a group of interdependent, highly trained employees who are responsible for managing themselves and the work they do. They set their own goals, in cooperation with management, and the team plans how to achieve those goals and how their work is to be accomplished. The central organizing fact of a team is that it has a common purpose and measurable goals for which the team can be held accountable, independent of its individual members. Employees on a self-directed team handle a wide array of functions and work with a minimum of direct supervision.

"It may be simple...but that does not mean it is necessarily easy," explains Barbara Wiley. As a team developer at Quaker Oats, she has lived the experience of making this transition to self-managed teams. She adds, "It is like potty training—simple does not mean easy!" She advises keeping a sense of humor and even expecting little thanks for the efforts of driving the change. While she and we have different styles in accomplishing the same end, we have worked together enough to know that we concur on the big picture. Wiley wisely takes her cue from the Hippocratic Oath that doctors take when she says that the first rule for anyone in her position is "Do no harm." The larger the change human beings consider, the more discomfort that change can generate. Wiley's advice is well taken by anyone active in considering, examining, or actually making a change in organizational structure.

Wiley is also correct when she says that the agent of change must begin by listening to the people of the organization. "Listen to the language, listen to their pronouns and the context in which things are said," she stresses.

There are right and wrong reasons for converting to self-directed teams. A careful examination of organizational motives will tell whether such a conversion is likely to be successfully implemented. This examination can only begin by listening to the voices within an organization. There must be a structure to this listening that will support a decision, regardless of what that final decision turns out to be. The first step is a *readiness review*. Is any organization ready for teams? Perhaps some amount of preparation is appropriate. Think of the readiness review as a checklist, like the one an airline pilot goes through before taking off. Listening is the method of going over that list. To continue the metaphor, the pilot is looking at, examining, listening *to* the airplane to ascertain its flight readiness. At the end of the pilot's process, the plane usually goes on its way. But if a problem, challenge, or contraindication is "heard," the adjustments and repairs are made, or the flight is canceled. The point to remember: no trip is begun without some questions being asked—and answered.

The questions to be asked are in the context of the above definition of a self-directed work team. This definition also fits the Type V group (self-led/task focused) discussed in Chap. 1. For an organization to make the transformation to self-directed work teams, major system changes in the organization are needed. True teams require these fundamental changes to ensure their long-term survival. These system changes cannot, and will not, come overnight. Switching metaphors from a plane to a supertanker, one can see how difficult the task of change can be. Like a supertanker at sea in a storm, the ship must be turned slowly and with great care into the wind or it may get out of control, even capsize. Sea captains will say, as will airplane pilots, that they have learned to listen to their ships and planes and to the environs that surround their journeys.

To sum up, be aware of the following:

- Simple is not the same as easy.
- Championing the change to self-directed teams may not make one popular.
- Do no harm.
- Listen well.

Ready for the review?

Readiness Review

The readiness review begins by looking at the reasons for making the transformation to self-directed work teams. There are right and wrong reasons for converting to self-directed teams. A careful examination of the organization's motives will tell whether that organization is likely to succeed, or not, in the implementation process.

Right reasons for converting an organization to teams are:

1. Total quality management efforts and employee involvement processes have shown the power of teamwork. People in the organization speak of these team efforts in favorable language and they engender more honest effort than discomfort. The organization has used Type IV groups (Self-led/time and task focused) many times and sees very positive results. Those results are referred to in words and actions that are positive and seem, by most of the organization's members, to be well received. An even higher level of employee involvement will reap greater rewards in customer responsiveness and organizational efficiency.

2. Competition has increased in the industry. The old command-and-control methods using Type I or II groups (leader centered/leader focused and leader centered/function focused, respectively) are too slow and cumbersome to effectively manage what the organization

wants to accomplish. Type V groups will give greater flexibility in responding to customers, constituents, and markets.

3. There is a great deal of potential in the work force that is being wasted or used inefficiently. This is frustrating to the work force because it wishes to produce a quality product and/or service as much as management does. The language used and the things said are about wanting to do more, be accountable for more, have a greater say in how their work is accomplished. Type V groups will help employees focus their efforts on value-added activities and take greater pride as they gain more control over the work they do. True teams will also give increased ownership in the products they make and the processes by which those products (or services) are created. Listen to the organization's many voices. Are the sounds of potential teams heard?

4. There is a visible need for stronger management-employee partnership. Can an emphasis on win-win cooperation, while reducing or eliminating adversarial labor-management relationships, be realized? If vast amounts of energy are focused on fighting among organization members, competitors gain a great advantage in the marketplace. Can management and labor find a way to work together toward accomplishing the work of the organization? If the answer seems to be yes, self-directed teams could be that new way.

The above are all strong reasons for making the change. More important, they are positive reasons, based on affirmative judgments, that suggest a proactive course of action. Any major change gains momentum if an organization and its employees all believe the change is being made for positive reasons. When the discomfort and challenges this change can bring are viewed in the light of the above, solutions can be found that assure everyone's benefit.

Just as there are positive, proactive, and *right* reasons for an organization to "team up," there are negative, reactionary, and wrong reasons for converting to teams.

Wrong reasons for converting to teams are:

1. The organization has downsized and there are not enough supervisors to supervise everyone. Thinking self-directed teams are an appropriate response to personnel shortfalls is the ultimate in organizational shortsightedness. With this attitude, it is impossible to create the systems in the organization which are needed to support teams, and an organization with this attitude which plunges into a true-team structure has a very high probability of failure. As subsequent chapters will show, the transition to self-managed teams requires a massive change in the subsystems of the organization; otherwise the teams will

rapidly wither and die on the vine. This will leave veteran managers with twice as much work as they had before!

2. "The boss," "headquarters," or "the corporate executives" told us to start self-directed work teams. A company president had given this directive to all his vice-presidents. As the VPs were going about implementing teams, chaos was breaking out throughout the organization, and middle managers were found to be actively undermining the process out of fear of losing their jobs. While teams were being formed by assigning people to them, there was no effort to effectively train the teams, or management, in how to use the new system. Worst of all, the president's own behaviors continued to be highly autocratic. This was the leader modeling the opposite behaviors to effective teamwork, which he expected of others. Most often, when there is a corporate edict, it comes from excitement over the prospect of increased productivity and with little thought given to the major changes actually required to get the increase.

3. The organization's management believes its people are already self-directed. With some minor changes it is believed it can move into self-directed work teams. In virtually every case where managers, without systemwide support, believe they have true teams, they are wrong. What they usually have is nothing more than a Type I (leader centered/leader focused) or Type II (leader centered/function focused) work group. While working with a major utility, the manager invited a readiness review, believing his group was primed for self-directed teams. Upon careful examination, it was found that there was a profoundly negative atmosphere in which results were achieved through highly structured and tightly controlled Type I groups. Virtually unbeknownst to the manager, the degree of mistrust and anger in the organization's environment precluded any attempt to form self-directed teams. This came as a complete surprise to the manager, as it does to many. Greater trust and a better dialogue between management and employees must be established as part of the structure to support the transition to teams.

4. The transition to teams may prevent unionization. Of all the wrong reasons, this one is the most sinister and can actually get the company into major legal troubles. If an organization seems fearful of unionization, there are issues that must be resolved before self-directed teams can be considered. Any effort to improve quality and market competitiveness will require the best of both labor and management. The energy expended in labor-management conflict puts a severe strain on the organization's ability to prepare, design, and support self-directed teams. Without positive labor relations before, an even

worse climate will be the result of an attempt to try self-directed work teams. Employees will see it for what it is—an attempt to preclude their right to collective bargaining. Establish strong, positive management-employee relationships which can be independently documented before beginning the team process. The transition will not be possible without them.

If any of the "right reasons" seems to fit an organization, then it is well positioned to begin the implementation of a self-directed work team structure. If any of the "wrong reasons" is a match, an organization is not ready to proceed. We emphasize that an organization unready for this substantial change will see real harm to the organization if it proceeds with self-directed teams.

The readiness review continues with an investigation of positive and negative signs within organizations which are good predictors of future success or failure. Note that the "rules" will not be so hard and fast here. For the right and wrong reasons listed above, a single positive means to consider proceeding and the presence of a single negative means "Halt." The situation is not as clear-cut in the case of the positive and negative indicators. The positive indicators show readiness to make a change; the negative indicators are organizational caution signals.

Positive indicators include:

- A recent history (at least a year) of positive and improving labor relations as documented by some reliable independent survey or assessment. Independent documentation is important. Most management teams have little idea about the real perceptions of the work force. Such things as decreasing grievances or improvement on an independent survey would help in assessing this area. Companies which are enjoying improving labor relations are also building greater trust and a fund of goodwill to draw upon when converting to teams.

- A history of management flexibility and willingness to implement employee empowerment processes (e.g., quality circles, total quality management) with objective results.

- A history of management ability to stick with a process for long periods of time (e.g., just-in-time manufacturing, problem-solving teams, quarterly employee meetings with top managers) until results are seen. Management which has a reputation for hopping on every bandwagon will not be taken seriously by the work force. This "flavor of the month" approach to change is deadly to long-term improvements because it inoculates the work force against any real efforts to improve the system.

- A strong new management team at the local level which has no history with the work force and has previously demonstrated skills in employee involvement processes. The work force is generally willing to give a new management team the benefit of the doubt if it moves methodically in the direction of teams while listening to, and consulting closely with, the work force.

- An already functioning "pay for performance," "pay for knowledge," or "skill-based" compensation system. Having such systems already in place makes it easier to adjust the rewards system to reinforce the new team behaviors early in the process. It is also a sign that management is aware of the shortcomings of traditional pay systems and has taken steps to bring pay in line with corporate team philosophy.

- A management group which has consistently involved the work force in strategic planning, workplace training, or multilevel problem solving. When management systematically gets workers in the same room with management to solve problems and make plans, there is an opportunity for growing trust and understanding which will make the transition to teams much smoother.

Negative indicators include:

- A continuing history of management-labor strife. Mutual trust and goodwill are essential in making the team transition as smooth as possible. Management cannot get employee involvement, trust, and "buy-in" by rule, edict, or coercion. If there is labor strife, work on fixing it now, before moving on to teams.

- A recent downsizing. Downsizing often leaves middle managers with the suspicion that the company is looking for ways to eliminate jobs—their jobs. Middle management will be a key ally in the process of changing to self-directed teams. If these managers are mistrustful, it will make the transition that much more difficult.

- A history of top-management inability to stay focused on a change process long enough to see results (that "flavor of the month" approach). The best indicator of future behavior is past behavior. If management has been unfocused and flighty in the past, it is likely to be the same with self-directed teams, jumping ship as soon as problems are encountered.

- Key local top managers are known by the work force to be unsupportive of employee involvement. The employees know these individuals well, most often unlike management. Management may even deny that such people are present and that they will exhibit any destructive behaviors. But employees are reluctant to follow corporate leadership if their own manager harbors animosity towards the process. Employees can also be placed in uncomfortable and even untenable situations, caught between corporate directives and the real-life sabotage they see from these well-known managers.

- Strong objections by corporate headquarters to allocating the full estimated resources required to implement self-directed work teams successfully. In the first two years of preparation, design, and implementation, the transition to true teams is expensive and time-consuming. If top management seems reluctant to allocate the resources, great care should be taken in proceeding. High-performance teams do not come on a shoestring budget. Even worse, if halfway into the process the corporate headquarters cuts resources, it will leave employees with a very cynical view of management. The next change will be many times harder and more expensive, if even possible, to achieve.

- Weak or nonsupportive human resources or labor relations departments. These two groups generally have tremendous power over employee involvement processes, especially labor relations. Bring them on board early and keep them posted on progress. If doing this seems problematic, it is a true negative indicator.

Do the positive indicators seem to ring true for the organization, or are the negative indicators closer to life in its workplace? If three or four of the positive indicators are present and none of the negative, there is a strong likelihood the organization is ready to go to the next steps in implementation of self-directed teams. If even one of the negative indicators is present, caution is advised. Addressing the issues presented in the negative indicators may well be a sound decision for the organization in general. It is crucial in considering a change in structure like the one to Type V teams. Careful planning, anticipation of problems, and the means to find solutions are necessary precursors that will pay off in the long run.

Wrong reasons and negative indicators are stop signs on the road to self-directed teams. Like their traffic counterparts, they really mean stop, examine the situation, and then proceed only when safe. The difference between the traffic sign and an organizational sign is that, in traffic, one need wait only seconds, or at worst, minutes. In the organization, waiting for these adverse reasons and unfavorable indicators to pass, as they do when you are driving, is folly at best. Honestly looking at the results of this readiness review should give any organization additional information about itself. Whether or not the decision is made to implement a transition, it should use this information. The simple, though not easy advice: address and ameliorate the negative; reward and accentuate the positive.

To repeat, if an honest assessment of an organization reveals no wrong reasons or negatives, and several right reasons and positives present, the transition to teams can be considered. If not, the help required may be beyond the scope of this text. Remember, the organization has just encountered a stop sign.

The New Human Infrastructure

Most organizations are not as ready as they think for the transition to teams. To help prepare for the change, a transition strategy has been devised which at once plows the ground and plants the seeds of involvement without disrupting the flow of the organization. Whether implementing self-directed work teams or a system using Type III groups (leader centered/integrated-task focus), a new and supportive human infrastructure must be in place before a system for quality can take hold. Chapter 4 will look more closely at "new ways to work" which can be implemented, and in fact must be implemented, prior to the transition to teams. Open meetings and leadership rotation are examples of the kind of management changes and new human infrastructure that support employee empowerment of all kinds.

Employee empowerment is more than a fad, buzzword, or current hip corporate jargon. The underlying point of the fable and moral in the Introduction reflects the belief that a management system that allows employees who do the work to manage how that work gets accomplished is crucial. Simple, yes. Easy, no! Employee empowerment, however it is structured, presented, and managed, is a good thing in most organizations at most times. To make this happen, the new human infrastructure is required within the organization.

> We define *human infrastructure* here as: the system of human interaction and communication within an organization. The human infrastructure is concerned with everything from how gossip is used in the system to how performance appraisals are conducted. It includes how meetings are run and who is kept informed of changes and how they are informed.

In the next two chapters, and throughout this book, much of the discussion is focused on how to realign an organization's human infrastructure in a way that supports employee empowerment and a team structure. But before looking at, and learning, new skills in organizing the human infrastructure, a bit more examination must take place. Those who run companies, agencies, and enterprises of all kinds are usually quite certain in their beliefs about their work force. Most managers and executives think they know what they need in order to assess their work force, the climate that exists between themselves and that work force, and even how that work force perceives itself and the management.

Most organizations are structured in ways that send a single clear message. That message is most often the primary difficulty management faces as it makes the transition to true employee involvement. That problem is a profound lack of trust in the ranks of the employees. Adversarial management styles have given employees very little reason to trust management. On any given day, stories appear in local media about the mistreatment of employees or arbitrary decisions by local managers which profoundly affect people's lives. Most employees have many personal experiences of apparently arbitrary and unreasonable behavior by management. Whether the unreasonableness is real or imagined, these experiences affect the level of trust between management and employees.

Look at employee trust as a bank account into which management makes deposits and from which it makes withdrawals. In the perception of employees, management tends to make meager deposits—but regular, substantial withdrawals. From the employees' point of view, management rarely recognizes, listens to, or rewards them. From management's point of view, they give what they can but have many more problems to worry about besides "rewarding or recognizing employees." The effort management makes towards employee recognition and involvement seems like a major deposit from the managers' perspective. The same effort looks like spare change to employees. The trust-building structures detailed in Chap. 4 can radically change these perceptions of both sides and contribute to a rapid and smooth transition to an empowered workplace. These are the tools an organization can use to more successfully manage the "trust accounts" of its members.

But first, really consider that tough organizational examination previously discussed. Is the organization's commitment to empowering employees genuine? Did discussion of these questions, reasons, and indicators take place with others in the organization? Do these "others" represent all of the varied voices who make up the organization? An organization must honestly look at these questions before it can proceed. If the organization is ready—or if the reader just wants to see what happens next—read on.

3

Top Management and Self-Direction

Analyzing Systems

At first glance, the emphatic assertion with which we begin this chapter may seem to introduce a jarring juxtaposition. The emphasis chronically, constantly, and continually placed on employee empowerment may seem at odds with this statement, which is: *The transition to teams must begin with upper management.*

The top level of management in any organization is *the only* place a transition this dramatic and encompassing can begin. Just as it is true that employee empowerment is the key to making true teams in an organization, it is also true that only those at the top of an organization can put a process this significant into action. This can alter the work life of everyone in the organization, but often those at the top experience the greatest change in their day-to-day activities, as well as their overall stature in an organization. (This issue will be discussed in greater detail later.) The change can be inspired by anyone and championed by everyone—but it can only begin when those at the top begin it. As mentioned previously, organizations operate with the newest in technology *except* when it comes to human infrastructure.

As the CEO in the fable learned, each employee is a successful manager at something. Many manage their finances, own a house and pay the mortgage on time, buy cars, bear and raise children, serve on boards of all manner of religious and civic organizations, run scout troops and bowling and softball leagues, organize fundraisers, and on and on with a literally endless list of other management duties. What prevents workers from using this same creativity and energy in their work?

Although few can even recall his name, most Americans remember when a Japanese prime minister made the comment that American workers are lazy. At that same time that inflammatory statement made the headlines, American workers were producing world-class products in companies owned by the Japanese themselves in the Nissan plant in Tennessee and Honda plant in Ohio. Americans were also producing world-class products in American-owned companies at Gaines Dog Food in Topeka, Kansas, and the Saturn automobile plant in Smyrna, Tennessee, and a host of other places. The issue is not which workers are more industrious, Japanese or American. Rather the critical issue, often unseen in current discussions, is: What system best utilizes the full resources of employees? American workers are not lazy and neither are their managers. But both are laboring under a system of human resource management which is antiquated, and most often punishing to those who must work within it.

Before any discussion of the change to a new technology in human infrastructure, the current technology must be examined. Here is an example that could come from a corporation, office, factory, organization, agency, government department—anywhere a group of people join together to accomplish work. The example could have been taken from experience in the armed forces, manufacturing, government, or not-for-profit sector. The example institution is an insurance company, but the universality of the situation is readily apparent. Remember, the focus is on examining the traditional—and for most organizations, current—technology in managing human infrastructure. Then things can be changed.

This insurance company is one in which applications come in for processing every day. The company is organized into Type I, leader-dependent groups (leader centered/leader focused). One person picks up the mail and sorts it, passing appropriate heaps of mail to four other people, each of whom has a very specific task to do in checking and approving each application. If all find the application correct, an underwriter examines the application and determines if it is acceptable and under what conditions. The application is then sent to a manager for approval and back to one of the original four clerks for filing, or inputting, to the computer system. In all, it takes one to two weeks for the entire process to be completed.

If an insurance agent calls this office to ask a question, the person who answers the phone rarely knows the answer, or, often more frustrating, is not authorized to give an answer. The agent is put on hold while the clerk who answered the phone puts down whatever work he or she was attending to and searches for the one person who might know the answer. If the answer-holder cannot be found, a message has to be taken with the promise that someone will call the agent back in a day or two.

What happens if one person in this office is sick, quits, or is in a meeting? The work assigned to that person does not get done. Upon coming back, the person might ask for help in attending to his or her swelling workload. But everyone else is busy, or at least acting busy so they will not be assigned more work.

This system has many punishments and few rewards for coordinating work activity with others in the office. Since only the underwriter is "trained" in underwriting, this position is a natural location for a bottleneck. For the work of this office to be accomplished, it must pass through the underwriter's hands. Other members of the office, the work group, may actually have a light load but would not be allowed to do this job. *Not allowed* here means that by tradition, convention, rule, or regulation, the work has been structured in such a way that it is often dictated to employees what they can and cannot do in accomplishing their work. Does any of this sound familiar?

Back in the example office, imagine that one of the clerks, Terry, was absent yesterday. Consequently, she will be loaded with work today; that mail comes in each day, regardless of how the human infrastructure works. Also imagine that Terry asks for help from her supervisor, Leslie. What consequences could this have? Before reading the list below, try and transpose this example to any office, work group, or organization you are familiar with. What list of consequences would you foresee there? One clue: the authors' list numbered eight consequences, and they all have at least one common element.

1. Leslie might think Terry is not able to handle her job.

2. The rest of the group might feel resentful toward both Terry and Leslie if they are asked to do part of Terry's job.

3. If Leslie is too busy, the work might never get reassigned, leaving Terry holding the bag.

4. If someone should volunteer to help Terry, Leslie might think that individual does not have enough work to do and assign that person more tomorrow.

5. If nothing is done to help Terry, the whole group gets behind in its work; Terry may begin to get blamed.

6. In order to get her work done, Terry may have to work overtime, adding to overhead costs.

7. Terry will work quickly, which usually means less accurately; she will make more mistakes than usual, causing others extra work in

correcting those mistakes and adding to resentment felt in the office.

8. If someone should quietly go over and help Terry, he or she might get behind in his or her work while also risking being perceived as socializing on the job, not to mention the expended anxiety over those perceptions.

Is the common element visible? While there may be others, the most significant is that no good or positive outcome can come from any of these consequences. None of the eight can be construed as constructive, in any reasonable light. If implemented, any of them will make the work of the office more difficult to accomplish. This situation is "normal" in that it occurs in one form or another in organizations across the land. Supervisors and employees are faced with a system and structure that has inefficiency and waste of effort built in, institutionalized, even sanctioned and sometimes sanctified. At least, those are the messages most often sent in the instructions and rewards most employees face.

Look at the instructions and rewards present in the example office above and ask "How closely does this example match the organization I am examining?"

There are so many more negative consequences for the employees in this office, and in many organizations. Contrary to management's beliefs, this system has little authentic accountability. Instead it has a system of blame. Whenever something goes wrong, someone is going to get blamed. The supervisor will identify a weak spot and try to correct the problem with coaching, training, discipline, or worse. And the employees who suffer in this system will tend to blame the supervisor.

Returning to the specifics of the example, to better understand who is truly to blame, do a simple experiment. Identify the problem, Terry in this case. Fire Terry and hire someone else with superb skills. Does this solve the problem? Perhaps some think Leslie is the problem. Fire Leslie and hire a super supervisor. Does this solve the problem? In both cases it was never the people who were the problem, but the system which punished people for doing what they could do quite well, if organized properly. In any Type I group, a simple work-flow analysis will reveal waste and inefficiency in every corner. In such examinations, it is *always* found to be the case.

In several analyses done by one of the authors (Darrel Ray) in both service and manufacturing organizations, he has documented over 80 percent wasted time in these groups. In the insurance company on which the example above is based, the group was under statutory limits of 15 days to process claims. Due to marketing initiatives that were quite successful, its work load had doubled over a three-month period. The system became overloaded. Overtime skyrocketed. Temporary employees were brought in. Still, the backlog of applications remained above 30 days. Yet, when an analysis of value-added time was done with the group, its own analysis was in excess of 96 percent waste. (For those unfamiliar with the term, *value-added time* is a self-defining concept. It is the time it takes to add value, or accomplish some part of the task in creating the product or providing the service, as it passes through whatever system an organization has chosen to manage its work.)

The insurance office could not possibly catch up. This office is not fictional. It is a client organization that made the transition from Type I groups to a true Type V team design implementing much of what you will read about herein. Once in place, the team was able to gain control and reduce the turnaround time to less than seven days. Now the group routinely does 2 to 4 times the work it could accomplish as a Type I group. In less than one-fourth the time and with much higher quality, it is able to accomplish what it did before the transition to a true team.

The insurance company's old human infrastructure, that found in Type I groups, rewarded inefficiency and punished efficiency. Only when the organizational technology was completely changed could the human beings in the system use their full capacity to accomplish the work they knew how to do. And this change, like most others, could only be accomplished systemwide when the upper management approved the necessary resources of time and training. Even if the people in the office could see and plan the transition, implementing it could only be done from the highest levels of the organization. Soon, the special challenges faced by managers and supervisors in the transition to teams will be contemplated. What we want to reemphasize here is the importance of upper-management belief in this process before it can take hold throughout an organization. Again: no systemwide change can take place without upper management's blessing and full support.

This is only on the third chapter, and still the book is just looking at the process. Think about all the questions and challenges so far. When looking at the steps that can be taken before the transition begins and when it commences, as well as the ground rules for living with it, people must engage in honest feedback about how to accomplish the work. It takes planning and training. But the process can only begin when those at the top of an organization agree.

There is more that must be considered by upper management, and any organization, before contemplating this type of change. Understanding systems and their impact on human behavior is critical when designing the self-directed team environment. Those looking into a true team must consider the different types of conflict which exist in organizations. We will do this in the next section.

Conflicts: System vs. Personality

System conflict is conflict whose fundamental cause is in the manner in which a system is configured. In other words, the human infrastructure is set up to monitor and control employee behavior rather than support task- and group-focused solutions to accomplishing work. A brief mental exercise can help one decide if one is in the midst of a system conflict. Imagine that you fire the person who is apparently "at fault," and hire a new person. If the problem reoccurs in some way, then it is probably caused by a system conflict.

Look at the example office again. If the supervisor Leslie is fired, and a new person hired, the problem will probably be back in a short time. What would, or could, the new person do to change *the way in which the work is accomplished?* The conflict is caused, not by Leslie, but by the manner in which this system is configured. Leslie did not create this system; Leslie only lives in it. In this system Leslie is responsible for making work assignments and making sure people do their job. The supervisor has guidelines about who is authorized to do certain tasks and some things can only be done by a supervisor. The entire system is based upon a fundamental assumption that people cannot be trusted to do the work. The system builds in conflict because it requires someone with greater authority to coordinate that work.

System conflicts are very common. In fact, most of the conflicts seen in any organization are largely system conflicts. Unfortunately, managers misdiagnose these conflicts and assume they are personality conflicts. *Personality conflicts* are based upon personality dysfunction, generally resolvable only with professional intervention. These conflicts may include those that arise because of psychological, substance abuse, or social problems of individuals in the workplace. While many people have a variety of emotional and behavioral problems, they do not manifest themselves in the workplace nearly as often as managers believe. When managers misdiagnose system conflicts as personality conflicts, they will intervene in inappropriate ways.

A system conflict can only be resolved in one way—by redesigning the system. A personality conflict requires individual intervention. Unfortunately, it is much easier to coach, counsel, fire, or discipline individuals than it is to change the system which caused the conflict. When an accountant gets in conflict with a purchasing manager, it is generally because they have conflicting goals, not because their personalities don't mesh. When the Labor Relations Department gets in conflict with a union vice president, it is the system which should be implicated, not the particular individuals. Of course, an unskilled labor relations manager can certainly make things worse, but replacing that manager will not make the conflict go away entirely. Over and over again, managers try to blame individuals, when it is the system that has created and perpetuated the conflict.

Endemic and Symbiotic System Conflicts

There are two kinds of system conflicts. The first is *endemic conflict*, sometimes referred to as "cats versus dogs." This is conflict which is rooted in the design of the interactions and work flow between two people or groups. Conflicts between sales and operations, purchasing and accounting, management and employees, maintenance and machine operators....Fill in a pair or two from any organization. Like cats and dogs, they seem to be natural adversaries, enemies for reasons that seem to make sense to those involved, even though no one recalls the enmity's source. They are not. In order for cats and dogs to get along, one need only raise them together. When introduced as puppy to kitten, they will live quite peacefully together.

Endemic problems in an organization require the same treatment. Sales and operations each have different goals and are rewarded for meeting those goals. Sales is rewarded for making sales; if that means promising an unrealistic time line, they will do it. Operations is rewarded for producing a quality product within a specified time; deviations from that time frame mean added costs and quality problems. And the overall system, the human infrastructure, more often than not supports the conflict.

The solution to endemic conflicts is to force these groups to live together and set mutually agreeable goals. In designing a self-directed work environment, teams and other groups should be configured in such a way that the cats and dogs are *forced* to live together. It can, and does, work.

In a manufacturing plant, the maintenance group was reassigned to teams on the production floor. After all, it is the production crews which actually are the internal customers of maintenance. Yet they were always complaining about one another. When a team structure was implemented, one of the design decisions was to assign maintenance personnel to the production groups. With the new design, downtime was reduced by half within a matter of months. Preventive maintenance became much more important in the eyes of the operators, and the maintenance persons got firsthand experience with the problems of downtime.

Another company redesigned itself into business units and broke up several traditional departments. Marketing, purchasing, accounting, and scheduling personnel were all placed on a team within a single business unit. This was an environment which prior to redesign had diehard dogs continually battling uncompromising and uncooperative cats. The redesign yielded dramatic results. Within a year, product development time was reduced dramatically and major cost savings in inventory control were in place.

The second kind of conflict is called *symbiotic*. A mischievous child once tied two cats' tails together. When the cats discovered they were tied, they immediately began to fight each other, much to the amusement of the boy. If the cats had analyzed the problem, they would have realized that theirs was a symbiotic conflict. Had they gone that far, they might have attacked the lad together! *Symbiotic conflicts* are conflicts between groups which cannot live without one another. These often take the form of legally binding agreements such as union contracts or customer-supplier agreements. The two sides need each other, or at least are required to live with one another.

Symbiotic relationships need not be adversarial, although they have traditionally been systematized to occur that way. To reduce or eliminate symbiotic conflicts, a system must be developed which requires both sides to work together closely toward mutual goals. This may take the form of regular meetings to solve problems or share data. The bakery team at Wolferman's, Inc., consistently experienced problems with packaging. It decided to call the vendor in and show him the problem. In the meeting, the package vendor heard directly from the team about a problem of which he was completely unaware. Within a week he was able to help it solve the problem. The success of the meeting was so apparent that the team decided to have other meetings with vendors to solve problems. But all this could take place only after Wolferman's altered its system to a true-team approach.

Union and management are mostly symbiotic—much of their existence is spent monitoring and dealing with each other. Traditionally, these have been adversarial relationships by custom, convention, and in some cases, borne of battles. In designing a self-directed team environment, union and management must *always* sit on a Steering Committee together. (More about this in Chap. 5, where beginning the process to reach a true-team system is described.) The effect is generally immediate when the transition to the team system is begun.

Grievances go down, contract issues get resolved more amiably, and the sides begin to develop mutual, rather than mutually exclusive, goals. The process aimed at getting the cats and dogs to live successfully and effectively together really does work.

The Special Case for Managers

There is one other special case of built-in systems conflict that must be examined before and during the transition to the team structure: the role of managers and supervisors. In the traditional technology, employees are seen as serving the manager. This allows the manager to set all priorities, to make job assignments, allocate available resources, and interrupt and change assignments without necessarily consulting the employees. And that manager has a manager, who has a boss, who has a vice president, who is considered a functionary of the president or CEO. This has been referred to as *top-down management,* and it is a system style which leads to a great deal of gratification for the managers and "bosses." Managers often manage, not for money alone, but for the ego gratification they receive and the feeling that they are contributing at a higher level in the system than those who work for—not generally with—them. Everyone knows managers who put in 50-hour weeks can actually earn less than those whom they "outrank" in the organization when overtime is included.

The entire system from the president down to the first-line supervisor is generally spoken of in military terms, as a "chain of command." This top-down approach allows for information to move generally "down" through the organization. Not only that, most systems like this discourage, hamper, and even punish those who attempt to move information up or across the command structure. How many people have been accused of insubordination, or intimidated by the fear of this accusation, for trying to impart honest information about how to accomplish their work?

To make an empowered team organization, the system must be redesigned to allow for orderly and efficient flow of communication in all directions. Often, communication links are discovered that cannot even be envisioned by the present structure. Think about our maintenance workers at Wolferman's. Prior to the transition to teams, no one would have envisioned them as members of production teams, communicating as a regular part of the job with the production people. Maintenance and production goals were placed together in the system when and where it made the most sense—where it was most effective.

No longer were these two groups adversaries. Their communication took place not through supervisors and memos but up, down, across, over—where it was most effective!

Eliminating the Top-Down Mentality

The first step to eliminating the top-down mentality and approach is to define—or in some cases, redefine—who is the customer. In traditional terms the customer is the manager or supervisor of the employee. It is that person of higher rank whom the employee seeks to satisfy in accomplishing his or her work. In a team environment, the team is the customer of management. Management exists to serve the team, which in turn serves the external customer, the end user of the service or purchaser of the product. (See Fig. 3-1.) This simple concept has major implications for the design of the organization. Information must now

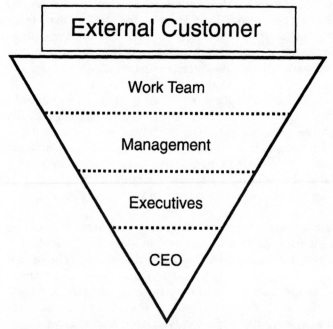

Figure 3-1 The team is the customer of management. "We will treat employees as we would have them treat our customers": senior executive, *Fortune* 500 corporation.

move in radically different ways throughout the organization. Where it has always moved in one direction, down, information must now get to those who need it. "Those who need it" are those who can use it to get the work accomplished faster, more accurately, and with as little waste of resources, including and especially time, as possible.

When organizations want to know how they are doing, they ask their customers. In a true-team environment, a management team that wants to know how it is doing will ask its customers, the teams. The movement in perception from the team working for the manager to the opposite can sometime be difficult for management personnel. This increases the burden on upper management to initiate and support the process.

The next chapter will examine more closely new ways to manage work and communication throughout an organization. Part 2 of the book will describe how the team structure can be designed and what has to be done to nurture, support, and implement it. Part 3 will continue and enhance the description of how to actually accomplish teaming up.

In other words, from this point on, this journey will turn outward. So far, all that has been asked can be accomplished in one's own head and heart. Chap. 4 begins the look at techniques, tasks, and strategies for making the transition to true teams. From this point forward, we go beyond cerebral examinations to actions that directly involve the organization.

Mark the next page; it is where one begins the process of teaming up.

4

New Ways to Work

Changing the
Communication Patterns

This chapter actually begins discussing the process—beyond thinking, considering, and pondering—of a transition to a true-team organizational structure. Here are ways to work that one can start to use tomorrow morning. These ideas can be implemented, whether or not an organization proceeds toward a total "team up" plan. Any organization acting on these ideas will be moving toward greater employee empowerment.

Before the specific "how to's" begin, consider the experience of Gary Henrie, formerly clinical director and currently Executive Director of South Central Counseling, a Nebraska mental health center. With a number of locations serving ten rural counties, the center provides rehabilitation and outpatient services to mental health clients, and runs substance abuse, foster care, and residential services programs—a full gamut of services in the social service field. Often, team structures are thought to apply only in manufacturing, although in fact they are growing in appeal to service industries. But in the social service fields, where there are often diverse missions within the organization, teams are often discarded as unwieldy and impossible.

But Henrie sought outside assistance just after assuming the top spot at an agency that was "floundering and in chaos. Bad morale was the only morale. I questioned my sanity in even taking the [Executive Director's] job. I knew I had to find a direction." Henrie was also concerned about the agency's survival in the wake of health care reform and how to be adequately prepared for the future. Henrie found himself wondering what he could do.

He called one of the authors (Darrel Ray) looking for total quality management. After a subsequent one-day training, Henrie did what is about to be described. In the end, he continued on through the process to a true self-directed work team structure. But he began with the team structures described in this chapter. For South Central Counseling, and *any* organization, these team structures help make the shift from a traditional top-down management system to one that supports a team approach. Gary Henrie began here, found these things worked, and continued on through the process, challenges notwithstanding.

How can any traditional organization transition from the nonsupportive top-down human infrastructure to high-involvement/high-performance management systems without creating chaos or damage? By developing the trust-building structures and using the meeting guidelines that will be described in this chapter over a six-month period, management can set the stage for increased employee empowerment and take the first steps toward self-directed work teams.

Management consultant Cheryl Highwarden has said, "If you change the patterns of communication, you change the culture of an organization." The trust-building structures are designed to change the patterns of communication within an organization. Destructive patterns of communication can be changed rapidly using these structures. This does not mean there will be no resistance or anger related to the changes, especially among more traditional employees and managers. Resistance is a fundamental aspect of any change effort.

Much of what this chapter deals with is meetings and "meeting behavior." Meetings are where a good deal of an organization's communication takes place. In any high-performance organization, meetings are an investment to ensure clear communication, educate the participants, coordinate activities, and make decisions. It is easy to see meetings as so many people do: a waste. The more positive, and team-supportive, meeting mien: an investment which must be managed, as must any good investment, to get the best return.

All three trust-building structures are based upon the notion that every employee should see the organization from one or more levels above their current position. Employees who see the organization as it is seen from a higher position (that of their boss or their boss' boss) are more able to fit their efforts to the needs of the organization. They have a broader view of the organization's mission, and better understand the challenges which management faces in making an organization efficient, effective, productive, and profitable.

Open Meetings

The first trust-building structure is *open meetings*. From the day they begin, managers will no longer go behind closed doors and make decisions that affect other team players without letting them into the meeting. For too long, management has closed its doors to employees when it came time to make decisions. This practice has led to much disaffection and mistrust. Under the guidelines to be outlined here, all management meetings should be open to employees. Employees need to see for themselves that managers deal with hard decisions and are working in the best interest of the employees and the organization. By immediately implementing this structure, managers learn to deal openly with the objections of employees during the decision making. This is the very essence of employee involvement, yet it is often omitted.

Managers who take this step report the presence of nonmanagers in the management meetings changes the nature of interactions and forces managers to take a more global look at the effect their decisions have on the work force. Tony Leonardi, Vice President of Sara Lee Bakery, reported, "Open meetings allow all points of view to be heard. In many instances the hourly workers have a better understanding of the issues and problems of the line than do their management."

In one glaring example, management at corporate headquarters promised a subsidiary company that if they made their highest profit goals in fiscal years 1991–1992, all the management staff would be treated to a Caribbean cruise. During an opened-up management staff meeting, one of the nonmanagers raised the embarrassing question "You mean we helped you make that profit, yet you are the only ones who benefit?" This question upset some of the managers who were eager to go on the cruise. But after lengthy discussion it became apparent that a cruise would send a very destructive message to all employees of the company and probably destroy much of what they had been trying to accomplish in the transition to the true-team concept.

The management group decided to take the money ($50,000) and let a committee of employees decide how to celebrate the company's success within some broad guidelines. The choice was a company-wide party given at a local luxury hotel for all employees and their families. The response was very positive and sent the message that management considers itself an integral part of the team. In the next fiscal year (1992–1993), amidst a poor economy and several negative external market factors, the company made profit improvement of 35 percent over the previous year. To add to these impressive results, profits were rising faster than sales. Such an achievement would not have been possible if the managers had taken the cruise and created widespread ill will. It was the open meeting format that made this possible.

Certain guidelines must be followed to make open meetings successful. First, meetings must be structured. There should be a system that guarantees that all employees have an opportunity to be involved in one or more management meetings each quarter. There should be at least two employees in each meeting. A single employee among managers will often be too intimidated to participate, especially when the open meetings are new to the organization. Employee representatives should be strongly encouraged to participate and give their views. They should be given the agenda in advance and be given a place on that agenda. Employees should be clearly advised of their important role and given guidelines on what is expected of them. Two particular guidelines should be explained before they come to any meeting: First, any discussion of proprietary information or personnel action may require that they leave the meeting. Second, these subjects will be reserved for the end of the meeting and management will do its best not to exclude the employees any more than necessary. Reports from companies who have implemented this procedure indicate that they rarely have to ask anyone to leave.

John Seymour, Manager of Human Resources at Standard Motor Products, Inc., Kansas Division, says, "We always have a nonmanagement person in our meetings. It engenders trust and the feeling of openness when people feel we are being honest about our business. They feel comfortable that we will be fair and aboveboard in all our dealings."

Ernest Lewis, chairperson of the United Auto Workers at Standard Motor Products (SMP) says, "Open meetings enhance communication. When the meeting is open we at least know what management is thinking, even if we don't agree with it. That means there are no hidden agendas. When you have no hidden agendas that creates more credibility for both sides."

Open meetings are an investment in educating line employees about the business while building bridges of understanding and trust. By instituting open meetings, management sends these positive messages to the work force:

1. We want your input.

2. We have no secrets from you.

3. We trust you and value your participation.

4. We want you to understand as much of the business as possible.

Shared Leadership

The second trust-building structure is *shared leadership*. Chances are, the same person always runs the same meeting; it is that individual's agenda that gets "worked," whether this is appropriate or not. All management groups which meet regularly should have a leadership rotation schedule. Each manager in the group takes his or her turn to lead the meeting for at least a month at a time. In some cases, a two- or three-month rotation schedule would be appropriate. Regardless of who is actually "in charge," the group takes primary responsibility for leading itself. This is a fundamental principle of self-directed work teams, yet it is rarely used in management circles. The chairperson for the meeting is responsible for collecting items for the agenda, facilitating the movement through the agenda during the meeting, following up on action items after the meeting, and any results that require follow-up. Shared leadership allows the top manager of the group to sit back and participate in the meeting as a team member rather than as "the boss." It deemphasizes his or her power and emphasizes the need for everyone to take greater responsibility for the decisions of the group. Managers report that this technique refreshes the group, makes meetings more effective, and increases awareness of problems the whole group shares. This approach also decreases territoriality and interdepartmental squabbling, while improving group problem-solving efforts.

Gary Henrie says,

> Leadership rotation has been very effective. I like it because I've learned the value of having an agenda and being prepared. It has also been a valuable lesson to the management team in learning the difficulty of managing our organization. What I value most is I get to "set back" and participate. I used to resent having to always run the meetings. Everyone says it's a better meeting, more efficient, more decisions get made and they look forward to coming. Most important, it has increased accountability.

Using shared leadership, the organization sends several positive messages:

1. We expect all managers to see the organization as a whole and not just from their narrow perspective.
2. We expect managers to involve supervisors and employees in all decision making wherever possible.
3. We expect all employees, management and nonmanagement alike, to look at the organization from one step above their own position.

Skip-Level Meetings

The third trust-building structure is *skip-level meetings*. Skip-level meetings help managers view the organization from at least two levels below them, avoiding the filtering effect of middle-management layers in a hierarchical and bureaucratic organization. This method has been widely practiced at General Electric with great success. At first glance the skip-level meeting appears to resemble a "focus group"—but it is not, and should not be treated as such. Focus groups are just that, "focused" on a particular issue and convened just for that narrow purpose. Skip-level meetings are not focused. They are broad information-generating opportunities. A group of five or six line workers from one or several areas is selected to attend this 90-minute meeting with the manager. No other managers or supervisors should be present.

The line workers are given an advance memo on the purpose and structure of the meeting and asked to attend. Attendance should be voluntary! Those invited are asked to talk with their coworkers and find out what they want upper management to hear. They will then bring this information to the meeting.

At the start of the meeting, the manager explains the purpose of the meeting and tells the assembled group that he or she is there to listen, not to solve problems or even to answer questions. The manager should be very clear that this is not a meeting to spy on their supervisors, nor is it a problem-solving meeting. It is an information and problem identification meeting.

During the meeting, the manager takes notes on a flip chart, so that everyone can see what is being noted. At the end of the meeting, he or she recaps the issues that seemed important to the group and promises to get back to them in writing on each and every item within 30 days. The manager may delegate some of the issues right back to the persons in the meeting, or to other supervisors or managers. After about three weeks, the manager writes up his or her answers to the employees' concerns and distributes it to everyone in the organization. The process then starts again with another employee group.

People can be selected randomly from many areas, or the manager may wish to concentrate on a different area each month. The manager should avoid answering questions or trying to solve problems on the spot. He or she should just listen and take notes. Skip-level meetings place management in the position of having to listen exclusively, rather than to talk, tell, or explain. A different skip-level meeting should be held every 30 days.

In the beginning, this process will be extremely threatening to middle management. They may feel they are being spied on, and often middle managers have even less trust of upper management than line employees. It is important for the upper management to stay focused on problems, *not* people. Middle management should be reassured of the purpose and intentions and encouraged to have their own skip-level meetings, if appropriate.

Above all, upper management should never use information gathered in skip-level meetings for discipline of a supervisor or manager. This will build great distrust among all concerned. Remember we are talking about an activity designed to build trust. If the information is handled competently by upper management, the process *will* breed trust, as well as faster resolution of organizational problems.

Managers and meeting makers should be warned that for the first three to four months the meetings will tend to be "moaning and complaining sessions." Many points of view and issues raised will appear to be petty grievances. Groups seem to need to get this stuff off their collective chests and at the same time are testing to see if management is truly listening. By about the fifth or sixth month, employees will stop complaining about petty things and "get serious." Managers are often very surprised at what they learn about their organization from these meetings.

Gary Henrie says this about skip-level meetings:

> I always thought I had a good relationship with staff but when I meet with them in a group setting with no managers around, it is amazing what I learn. I think it has done a lot to build integrity between management and line staff and it gives me a different perspective. They see action on the issues they bring up and that also reinforces the integrity. It's not just promise and forget.

Skip-level meetings are an investment in direct and more effective communication between management and management's internal customers. In addition they provide significant intelligence gathering about how the organization is performing in the eyes of those who produce the service or product. Copies of all skip-level meeting responses go out to every team or are available to each person in the organization. Skip-level meetings send many positive messages to the organization:

1. We want to hear from you about your concerns.

2. We will get back to you—in writing—and everyone will know the results because we have nothing to hide.

3. We will not solve every problem, but we will acknowledge your concern.

4. Management no longer will remain isolated from the hassles of the system it has created.

5. We want to identify and solve problems, not blame people.

Meeting Guidelines, Including the 59:59 Rule

The fourth practice, implementation of *meeting guidelines*, concerns management of the investment in meetings. Effective meetings are a discipline which should pervade the organization. The guidelines, listed below, are intended to help all managers and meeting-makers gain control of their meetings and use the time effectively.

1. This first guideline is called the *59:59 Rule*. Using it can cause some startling changes, but it sets an important tone in making new communication patterns. The rule is this: All meetings will conclude in no more than 59 minutes and 59 seconds, at which time all persons are expected (not encouraged) to leave. All too frequently, meetings run 10, 20, even 30 minutes overtime, causing many small disruptions in everyone's schedule, which then cause other problems to ripple through the system. Overtime meetings alone cause vast amounts of hidden waste. As self-directed teams begin to function, they will be expected to have weekly meetings. Management must model this practice if it expects the teams to do the same.

2. All meetings will start on time. Period. Once promptness is the only expectation, everyone will be prompt.

3. Should a meeting require more than 59:59, the specific amount of time will be agreed upon in advance (e.g., 1:59:59) and all will be expected to leave at the end of that time.

4. All meetings will have a written agenda in advance. Anyone in the meeting may put items on the agenda with the chairperson.

5. Any discussion of items not on the agenda will be left for the end, if time permits.

6. Specific problems which need to be addressed should be given to subgroups who develop a proposal for presentation to the whole group. Do not waste time solving a problem in the large group, when a smaller group could resolve it just as effectively.

7. Do not waste time discussing issues which concern less than 70 percent of the people present.

8. A meeting can last less than 59:59.

Management must demonstrate an ability and willingness to use these less sophisticated tools before self-directed teams can proceed effectively. An organization which cannot learn to practice these, or similar tools, diligently over at least six months has no business trying to implement self-directed work teams. Conversely, using these trust-building structures and meeting guidelines, a company can go through the transition from traditional management to high involvement with much less turmoil, while building a strong foundation for self-directed teams.

The latter is exactly what Gary Henrie did. After a one-day training at his agency he began to institute the trust-building structures and meeting guidelines. After they were in place and showing clearly positive results, Henrie believed he had begun a process of employee empowerment that he wanted to see through to its conclusion of true teams. His organization moved forward with structures in place that supported a new human infrastructure.

To recap, so far this chapter has discussed steps which can, and should, be taken before implementing self-directed work teams: developing a tradition of open meetings, practicing shared leadership, using skip-level meetings to encourage better information flow to the top, structuring meetings and using the 59:59 Rule. Also important is changing the system of performance appraisal for managers (this will be covered in Chapter 6). Taken alone, these are useful and often effective techniques. Taken as a whole, they are a technology designed to support highly effective communications within an organization. Dale Hughes, purchaser at Standard Motor Products, Inc., summed it up this way: "It's like going from a string and two tin cans to fiber optics. We communicate far better now."

If this level of technology seems impossible to an organization, self-directed work team technology will be even more difficult to implement. Think twice before going beyond this level. When management demonstrates its ability to open up the communication structure within the organization, the work force will become a more active and positive ally in the change process. Workers are much more impressed with managers who "get in the boat" with them than those who try to keep one foot on the shore while *talking* about getting in the boat.

Before the boat sails toward a team structure, and perhaps about the same time an organization begins using the trust-building structures, two issues will surface.

Two Key Issues: Pilots and Consultants

Managers often ask, "Is a pilot program a good way to begin the process?" The response is simple, though not often well received: No!

Pilot programs generally do not work over the long run. The idea implied by the term *pilot program* is "If it does not work, we will scrap it." This is not a message of commitment from management.

Pilot teams have been successful over as much as three years time. However, in virtually all organizations, efforts to develop other self-directed areas never took hold until the organization made a major commitment to the process and began changing the human infrastructure so that it would support the team concept. Implementation of the trust-building structures and meeting guidelines begins the changes that need to be made to establish the new human infrastructure. They are the beginning of a process that takes commitment and time on the part of the organization. To expect one small corner or single unit, even if it experiences success, to be a "laboratory" for the entire organization is to expect the impossible, for reasons that will be detailed below. Further, without the support of changes in the entire infrastructure, any conclusions based on the "pilot" experience, whether positive or negative, are just not useful enough.

Pilot programs generally work in a limited area or time frame, but not for the reasons management believes. A pilot program has the blessing and protection of management. Participants are often volunteers or are hand selected by management. The pilot is given resources and latitude which no Type I group (leader centered/leader focused) is allowed (see Chap. 1). However, a pilot group often looks and functions more like a Type IV group (self-led/time focused) than a true Type V self-directed team. The positive results these teams get are real, but this does not mean that these results can be reproduced in the larger organization.

Often the results a pilot group shows in 4 to 8 months are largely the result of the Hawthorne effect. This term refers to research done in the 1930s at the Westinghouse Hawthorne plant. The researchers discovered that simply paying special attention to workers can get strong positive production results, and they dubbed the phenomenon they observed the *Hawthorne effect*—something like the placebo effect in medicine. In a pilot program, it is often impossible to tell what part of the results are real and what part are Hawthorne effect. If the pilot goes on for 18 months or more, true results may become clearer. However, in 18 months an entire organization could be well down the road to implementing self-directed teams and showing concrete results. Why waste 18 months on a test that does not really test anything?

Management frequently uses pilot programs to hedge their bets. If it works, great! If it fails, then they can disavow responsibility for it. The work force and middle management sense this lack of strong commitment to a pilot program. This can sour the entire environment. The employee sees management saying "Get in the boat and go across the river; if it is safe, then we may all get in with you." This sets others up for risk of failure which management is not itself willing to take.

The most important success component is one or more key top managers who are willing to put themselves in the boat with the work force with an unequivocal commitment to true self-directed teams, and all that is required to make them work. As ODT, Inc., Senior Associate Gil Gonzalez is fond of saying, "You can read all the books on swimming, but sooner or later you have to get in the water if you want to learn how to swim." Until employees see management right in the water with them, they will not believe management really wants to learn how to swim.

The most harmful part of a pilot program is its negative impact on the rest of the organization. To understand this is to understand the nature of resistance in organizations. Organizations are similar to organisms. Organisms resist harmful viruses and bacteria to protect the body. This is the best strategy in virtually all cases. Unfortunately, the body does not always discriminate between harmful, benign, and helpful environmental agents. Allergies are an example of the body resisting something which is not harmful. In a more critical example, an organ transplant, the body may actually die without the new kidney, bone, or heart. Yet the body will attack this intruder as vigorously as any deadly bacterium or virus. Resistance is good most of the time, but can occasionally be harmful to the overall health of the organism—or even fatal.

Organizations are the same. When a new idea is introduced it is resisted. Ideas, like germs, can be harmful or helpful to the organization. Even if only every good idea was adopted, there would be chaos. But, some ideas really are good for the organization. Self-directed work teams may be the best thing for an organization, but a pilot program is one way for the whole organization to develop effective antibodies before the idea spreads. As the pilot program is in progress, middle managers, union officials, and even resistance-prone upper managers, watch it to learn weak points. They often use this information to build alliances within the organization. Entire groups of middle managers can become convinced that self-directed work teams will not work in their area and will effectively sour the work force on the idea long before it ever arrives.

There is a more effective way to implement self-directed teams. First, if management is truly committed to the concept, then the issue of working or not is a moot question. The more important question is "How committed is management to the process?" A large high-tech firm has developed a plan of implementation which identifies entire offices of 100 people or more. These are called *first application areas.* The company has made a clear commitment to the method, indicating that this is the direction the company will be going, although some offices will go before others. This rollout method, with clear management direction from the start, is much more likely to succeed. The company had tried isolated pilot teams for three years with great success for those individual teams, but less success in gaining acceptance in other areas. By using first application areas, the company gains valuable experience with the process in these areas, which will be useful as the second application areas begin six months later. In this way the company gains the benefits of a pilot project, without the negative messages that engender strong organizational resistance.

But there will be resistance. No matter what method is used, there will be resistance. Much of this opposition can be avoided or reduced by clearly demonstrating management's strong commitment to the process through the use of the trust-building structures, and of other structures to be discussed later. These steps are more effective than any pilot program, as they cut a wider swath through any organization.

When the process actually begins, many organizational leaders will advise selection of a strong, experienced outside consultant. Very few organizations have the experience and expertise required to implement self-directed work teams without assistance. Implementing true teams without outside expert guidance can be like trying to do major surgery on yourself. It doesn't work well. In an effort to keep brief a discussion that may be perceived as self-serving, consider the following:

- Upper managers are not able to see how their behavior affects the process. The change to teams is a form of organizational surgery. It is impossible to be objective about one's own body. Remember the old saying "A lawyer who defends himself has a fool for a client." What looks easy to an observer is fraught with hidden steps and procedures. Objectivity is essential.

- Few people in management have had extensive experience with teaming up. There are some good books on the subject. But would anyone get into an airplane with a pilot who had read all the books but had no practical flying experience?

- Without guidance some things will be emphasized too much, others not enough. A good consultant can help level out this process and ensure a smoother transition. Lack of experience can lead to over-simplification and missing important ingredients.

- Even those internal consultants with much expertise have a hard time instructing management in the process. Strong internal consultants are a great asset—in fact, are essential to make the transition— but they generally have difficulty telling their bosses what those bosses may not want to hear. Internal consultants want to keep their jobs as much as anyone.

- Outside consultants can remain objective about management-union issues. A consultant can also help management and union negotiate the tricky contract issues which arise in the transition before a new contract is actually negotiated.

An experienced and strong outside consultant, who has seen myriad variations of and challenges to implementation, will save an organization thousands of dollars, hundreds of hours, and much heartache.

How does one choose an outside consultant? At this time in the development of self-directed work team technology, there are few people who have actually seen the process from start to finish. Since the true-team concept has only penetrated the organizational universe in large numbers in the last six to eight years, few people can have seen the process many times. While there are many consultants in the United States, there are very few who have sufficient experience with a total team management structure to guide an organization successfully through the process.

Here are some simple guidelines in looking for a consultant:

- Look first, and most importantly, at their practical credentials, *not* just academic degrees. Where have they implemented teams in the past?

- Interview some of the companies where they have already implemented self-directed work teams. Find out the process they used, and how successful it has been.

- If there is a union, make sure the consultant has experience implementing in a union environment. Many unions have become very supportive of the process, but only if they see the ultimate goal as fair to their members.

- Look for concrete results in less than two years time. Ask to see documentation that clients have in fact improved performance in some meaningful way. Many companies publish in-house newsletters which chronicle the process quite clearly for their organization. If these are available, look them over to get a sense of the way the process will unfold.

- Before the consultant is hired, know who will actually be doing the work. Some consulting firms show the "big guns" when selling the job, then send in others to do the work. There is nothing wrong with this, since many of the top consultants will not be able to be involved in all aspects of a project. But make sure there is trust with the people who will actually be doing much of the daily work. Find out their experience level with the process, not just that of the senior consultant.

Enough said about hiring an outsider to help with this transition. With or without—now it begins.

PART 2

Designing for Self-Direction

5
The Steering Committee

Successful Listening: All the Voices

"The Steering Committee"; how often does a title so aptly describe its subject?

The planning, preparation, and pleading have placed the organization at the brink of a monumental change. Contemplation of self-directed work teams, upper-management soul searching, selling the idea internally, and examining new ways to work have been accomplished. The journey has been contemplated long enough. Examination of where to go and ways to get there is as complete as can be. Continuing the metaphor, everything has been accomplished that can be done on land prior to leaving on a journey across the sea. The ship is stocked, the course is set. Now is the time to set off.

The Steering Committee takes the helm and is, especially at the outset, responsible for navigating the entire organization in these new waters. Its leadership will steer the organization through experiences that are new, often difficult, sometimes scary, and a big change for all. Steering Committee members should know at the outset that the waters may become quite choppy!

As the guiding conscience of the transition to this new way to work, the committee must represent all competing interests in the organization. All stakeholders must feel their voices will be heard, and that the choices made will be made on behalf of everyone and will be credible, with livable outcomes. When meetings are open, when meeting leadership is rotated, when skip-level meetings are convened—when the organization can live the trust-building structures and meeting guidelines described in Chap. 4—then the organization will have heard many of the voices within it.

When the organization moves beyond traditional top-down-only information flow, the true transition to teams begins with the Steering Committee. This chapter will examine differences of forms, memberships, and strategies Steering Committees can, and do, embrace, as well as examine the four tasks central to all Steering Committee efforts. It concludes with a profile of the first two years of the Steering Committee experience at Standard Motor Products, Inc.

At the outset, there is one component all successful Steering Committees must have in common. The importance of total representation of all organizational constituencies cannot be overemphasized. Any group of human beings will have an incredible range of reactions, feelings, and perceptions. And a change as fundamental and nontraditional as the one to self-direction invites people to let their feelings be known. Since the more traditional structures are less likely to solicit opinions from a variety of places, moving to self-direction can yield new and sometimes surprising voices, as the information in Chap. 4 should have clearly illustrated.

All voices must feel that they are at least being heard, considered, and acknowledged. Even when there is a union representing a large segment of workers, there is no guarantee that on an issue this large the union will speak with one—or even two or three—voices. (The Standard Motor Products profile will show that this challenge can surface and be dealt with successfully.)

Management may also feel a tug between competing points of view. There is often a temptation on the part of management to "stack the deck" when choosing Steering Committee members. The union may also feel that all their officers must be involved, if just to counter the "usual" practices of its adversary, management. Lacking a union, workers may be even more inclined to see the Steering Committee as a tool of management. But the Steering Committee is where the change from traditional, adversarial relationships must shift to cooperation, empowerment, and self-direction. The way to begin building cooperation is by making sure that all voices will be heard.

If the choice of committee makeup becomes a power struggle between union and management, employees and managers, "our side and their side," the organization does little to move from traditional, top-down management to empowerment and self-direction. Approaching the choice of Steering Committee membership as a power struggle between any of the organization's constituents will result in unceasing difficulties. In Part 1, we saw how the groundwork is laid for this change; now it must be given the best possible chance of success.

Selection of Steering Committee Members

Selection of members can be done in a variety of ways. The overriding principle should be broad representation of all views and voices in the organization. Organizations can call for volunteers from throughout, and from the volunteer list have everyone in the company vote for four, six, or eight, depending on how many open slots have been determined. While management will begin the movement to install the Steering Committee, participation must be opened up as soon as feasible throughout the organization. Voting can also be done in constituent blocs, rather than at-large elections. Bloc voting tends to protect the many—often competing—voices that must be involved. For example, the three highest vote-getters from management and the three from union members will become six of the committee. Establishing blocs can ensure opportunity for representation, but the voting should be done by everyone, for everyone, whenever and however possible. Keep in mind that the mechanics of how the votes are taken are less critical than efforts to ensure that all levels and groups in the company are represented. An effective plan is to have half of the committee replaced every six months, and to make clear at the beginning that this will be done. This gives everyone the opportunity to see that voices will be changed on an announced and agreed upon schedule. In this case, whatever voting process is implemented is conducted again when it is time to replace committee members.

It is rare that all Steering Committee slots will be elective. To ensure stability, consistency, and momentum of effort, a corporate vice president and union president (or those in comparable positions from the traditional adversarial groups) are always on the Steering Committee, as well as one other manager and shop steward. This ensures that everyone has some say in who is on the guiding body, while the guiding body retains a mix of experience and knowledge as well as the range of voices. At the same time, management and union are closely involved in the process. Especially in organizations that choose to set a schedule ahead of time for elections or replacements on the committee, retaining key members helps avoid too much retrenching, reeducation, and repetition on behalf of the committee.

For the manager reading this for the first time, turning the organizational helm over to the Steering Committee appears a very intimidating and time-consuming task. The process of letting go of traditional management control and holding the Steering Committee accountable is difficult to grasp. The role of the manager is to determine with the Steering Committee what areas are to be given over to its governance and which will stay in the hands of management. This negotiation process will favor management in the first year, as it is management that must give up its unilateral "right to rule." As the Steering Committee gains more experience with the process, management will need to renegotiate with the committee what areas fall under its guidance. This is a dynamic process that will sometimes change from month to month, and could even change day to day. This dynamism is more reason to be sure the committees have credibility by representing the full spectrum of the organization. This enables the committee to communicate its messages to that full spectrum, as well as hear from that same wide band of interests.

Large organizations with many layers of management and bureaucracy may have difficulty maintaining the thrust for employee empowerment. "Management creep" will often take over within 18 to 24 months; this is the tendency of managers to create excuses for taking back control of bits and pieces of the process. Management creep will then go on steadily, even if slowly, until there is little or nothing left of the original empowerment initiative except bitterness and cynicism on the part of the workers. Think about losing weight. In the first few weeks of a diet it is easy to maintain enthusiasm as pounds begin to melt away, and the excitement of loosening clothing keeps resolve and will power at a high level. When the first plateau is encountered and melting pounds become weight maintained, or a pound or three regained, discouragement sets in. One stops looking at the scales and slowly slips back into the old eating habits. Management must establish clear benchmarks for its behavior so that it will be known if weight is being gained or lost. Over and over the greatest threat to empowerment processes is management's own tendency to reassert its control.

Coming up—after a look at some key considerations related to the formation and operation of steering committees—the committees' "four tasks." And, like an effective weight control system, these tasks can serve as criteria, framework, and control for management, employees, teams, and the Steering Committee as everyone discovers a new way to live at work.

Key Considerations: Size, Structure, and Consensus

A large organization will require several steering committees. Perhaps there will be a single committee for the entire organization with others for various local units. To give a general guideline, a single steering committee can effectively govern no more than about 300 to 400 people and probably works best with groups in the 100 to 150 range. As part of the redesign, the organization should look at ways to stream-line into business units or groups with less than 150 employees. (Remember, as mentioned already, streamline the groups and whom they work with rather than cut, fire, lay off, or reduce the work force. The credibility of the change to teams lies in making the entire family a more effective organization, not a smaller one.)

The size of the steering committees themselves is a crucial issue. They should be no larger than 8 to 10 people. In listening to all the voices, there must also be a new way of reaching decisions. No longer will votes, majorities, and head counts be used in reaching decisions. The key concept for *all* decisions made by all committees and teams is *consensus*. And it is far easier to gain consensus with a committee of 8 than a group of 15.

For those who have always seen the workplace as an adversarial arena, consensus can be a challenge that may even seem unattainable. For many people, both those in charge and those whom others have always been in charge of, consensus may take some adjustment. Consensus means that there is agreement among the group on any decision reached. Consensus does not necessarily mean that everyone agrees. Sound contradictory?

What one learns when exposed to consensus is that agreement can be reached across varying levels of enthusiasm and comfort, but still be reached. When an issue is confronted and a solution proffered it will be common for some to love the idea and some to be wary of it. Consensus does not mean "back to the drawing board" to find a "bet-ter" solution that makes everyone happy. Consensus means that everyone is willing and comfortable *enough* to give the idea a chance. Some may do it with reluctance and some with glee—as long as all members can muster any level of support, the idea can be tried. When people understand the latitude that can exist within the perceptions of the group, a decision can be reached that everyone will, at least, be willing to give a chance. For some, it may mean agreeing to disagree; for others, it will mean making a different decision due to input from group members. After all, the opportunity exists for the Steering Committee to alter its decisions (by consensus) once the results of the change are known.

The committee should have several days of training in problem solving, and in running meetings, as well as planning and presenta-tions. The selection should be made far enough in advance to give the committee time to work together, learn together, and become at least somewhat comfortable with consensus reaching. It is not appropriate, or even reasonable, to set out a specific yet generic training agenda here: each committee must be left to find its own way. And this "finding its own way" is an important part of the members' initial work. There is no formula for how to train, or even how often to meet—therefore, it is crucial that the committee keep its commitment to listen to all the voices and to reach consensus. Listening, consensus, and accomplishing the "four tasks" will yield each Steering Committee precepts, practices, and procedures that enable it to succeed at directing the change to self-directed teams. The details may differ, but each committee will find its way by implementing the principles outlined in this book. It will be extremely helpful if individual members are able to understand the concepts in this chapter as well as those in Chaps. 2, 3, and 4—whether or not they embrace Chap. 1.

The Steering Committee will take two to three days per year to develop a mission for the organization. Other strategic planning meetings may be held throughout the year, according to the consensus reached by the committee. Members will be expected to carry out the plans of the committee and communicate them to all the teams. As the Steering Committee matures, it will be able to take on greater responsibilities and solve problems efficiently. It will take two to three years for the Steering Committee to develop fully as a decision-making group. During this time the interest in the committee will wax and wane. Both union and management must be aware of their tendencies to revert to old habits of adversarial posturing. The Steering Committee is the vehicle through which differences should be worked out openly, with as much good faith as possible. When the Steering Committee makes decisions by consensus and is broadly representative, all the challenges discussed in this book can be met, dealt with, and incorporated into the organization's development.

The Four Tasks

While the Steering Committee will face a number of varied challenges, there are four major tasks facing all Steering Committees. Remember, each committee may find different solutions to accomplishing these tasks, and the time lines mentioned here can only be general. Each committee will find its own pace and rhythm. Now, the four tasks.

Within the first few weeks the Steering Committee should establish a charter and develop a code of conduct for its members. This is the *first task*. The example of the Steering Committee will be followed by the entire organization; the charter and code serve notice from the start about how the committee will conduct its business. Even those who are uncomfortable with the change are more likely to respect the work done by a group that defines from the outset its mission and standards of behavior. It is important to establish a good model. This first task is also one that must be defined individually for and by each committee. With consensus, common sense, and knowledge of the environment in its organization, the code of conduct is a strong initial activity for the committee.

Moving on to the drafting of their charter, each Steering Committee will consider similar issues as it looks for its own way. The members must realize as they write their charter that it is up to them to guide a process which results in authentic employee empowerment, in work groups that assume and share all the responsibility once handled for them by managers and supervisors. As the team developers begin their tasks, the committee will need to monitor progress of developers and teams, and coordinate and develop the training resources as mandated. In a union environment, there is a mandatory addition to the Steering Committee's charter: to determine the issues that will be negotiable in the next contract. This is where the challenge of moving away from the traditional adversarial approach is often formidable. When they have finished the "first task," the Steering Committee is armed with a charter and code of conduct developed on their own, and has gained valuable experience and credibility at the same time. No example can really help them, as *the process* is part of accomplishing this first task.

The *second task* of the Steering Committee is developing the *levels of empowerment*. The example we will look at soon is proffered with this caveat: expect each steering committee, and each team, to develop these empowerment levels in its own way. But remember that once set, the sequence must be honored. Level 1 must be fully implemented before moving to Level 2; Level 3 cannot be begun until Level 2 is completed; Level 4 must be addressed only after Level 3 is implemented. As already alluded to, the Steering Committee is the first group responsible for developing levels of empowerment, and each team must also accomplish this second task.

Experience teaches that there are common threads in development; human development tends to follow a pattern. Competent human beings develop over time, learning to crawl first, then walk, then run. A useful, although not firm, rule of thumb: a month of team development roughly equals a year of an individual human's life. At 2 months, committees and teams are toddlers, at 12 months they are adolescent. Sometimes teams get ahead of their development and think, like adolescents, "We can do it all!"

Here is an example of the levels of empowerment; they are the ones devised by the Standard Motor Products, Inc., Steering Committee, which we'll profile later in the chapter.

1. First level of empowerment
    a. Select team leader and other team management position.
    b. Review and/or redesign layout of the work area.
    c. Establish functional job assignments for committee/team members.
    d. Set performance goals.
    e. Begin feedback process.
    f. Establish ground rules.

2. Second level of empowerment
    a. Develop mission statement.
    b. Start cross-training and support training.
    c. Start tracking performance against performance goals.
    d. Conduct regular feedback meetings.
    e. Establish team/committee self-discipline to enforce ground rules.
    f. Establish self-assessment process.

3. Third level of empowerment
    a. Schedule workload and normal hours of work.
    b. Practice frequent and direct feedback.
    c. Conduct regular communications with other teams/management.
    d. Interview/orientation of new team members from internal bids.
    e. Establish hiring guidelines for new team members with management.
    f. Team members' performance appraisals.

4. Fourth level of empowerment
    a. Committee/team makes most of their own decisions.
    b. Schedule workloads and assignments.
    c. Schedule hours needed, including overtime.
    d. Team takes part in hiring new team members.
    e. Team is responsible for some part of budget.

This list is the road map one organization developed for empowerment. The Steering Committee goes first; what the committee does, the teams will learn to do as well. Although there may be things on this list that are actually tasks of the teams, the committee must monitor what the teams accomplish. The levels of empowerment become a checklist of skills which the organization, and each team, should work on. As teams show higher levels of skill and responsibility, they can be given higher levels of authority. The Steering Committee authorizes teams to go to the next level of empowerment only when they have demonstrated mastery at their current level. This developmental approach ensures that the organization makes the transition to self-directed teams in a developmentally sound, rational, and reasonable fashion. Teams really do act like children along their developmental path! A young team, like a young person, is only concerned with its own needs; a mature team, like a mature person, is concerned with the wider needs of the entire organization/community first, the team needs second, and personal needs last.

The *third task* of the Steering Committee is strategic planning, which includes training and positioning the work force to be competitive in skills and knowledge. Each year the Steering Committee should take a hard look at the organization and the challenges of the marketplace. From this, a development plan is drawn up and shared with all the teams. Teams are held accountable for implementing the development plan, including upgrading skills and developing new ones. Targets for reduction in product development time, customer responsiveness, quality, productivity, safety, or attendance may be set by the Steering Committee.

This important annual exercise should be implemented through an off-site experience where the Steering Committee has the opportunity to focus on what has been done to date and what needs to be done. Here is a specific suggestion for how to accomplish this important task. Someone should make a sign with these words on it:

What are we trying to do? How are our Human Resources positioned for the marketplace we are in?

Bring that sign to each of these annual meetings and place prominently. When the answers to these two questions are reached, this task is accomplished for the year.

The *fourth task* of the Steering Committee has already been mentioned, but it is important enough to get its own listing—oversight. To oversee the process, and provide guidance and praise, the Steering Committee provides the opportunity for each team to make a 20- to 30-minute presentation to the committee one or two times per year. These presentations send the message throughout the organization that progress is expected and recognized. Through these regular presentations, the Steering Committee gains a wide-ranging view of the entire organization and is better able to coordinate change and redesign efforts. At the same time, the committee is able to monitor the maturation level of teams, and to ensure that the training is moving them forward and that the plan is being implemented effectively.

There actually is a fifth task for the Steering Committee, but discussion of it is deferred to Chap. 7. To save scanning forward or consulting the Contents, the fifth task is the selection of the design team.

Now, on to the look at a Steering Committee from the points of view of two of its members.

Profile of a Steering Committee

"I was a believer," says Tom Norbury of the self-direction concept. He further explains that management at his previous organization—Norbury came to Standard Motor Products, Inc. (SMP), in 1988—used many aspects of the same approach, though not in as structured a format as at SMP.

"We heard about it in the 1991 contract negotiations," says Ernest Lewis. He added, "We thought it was a flim-flam. The explanation made us skeptical; more work by less people."

These attitudes are fairly typical when self-direction first surfaces in a plant environment where union and management have been adversaries for as long as, or longer than, anyone can remember. Therefore, it should come as no surprise that Tom Norbury, a business unit manager, was the highest-ranking management member of SMP's Steering Committee. Or that Ernest Lewis is the chairperson of union Local 710 of the United Auto Workers, the union that represents the workers at SMP.

Norbury began working on employee participation when he began at SMP. "This change cannot be accomplished without top management, but top-down force won't work either," he says. Management was also concerned that the adversarial relationship between management and the union was threatening the company's ability to compete and even survive in the contemporary marketplace.

It has been more than three years at this writing, and the Steering Committee still guides the process. Lewis says that there are still union members who maintain the initial skepticism. But there are many who, like himself, have been convinced over time that self-direction is a change that has benefited all members of the SMP community. Lewis explains that when he first saw the commitment on the part of management to this new way to work, he began doing his own research. And what he learned was enough to at least get him to listen, while convincing others in the union that they should do the same.

The first breakthrough was an agreement added to the 1991 contract that would allow for changes to be tried, if both union and management could agree. Norbury calls this the "trust me letter." Lewis says the union members had varying levels of discomfort with this approach, but that the bottom line for the union members was seeing the commitment from management, coupled with the agreement that only those changes agreed upon by both sides would be implemented. And Norbury had a real understanding of the difficulty for union representatives in reaching agreement with one voice. "I know the union reps are running for office each day they're on the job," says Norbury. There was also the added pressure of competition, market share, customer satisfaction—of the need to meet these challenges and keep the company viable. All the competing voices agreed they wanted a strong company regardless of the differences in how they felt that goal should be met.

The plant's top human resources official sat down with union leader Lewis to pick the members of the Steering Committee. The original plan was to include the plant's manager and comptroller, the four individual business unit managers—i.e., Norbury and his three peers—and four union representatives. The selection process presented the first difficult challenge, as the union wanted larger representation on the Steering Committee. Both Lewis and Norbury realized that it is far easier for management to speak with a single consistent voice. Norbury says that their vice president, Joe Forlenza, believed strongly in the change to self-direction. Thus, especially at the outset, management representatives felt it their role to represent that management position. For Norbury, this was easy as he was a believer prior to coming to SMP. The remainder of management, regardless of their own feelings, provided an almost unitary voice of support. But the union had people on three shifts with different interests and concerns, speaking with diverse voices. Therefore, it was decided to allow the entire seven-member union bargaining committee to become Steering Committee members. In the fall of 1992 the Steering Committee was convened. From that day the potential for life at SMP to be altered forever was there.

Norbury says management believed that changes had to be made to ensure SMP's survival, which was constantly being threatened by the traditional ways of work. Management believed the adversarial climate, so common and even tightly woven into the fabric of many American workplaces, was the biggest threat to a successful future at SMP. Management was truly anxious, both about the way things were and how they could be.

Norbury, who began as director of manufacturing at SMP, explains that the change to self-direction coincided with the move to four separate business units. And both changes have made vast improvements in SMP's ability to meet customer needs, the key to any organization's success. With the change to four separate business units, each unit is responsible for its own product line, from design to distribution. A single sales force handles all the automobile aftermarket parts that the four units make and distribute; otherwise each unit functions independently. However, they are all bound by the same union contract and work rules.

"Quicker turnaround and more customer responsiveness" is Norbury's quick description of the aftermath of the two simultaneous changes. The move to the independent business units was planned and would have been implemented, whether or not the move to self-direction and employee empowerment happened. But the two changes occurring relatively close together in time has had a positive impact on life at SMP, according to Norbury.

Lewis, too, has a succinct description—business has improved. "Everybody participates now, while before there were assigned jobs. Everybody helps out, so that first we serve our internal and then our external customers." Both men agree that both changes are now firmly part of the organization's plan for operations. But getting to this point has required some new and different ways to work.

In the beginning, especially at the first three-day training of the Steering Committee, there were communication barriers that needed breaking down. Everyone knew the old-style adversarial relationship, so it took time to adapt to meeting consensus and working together. Norbury said that time and patience were required, especially among the management members, as it took much discussion with the union members to make changes. As has been said, management speaks more easily with a single voice, while the union speaks with many. Lewis describes the work force as diverse, and communication problems were exacerbated by language and cultural barriers, since the SMP work force included recent immigrants from Vietnam and Korea, whose comfort levels and customs created an even greater range of voices the union had to represent.

At first, according to Lewis, committee members had to get to know each other and learn to work together while updating plans, sharing general information, and monitoring progress as teams were established.

At present the Steering Committee usually meets every other week and has now learned to work well together. Part of the Steering Committee's success, both men agree, is due to the fact that everyone has seen the positive effects of the change to self-direction. While there are still those who resist the change, Lewis says that this group has continued to shrink. Norbury explains that decisions reached through the committees and teams often take longer to reach. And sometimes it will seem consensus has been reached and then a problem will arise that requires more discussion as new voices pose opposition that was not initially considered.

"The old top-down system was autocratic. Now we have true participation. It takes more time now, but we get better decisions," says Norbury. He adds that a plantwide survey taken about two years after the Steering Committee began its work showed that the majority approves and only a small minority would eschew the changes that have taken place. "It took two years, but we have passed a turning point," Norbury says.

The Steering Committee becomes the crucial forum—not only to negotiate what changes will be tried and how—but, as teams are established, as the reviewer of what the teams actually do. (How teams operate will be covered in greater detail in subsequent chapters.) The process includes each team making at least one report per year to the committee, beyond the initial report which sets the team's ground rules for operation. The details of what steering committees may deal with can vary. Each organization will face its own voices, challenges, and situations. Often, those facing change want to be armed with a grid or matrix to dictate decisions. These folks want a chart with the problems ranged on the top and side, and the proper "problem coordinates" in the middle showing the correct responses. But the key is in the process. Any steering committee that learns to communicate honestly, reach consensus, solve problems, run open and effective meetings, make and review presentations and plans—skills that must be identified and incorporated into the first few days of committee training—will be able to succeed. Both Norbury and Lewis agree that SMP's Steering Committee may have struggled, but that it has succeeded.

Prior to 1991 and the changes in SMP's organizational structure, training for most workers was technical only. Not only do the teams need to learn the skills that steering committees must also learn, Norbury considers the weekly team meetings as "training time." There are also "team huddles" for 5 to 10 minutes at least at the start of each shift. Figures are available to prove that the changes have increased productivity. "Our output per man-hour is up 5 to 10% at the same time people are receiving training and meeting times," says Norbury.

There have also been other reinforcers, including cash. In the first quarter of 1993 SMP made its first "gainsharing" payout, which was about 7 to 10% of base pay for most employees. The only formula: a 50:50 split between the company and employees of profits placed in the gainshare pool. Again, more important than the details is that the gainshare pool exists and that it is evenly shared between the company and the employees.

The Steering Committee is the front line, the cutting edge, the medium that embodies the message in creating organizational change. For Ernest Lewis, management's commitment coupled with his own personal drive to "be in the know" led him to spearhead an effort to at least consider the new way to work. For Tom Norbury, the change to self-directed teams needed to be made to keep his company alive. There are people like Norbury and Lewis, and the rest of the SMP Steering Committee, in every organization. And now SMP's other plants are looking for those people as the company's commitment to self-direction goes beyond this one Kansas plant. And the Steering Committee is the beacon, the guide, the captain at the helm of this journey of change.

6

Assessing the Organization

Assessments: The Last First Step

The poet Robert Burns said:

> O' would some power the Giver give us
> To see ourselves as others see us!
> It would from many a blunder and foolish notion free us.

Burns might have been trying to summarize the case for moving away from traditional top-down organizational structures. When the information, goals, resources, and plans of any organization are managed only from the top down, that limited perspective restricts everybody's participation—and impact. Those few who make decisions do so based on limited information which they will always swear to be authentic. But one person's "authentic"—especially that of a senior manager in a top-down setting—is another's artificial. The difficulty of "seeing ourselves as others see us" raises some of the greatest challenges of all human life.

But the concern here is more specific than all human experience. Organizations, and how the work they do can be accomplished more effectively, is the subject. In Chap. 2, the questions posed are about the organization and its members' true attitudes toward their work environment. In Chap. 4, several techniques are suggested that begin the transition to a new and empowered human infrastructure. This book follows, as much as possible, the sequence implemented in bringing self-managed teams to client corporations. Chapter 5 shows how the process of change to self-directed teams begins with the work of the steering committees. At the same time, other efforts must be in process.

It is important to assess the entire organization at the outset of the change to self-managed teams. The organization *and* the Steering Committee must have current, accurate, and useful information from throughout the organization. Compelling all levels of an organization to listen to all other levels is a huge and crucial step. When an organization listens to all its varied voices, empowerment, trust, and the new human infrastructure begin to flourish and grow.

For an individual, physicians strongly recommend a physical checkup before beginning an exercise program. This is especially important when the individual will be involved in a change to new activities that, while beneficial, will stress the body and all its systems. And it is also important to monitor the program as activity and performance are increased over time. Constant monitoring insures safety. An organization, like an individual, needs assessment information when beginning a serious, long-term empowerment process. This information gathering should allow the organization to take thoughtful and careful stock of itself. As our consulting poet Mr. Burns advised, if people could see themselves as others do, they would be saved from blunders and foolishness. Like the one that precedes the new exercise program, this assessment begins a process of change that is both difficult and propitious.

The empowerment process is the means by which thousands of old habits are broken and replaced by new ways to support the team-based management structure. Open meetings, leadership rotation, and other techniques mentioned in Chap. 4 set in motion the building of support for the team-based organization. Managers must change their habit of planning for others and develop a new habit of teaching others to plan for themselves. Employees must change the habit of waiting to be told what to do and learn the habit of thinking ahead and planning their own work activities. For everyone, the change means that work, and how it is accomplished, will be different.

Allen Fulford is the manager at Bell Atlantic's South Virginia Collection Centers. His office was one of several "first application areas" chosen within Bell Atlantic for the transition to a team-based organization. Fulford is a member of the Steering Committee and has been working on the transition to teams since the effort began in early 1993. When contacted for feedback for this book he said, "I'd like to run this request by the Steering Committee....I have to get out of the habit of making decisions myself. That's what I'm learning!" Alan Fulford demonstrated by that one simple statement that he is ready to begin the change process. While the Steering Committee was enthusiastic and endorsed Fulford and others' discussions with us, his insistence on taking our request to the group underscored that he "gets it."

Fulford will also say that, for him, the transition was a welcome extension of his own management style, which he describes with terms such as "open door," "empowered," and "always involving people in decision making." Once the decision had been made between upper management and union officials to try team-based work groups in the selected first application areas, a Steering Committee was formed for each area and the process begun. "We are still infants at this," Fulford explained in early 1994, after he and his work unit had completed the appraisal process that begins the transition to teams.

For any organization or work unit, assessment is the final step to both determine readiness and begin the process of change. If the readiness review of Chap. 2 indicates that an organization is ready to change, the journey may already have begun. Before proceeding, one should understand the systems conflicts elucidated in Chap. 3, as it is the systems which most often need replacing, not the people in the organization. In Chap. 4, we saw how the new ways to work create a framework and context for the new human infrastructure. These processes described in these chapters represent steps and stages required to begin the change to self-managed teams. If not feasible in an organization, that organization is not ready to begin *any* major change—certainly not a change to self-managed teams.

A surprising number of organizations cannot seem to accomplish the simple tasks outlined in Chaps. 2 and 4. Any organization which cannot discipline itself enough to accomplish these things is unlikely to succeed in implementing teams. The assessment process is designed to determine how disciplined management has been in preparing the organization for teams.

It is necessary to determine the level of goodwill and trust in the environment. If employees have seen no change in management or are suspicious of management motives, this does not bode well for the team effort. The trust-building activities described earlier are designed to begin building goodwill and a sense of common purpose between management and employees. This is the beginning of the shift from traditional adversarial relationships to cooperative and team alliances. Without comprehensive and objective assessment, there is no way to know if this objective has been accomplished. Unfortunately, management often believes it has generated far more trust than it actually has.

Assessment helps the organization understand itself from several different angles. First, all managers in the organization should be assessed. Second, the environment should be examined. Finally, employees should be asked about their perceptions of the organization. Each of these three will be discussed in detail.

Everyone and 360-Degree Feedback

Why should top management be assessed? Since it is the upper-level managers in any organization who will need to lead the change to self-directed teams, it is very important that they get current and accurate feedback on how they are perceived. A manager who is seen as autocratic and unable to listen will need to come to terms with these perceptions before he or she can seriously participate in developing the team concept. It is not that this individual cannot participate, but rather that the individual needs to know that the common perception will make his or her "team talk" suspect. In other words, credibility is going to be an issue.

Often one or more top managers clearly stand out as unparticipative and autocratic. Other managers are seen as disorganized and not focused on goals. Without clear and objective assessment, there is little hope that any manager will perceive the need or make important, team-supporting behavior changes. Some managers are like Fulford, ready to embrace these changes as a way of institutionalizing an organizational structure they have always believed in. But every manager must gaze into the looking glass and take stock.

The "looking glass" used must include a *360-degree assessment method* which asks each manager's subordinates, peers, and boss to evaluate him or her. One of the authors of this book (Darrel Ray) employs a 160-item objective questionnaire for this assessment, but several instruments are available that can generate the feedback required. With this confidential information, the manager is able to understand how others see him or her. This also allows each individual in the management team to create an action plan for change.

There are five sources of information about a manager's performance: the boss, subordinates, self, peers, and customers. Of these, self is the least reliable source of information. The second source of information, the boss, is not much more reliable than self. The boss has her own work to do as well as supervising others. Her time is rarely devoted to studying or understanding the subordinate's performance. As a result her assessment is sketchy at best, frequently limited in scope and perspective, and often inaccurate.

The best sources of information on a manager's performance are subordinates and peers. Subordinates are acutely aware of their manager's shortcomings and strengths. They know if a manager is a good listener, a poor planner, a strong delegator or a glory seeker. An employee has only one manager to learn about, while a manager has many subordinates to learn about. In addition, employees are constantly sharing information about the manager and comparing notes informally, regardless of the formal appraisal systems the organization has in place. This gives employees a much broader base of information from which to draw conclusions. Managers, for their part, have a hard time getting accurate and unfiltered information about their subordinates.

Finally, customers can be a good source of information, but few managers deal directly with external customers. More often, internal customers of the manager's groups would be useful in gathering performance feedback. Comparing this 360-degree appraisal approach with the more traditional performance appraisal technology reveals that the traditional top-down performance appraisal system gathers information from the least reliable sources and generally ignores the most reliable. If an organization, or individual, wants to be in a continually improving environment, all sources of information must be put into the equation. High-performance team environments use 360-degree evaluations of all managers and teams. All sources of information are used and given serious consideration in the appraisal process.

The effect of this redesign of appraisal is to radically and rapidly change the communication patterns of the organization. When team members and peers of the manager are put in a position to evaluate the manager, it places the manager in the position of treating teams and peers as customers. The manager must listen much more carefully, coordinate more closely with peers, train more thoroughly, and help teams learn to set and achieve goals congruent with the company's market strategy. Many organizations and corporations are already using 360-degree feedback. These organizations are already closer to the new human infrastructure which will support and nurture employee empowerment, and position them closer to a true team environment.

The 360-degree evaluation processes can be perceived as a potent threat, especially by those executives more comfortable with the traditional system. These managers, insulated from the problems they cause through poor planning, poor listening, poor training, and poor leadership, do not see and do not want to see their own blunders and foolishness. This part of the system should not be expected to change immediately, but the change should certainly be well on the way to completion within 12 to 18 months after planning for self-directed teams begins. In Chap. 8, the new management "mantle" in an organization that is becoming, and will remain, a self-directed team-based organization will be discussed in detail.

There are also times when the changes do not take that long. Fulford says his management group experienced immediate impact. At the management retreat where the process was first discussed and assistant managers received the results of their 360-degree evaluations, the initial feedback from peers and subordinates provided "some very valuable data." The directness and specificity of the information yielded "some real whipped puppies" on the first night of his management retreat. But the outcome over the next few days, and then months, was the creation of development action plans that have yielded true growth on the part of these one-time whipped pups!

Fulford is quick to point out that the acceptance and growth were due to a number of factors, which included the process and plans brought to the retreat and his management team. The corporate values were changing at the same time, and that was evident to everyone. Fulford describes an assistant manager who had developed a strong and controlling management style. This individual had never sought feedback from peers and subordinates, and rather did the job of being "the boss." And this management style, where the manager's role *is* control, was once the one expected of a manager in the corporate culture.

But controlling behavior was clearly counterproductive to the transition to teams.

Fulford says this information was not only received but put into practice by this assistant manager. An action plan developed around new insights created almost immediate growth. Fulford had given similar feedback to this manager in the past, but there had been little change in behavior. But when put in the context of feedback from peers and subordinates, coupled with awareness of Bell Atlantic's plans to bring teams to several areas, the information had instant impact. This individual grew, developed, changed, to someone who gave up the control method of management and now finds ways to support the new structure. The information, and the process through which it is gleaned, helps move along the transition to true teams.

While individual profiles are confidential, the overall group profile is shared with the Steering Committee and management group. From this revelation comes an open and frank discussion of management's strengths and soft spots. Such openness is necessary to ensure the development of trust among the entire group. The results of this assessment process become an important resource for the Steering Committee, and for the entire organization.

Assessing the Environment

The second essential appraisal is an assessment of the organization's environment. Like the management assessment, this both adds to understanding and fosters a sense of participation by all employees. The objective in assessing the environment is to determine the characteristics of a given organization. Is the organization highly task-focused yet poorly organized? Are supervisors supportive but poor at clarifying policies and procedures? How much are employees currently involved in the organization? This is important information which helps get the Steering Committee and the team transition under way.

There are many good instruments on the market which can provide a useful picture of the environment. Author Darrel Ray uses a comprehensive environment survey which is both simple and inexpensive, and Figs. 6-1 through 6-3 summarize an assessment done using this survey instrument. The "environment" was that of a single work group within a larger corporate client. Figure 6-1 lists and defines the environmental categories the group members were asked to assess. The survey was taken twice, at the beginning and end of a 12-month period during which the work group implemented the trust-building structures. Figure 6-2 graphs the results of the two surveys; it compares the "before" and the "after." Figure 6-3 shows the written survey report.

The report shows how this critical assessment is made into a valuable tool. Look at what the work environment scale measures, the changes over the year of using the trust-building structures, and the information available to include in the report. Keep in mind that the job at hand is both to gather useful information and to encourage development of the new human infrastructure, which must include increased employee empowerment.

Figures 6-1 through 6-3 illustrate how assessment information is gathered, synthesized, and utilized. This example illustrates the effects that the trust-building structures yielded over the year between assessments. The value of establishing a benchmark assessment before any type of change program commences can also be seen. With an objective assessment of the environment, a benchmark is established for assessing organizational progress over time.

Interviews and Employee Perceptions

The third leg of the assessment involves private interviews with a sample of managers, employees, and, where applicable, union representatives. This process includes structured interviews done by indi-

Relationship Dimensions

1. Involvement   The extent to which employees are con-
                        cerned about and committed to their jobs

2. Peer cohesion   The extent to which employees are
                        friendly and supportive of one another

3. Supervisor support   The extent to which management is
                        supportive of employees and encour-
                        ages employees to be supportive of one
                        another

Personal Growth Dimensions

4. Autonomy   The extent to which employees are
                        encouraged to be self-sufficient and to
                        make their own decisions

5. Task orientation   The degree of emphasis on good plan-
                        ning, efficiency, and getting the job done

6. Work pressure   The degree to which the press of work
                        and time urgency dominate the job milieu

Systems Maintenance and System Change Dimensions

7. Clarity   The extent to which employees know
                        what to expect in their daily routine
                        and how explicitly rules and policies
                        are communicated

8. Control   The extent to which management uses
                        rules and pressures to keep employees
                        under control

9. Innovation   The degree of emphasis on variety,
                        change, and new approaches

10. Physical comfort   The extent to which the physical sur-
                        roundings contribute to a pleasant work
                        environment

Figure 6-1 Work environment scale descriptions. (*Modified and reproduced by special permission of the publisher, Consulting Psychologists Press, Inc., Palo Alto, CA 94303, from* Work Environment Scale *by Paul M. Insel and Rudolf Moos. Copyright 1974 by Consulting Psychologists Press, Inc. All rights reserved. Further reproduction is prohibited without publisher's written consent.*)

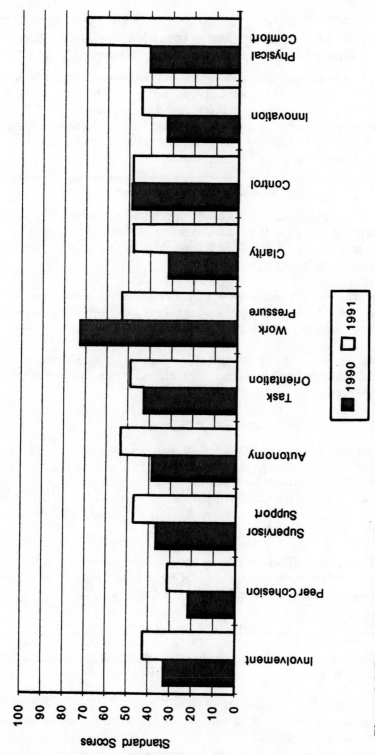

Figure 6-2 Bar graph showing results of work environment surveys taken before and after implementation of trust-building structures.

81

An Accounting Department after One Year
Work Environment Survey Report, 1991

The work environment scale (WES) survey shows across-the-board improvement in all relevant areas. The overall perceptions of the members of this work group are that this is a more pleasant place to work than a year ago. While there has been remarkable improvement in the last year, there is a consensus that there is still room for a good deal more.

Relationship Dimensions

Involvement: Employees feel more involved with more input and ownership for what they do. The score has improved over 13 percent (one standard deviation). It remains below average for most workplaces when compared to the national norms.

Peer cohesion: Has improved an equal amount but it too remains well below average. It appears that there has been some improvement in the teamwork and interpersonal cooperation.

Supervisor support: The change in this area is about 34 percent (one standard deviation), showing a great deal of improvement in the way supervisors are interacting with employees.

Growth Dimensions

Autonomy: Employees believe there has been remarkable improvement in the trust and freedom they are given to do their job and carry out their duties (one and one-half deviations). They feel they are given more responsibility and supervisors oversee their work much less. Again there is room for improvement, but this shows some very positive change in the last year.

Task orientation: There has been marginal improvement in the efficiency of the group. It appears that there is less time being wasted and better planning being done.

Work pressure: This area has dropped dramatically. People feel that the pressure at work is more reasonable and normal. They feel less harried and believe that there is less time being wasted on unimportant things.

Clarity: Has shown a large increase. There is a perception that the expectations, policies, and procedures are much more understandable and fairly enforced.

Figure 6-3 Report on work environment surveys taken before and after implementation of trust-building structures.

System Maintenance Dimensions

Control: This has not changed. The current level is probably good for the type of environment management is trying to create. No change would be desired.

Innovation: Employees believe there is more room for ideas and new ways of doing things. It is still low and would need to greatly increase to create a high-performing environment.

Physical comfort: This has increased more than any other scale. The comfort level of the employees is exceptionally good by any standards. It appears that the new office arrangement is far better and people are very satisfied.

Summary: There has been marked improvement in the environment, about as much as would be expected in a single year. Unfortunately, the starting point was exceptionally low last year (1990). This means that while there have been strong gains there is also a long way to go. There is no doubt that this group has turned the corner and is doing better, but it will take a concerted effort to keep moving forward and remain focused on continuous improvement. To continue the momentum toward increased gains, productivity, and teamwork, a program of team development is strongly recommended.

Figure 6-3 (*Continued*)

viduals outside the organization. It is important that this process be done by someone who is trained in interviewing and is not directly connected to the local organization. These interviewers give all interviewees a set of questions a few days in advance and then have a 30- to 45-minute interview with each. Through this process a large amount of very useful information can be gathered and collated into themes. The interviews, the management assessments, and the environment assessments create an in-depth resource.

Fulford approached these interviews as he had the process from the beginning, according to the agreement with the union. That agreement said that all those involved in the self-directed team process would be volunteers. When it came to the third assessment process, the in-depth interviews, there were volunteers aplenty. This was an omen, as will be revealed in the next chapter. Again, Fulford was candid in pointing out that the team concept was in keeping with his organizational philosophy. Fulford's enthusiasm for the process notwithstanding, he understood that information had to be generated at the outset to make the process credible and acceptable.

All of the information generated by the management, environmental, and employee perception assessments is given to the organization during the initial retreat for planning the transition to self-managed teams. All those participating in the planning retreat see all of the information and are encouraged to discuss their own ideas and perceptions about the data. No effort is made to interpret the data extensively. Instead, retreat participants are asked only to do their own assessment and draw their own conclusions from the data.

During the three-day retreat, people refer to the data constantly and explore its ramifications. During the third day of the retreat the group is asked to make a decision: Are they as an organization ready to move forward in the process? Twenty percent or more of organizations are not ready at this time and require more work. For organizations that are ready, everyone present at the retreat must make a major commitment to make this process work. People are given assignments, and plans are made to move forward. Imagine if this retreat group were to consider the commitment to a change this dramatic *without* the assessment information! Picture how difficult it would be for the group to make any useful decisions if participants had only their own perceptions as data.

These assessments are an integral part of the decision on how to proceed toward teams. The next chapter will present a look at what happened at Bell Atlantic's South Virginia Collection Centers when they completed the assessment process. Fulford agrees that these assessments are an integral, initial ingredient in the process of teaming up.

7

Redesigning Work and the Team Concept

A Suppertime Story and Reengineering

The organization has reviewed its readiness, convened its Steering Committee, done its assessments. Upper management and the Steering Committee have gone on their intense retreats. Now the transition to true teams is poised to begin its sweep through the organization. This sounds great—maybe. But what really happens next? The *design team* is formed, and the new ways, the team ways, to accomplish the work are designed. This is done by looking closely at how work has been done, what jobs and tasks have always been done, and asking how they can be redesigned to fit a true-team model in an employee-empowered environment.

At the outset it is important to understand that redesign is not a one-time project, but an ongoing process. Even after the initial design team has disbanded, teams will continue the redesign process through refinements, changes in work flow, adjustments and changes in team makeup and functions, even by forming new design teams ad hoc when necessary. Remember, this is the beginning of a process, and that process will become the way in which the organization functions. Many of the refinements the teams will develop over time could not even have been anticipated by the first design team. That is why it is important not to try for perfection in design before getting on with the process. But it is crucial that the process at this point begin with redesign.

Why are redesigned teams more effective and efficient? The experiences of real design teams and how they achieved their team designs are about to be presented. The importance of redesign efforts, and strategies for guiding the process, is part of that discussion. But first, a story from one of the authors' (Darrel Ray's) childhood which illustrates his earliest understanding of the need to redesign work to meet a goal more efficiently and effectively:

> When I was eleven years old my three brothers and I returned home for supper with the goal of eating quickly and returning to the neighborhood baseball game, which had been adjourned in the fourth inning on the previous evening. We sat down to dinner only to find our mother had prepared a meal that had something to deeply offend each of our taste buds! In addition to the mean menu, we had to cope with Mother's standing house rule: *Everyone takes a helping of everything and no one leaves the table until everyone is finished.* My heart sank as I saw the peas, to me a most hated food and universally scorned by all. Brother Brad despised the broccoli; Jeff got visibly ill at the thought of meatloaf, much less its presence on his plate; David could not separate the descriptor from the name of his hated rations, "yucky-yams," as he always termed them. We decided as a group to take a stand that night. Each would eat only what he liked. Two hours later, still seated at the table, we were crying and complaining about the unfairness of Mother's table rules, while our plates displayed that which we each loathed. To add insult to our injuries, we could see the field across the street and all the other kids completing *our* game.
>
> Following up on the standoff of that night, Mother made the exact same meal the next night; she could be a strict supervisor! But she did not have the patience to stand over us on this reprise. So while she was gone, we conspired to get the job done rapidly. I like broccoli; Jeff loves yams; David and Brad have carnivores' taste for all meats. That left only the challenge of my peas, which no one really liked. I parceled out exactly 16 peas to each of us, and everything else was distributed according to tastes! The meal that could not be completed the previous evening disappeared rapidly and we were ready to get out and play. Mother was suspicious but proclaimed, "As long as no food was wasted or given to the dog, I'm satisfied!" As we dashed out to play, we, too, were pleased with our solution.

This parable raises questions about work design:

How was the process redesigned?

Who redesigned?

How did supervision impede the process?

What were the outcomes before and after our redesign?

Were management's (i.e., Mother's) goals met?

The importance of redesign to the long-term health of the entire team-up process is well known. A number of books and articles have been written on the need for redesign in conjunction with the team process. Virtually all organizations require a significant degree of redesign, and many work processes require reengineering due to the constant change in work environments. *Redesign* is defined as organized and close examination of all the human aspects of accomplishing the organization's work. *Reengineering* refers to alterations of the processes that humans work with. The two are closely tied, and often must be done in tandem. The goal of both redesign and reengineering is to create an environment that supports teams.

Before Design Teams

Some of the greatest disasters in team implementation have been in organizations which did not believe redesign was necessary and tried to skip this step. Redesign is necessary in most organizations simply because the current organizational design supports a hierarchical, non-team-oriented system. The human infrastructure must be altered to support the new way to work. The design team is the vanguard bringing these changes to the day-to-day operation of the organization.

The existing system before a transition to teams is as different from a true-team design as the first plane the Wright brothers flew at Kittyhawk is from a modern jetliner. One would never dream of expecting that vehicle of first flight to perform like the jet, nor could putting a jet engine into the first plane turn it into a high-performance aircraft. The team process is a very different model and must be treated as such. Merely tinkering with the old processes is not sufficient. As Ketchum and Trist note,

> Gradualism ignores the conditional aspect of commitment and modest change does not produce the conditions for discovery. Lacking the opportunity to experience a new kind of work and discover that they like it better and that it changes them, people do not respond in the desired and expected way. With the workers behaving in the same ways as before, the supervisor is forced to maintain the coercive role of the old paradigm. The discrepancy between the stated and desired condition and the actual is clear for all to see. Dramatic bottom-line improvements are not forthcoming and fade-out is not far off.*

*Lyman D. Ketchum and Eric Trist, *All Teams Are Not Created Equal*, Sage Publications, Thousand Oaks, CA, 1992, p. 86.

In other words, take redesign very seriously before beginning the team process!

Many processes in organizations are not team-friendly. They are predicated on central decision making, hierarchical systems, and top-down authority. Without redesign and reengineering, the process will get undermined by the old organizational systems, which focus on individuals rather than teams.

Note that redesign itself can be an impediment to the process if it is not a part of the larger employee empowerment process. One major mail order insurance company gave the job of redesign to the managers and supervisors, who floundered as they tried to redesign work they did not actually do themselves. The project dragged on for three years with no appreciable changes made. As employees were never seriously brought into the process and no organizationwide goals were firmly set, teams never got off the ground. The process wasted vast amounts of time and resources; middle management was never held accountable, nor did upper management show a clear commitment to the process. They were warned their efforts would fail. It was, given the way they went about it, an easy call. The people who do the work *must* be involved in its redesign.

For teams to survive, there must be a friendly organizational structure, the new human infrastructure that supports the true-team approach. Simply putting groups of people together into teams does not work. Once again, we repeat: The importance of a total approach to the transition to teams cannot be overemphasized.

The Steering Committee and/or the design team (or teams, depending on the size of the organization) must look at how large the organization is, and how its size is likely to impact the changes. Size of the business unit is a major consideration. Some companies reorganize into business units of around 150 people. The larger a business unit, the higher the process losses to that unit. It is more difficult for people to focus on meaningful goals if their unit is too large. It takes longer to get decisions made, and bureaucracy becomes a substitute for direct human communication.

Before Standard Motor Products Inc. (SMP) began the team process, it reorganized into four business units. As Thomas Norbury, manager of one of the units, explained in Chap. 5, the change to self-direction at SMP conformed with the move to the four separate business units, each with more than 60 people, none larger than 150. SMP was seeking a greater responsiveness to challenges within and outside the company, and the move to the independent business units would have been implemented whether or not the move to teams happened. But the two changes occurring relatively close together has had a positive impact on life at SMP, according to Norbury. The subsequent redesign of the organization into teams was accomplished more efficiently because of the breakup into units of more manageable size.

The key fact that top management, and subsequently the entire organization, must acknowledge is that the current structure is generally not well designed for employee empowerment or for teams. As the readiness review already indicated, human infrastructure must begin to reflect a commitment to nurture, support, grow, and maintain an employee-empowered management structure. This new framework is one where information and responsibility move as is appropriate and effective. Information no longer follows a top-down path—one which seems to be maintained more for tradition than usefulness.

Many may be quick to assume that the traditional methods may be at odds with a transition to team structure. If an organization has a union, there may be doubts about the practicality of mixing unions with true teams. In fact, if the process of change has union involvement from the very start, and both sides clearly understand the goal, unions have been found to be a strong asset. Ketchum and Trist succinctly sum up what most experience shows:

> Work redesign can be done with unions and on more than one occasion during the redesign process the local union has become the major stimulus for continuing when management flagged. When there is a union it is highly unlikely that redesign can be successful without their involvement.*

As we have noted, the union represents many voices and may never be a unanimous force. But where the union will agree to try, and will bring along enough trust to let the change to teams take place—as the union did at SMP—its presence will be a positive for the process.

To go one step farther, unionized organizations have often completed the process faster and as effectively, with less management backsliding than nonunion organizations. With a union present, management takes its role much more seriously. Management knows that it must stick to what it says, and is less likely to make rash promises only to recant them when the going gets tough. In a nonunion organization, management often fails to follow through on agreements and finds it easy to revert to more dictatorial methods. Because employees do not feel empowered to confront management with these incongruent messages, it often takes much longer for an atmosphere of trust to

*Ibid., p. 72.

develop. At SMP, because the Steering Committee and design teams dealt in an open and honest way and built the trust required to make teams a reality, they were able to overcome initial union skepticism. When workers saw that their input was important in making changes, that suggestions they generated did affect how their work was organized and accomplished, trust was built and the transition has created a stronger, more competitive, and more profitable company.

At the Bell Atlantic Collection Center introduced in Chap. 6, Thomas Whitmore volunteered to be on the design team. He, too, stresses that the transition to teams must be an honest and open process. Although hired as an assistant manager, Whitmore is now a team developer. He says, "This is a change in the way we have done business. Everything the design team does must be fair, open and up front. It's the only way to get it done!"

Elaine Vaughan, a veteran with more than 26 years seniority as a collections associate also volunteered, and was on the design team with Whitmore. As a volunteer, Vaughan had the choice of serving on the Steering Committee or the design team. She chose the design team, and was glad of her choice. Vaughan made her decision based on where she would have the most impact on the work she would actually be doing. The Steering Committee did not seem hands-on enough for her. The design team surely was. But before you hear about Vaughan's design team experience, our examination of the preliminaries to the actual design work must be completed.

It is not reasonable to tell an organization exactly how to redesign itself. As with any process, the details will differ from organization to organization. Bell Atlantic's Allen Fulford insists, "There is no blueprint, no menu. You just have to get into it and plan." An effective and reasonable approach to design teams is to take the team of managers, union representatives, and employees to a one-day, off-site retreat. This group receives special training in design principles and is given a tight deadline to do their research and submit a plan to the Steering Committee. If the organization is large, there may be several design teams working on major sections of the organization. The design team deals with much of the local, structural change required to make the transition. No one can develop a perfect design, especially early in the process when few have any experience. Design teams are asked to "get it 80 percent right" for now; adjustments can be made along the way as management, the Steering Committee, and the organization gain experience. It is also important to reconvene a design team in 15 to 18 months to revisit the design and make other recommendations for change, based on the experience of the teams and the organization.

Jane Plous of Wolferman's explains that after the first year it convened a second design team to examine "how it was working. People who do the work know what the issues are and how to improve." But by then the organization was committed to the process. She notes, "I have seen it work. We have seen people do things with teams that we were not able to make happen without teams." The second time around at Wolferman's the design team made adjustments in how work was done and even how equipment in the bakery was configured. The key is that the "they" in charge of changes represented all levels and functions within the organization.

In implementations of the transition to self-managed teams, the one-day training for the initial design team focuses on specifics, including the following guideline: The design team should have 6 to 8 weeks to do its work and must then make a recommendation to the Steering Committee. Team members may spend up to half of their time on the redesign project. Many spend a full day each week working together with 8 to 10 hours during the rest of the week spent collecting data and working on ideas. When the design team is given a clear mandate and a tight schedule, the members come up with some remarkable plans and recommendations.

Allen Fulford's charge—"There is no blueprint, no menu"—is crucial to hear before looking closely at what the design team actually does. Managers must keep this important point in mind. Once the commitment to teams begins, the process of looking at work differently begins. And this new process yields surprises. "What I've seen is people stepping up and accepting leadership! People who *never* stood out before now want to take on the role." It is human nature to be bound by expectations and experience of the people around us. What Fulford is saying reflects what many other managers have found: When the structure begins to change, the old expectations of who can and will do what must also change.

Fulford's counsel on preparing for the team transition is significant enough to reiterate: People will do surprising things when given new opportunities; there is no blueprint or menu. These are the appropriate admonitions and preparations before embarking on the details of design team training.

The Design Team:
Techniques and Strategies

We begin the discussion with the charge to a design team:

> Closely examine all aspects of work and work flow as well as the organization of people and technology. The goal is to reorganize the work into whole processes, which can be given to teams. Teams

will be highly trained to serve the whole customer or work on a whole process. Wherever possible the design team will try to eliminate handoffs outside of a team. Serving most of the customer's needs in a single call reduces non-value-added time to the company, pleases customers, reduces conflict between associates, and creates the conditions for high performance. If you make a product right the first time, it increases customer satisfaction and loyalty to our company. Both make our jobs more secure.

Bell Atlantic's Whitmore and Vaughan began the redesign process by listing *everything* a collector must do. Whitmore said the list continued to grow as more and more Post-it™ notes were stuck to the wall. "Until we began to put it down on paper, no one had really realized all the things that collectors do!" The design team went through the same exercise for the other jobs at the center: assistant managers, clerks, and Allen Fulford's job as manager. In each case, the list of tasks each person did was astounding. The union contract did require that certain functions remain in the hands of assigned positions. Assistant managers were still required to keep attendance records and clerks were responsible for certain record keeping. This design team first listed the work, and then looked at how it could be accomplished.

At Bell Atlantic the decision was made to allow participation in self-directed teams to be strictly on a volunteer basis. There was a potential pool of 74 people, each of whom would decide whether to join a team or remain in a traditional supervision structure. This was to happen after the design team did its job and made a presentation to the entire group. It will be revealed how—shortly. First, let's look at the rest of the design team's process.

Design Team Code of Conduct. One of the first tasks of the design team is to establish its own Code of Conduct. Suggestions for a design team Code of Conduct follow. Of course, these are guidelines only— codes will vary from organization to organization.

- Keep discussions of problems within the team. Maintain a high level of confidentiality and trust; thus all can express themselves and explore ideas without fear of someone taking words from the team to the rest of the office.

- Avoid taking ideas you don't like outside of the team to people in the work unit. There may be a temptation to get people stirred up against an idea. Avoid these kinds of diversions.

- Talk to people throughout the organization to learn and understand but *do not* share plans or send up trial balloons. Until your recommendations are complete, you really don't know what they will look like. Sharing preliminary plans can get people very upset about something which might never happen.

- Testing of ideas and trial balloons should be done only with the entire design team's agreement.
- Ask that everyone try to agree to 80 percent or more of the plan before it is considered finished.
- Ask everyone on the team to sign the final recommendations.
- Be patient and respectful of fellow team members. All teams have conflicts and disagreements. As adults, we are committed to working differences out in a mature manner.

Design Team Sequence of Activities.　Given below is a suggested order of business for the design team:

1. Begin by doing a global task analysis of the whole local organization.
   a. Ask individuals to work on different parts and collect data.
   b. Examine each "handoff" and determine what negative effects it has for the customer, for the associate, and for the company.
   c. Use carefully gathered data to make decisions. Avoid making decisions based on personal opinion and pet ideas.
   d. If appropriate, do a rough work-flow analysis. Don't get too detailed.
   e. Be aware of "false specialists" versus "true specialists." (A true specialist is a person whose skills cannot easily be distributed or shared among other members of the team. For example, a psychiatrist's skills cannot legally or ethically be shared with other members of a team in a psychiatric hospital. But clerical tasks can often be done by any number of people, making this a prime area for false specialization.) Eliminate false specialties where possible and distribute true specialties among the teams in a rational way.

2. Build the team design.
   a. Identify the task clusters for a single team.
   b. Identify the mission for each team.
   c. Identify the specific physical location of each team.
   d. Design as if everyone were going to be on a team.

Each group, whether a team or not, will have a mission and tasks to accomplish. Teams should have more skill integration; traditional groups are more segmented and less able to provide one-call service to the customer or a perfect product the first time.

3. Publish each team's tasks and each team's mission to the entire organization well before the actual reorganization begins. Publish criteria for selection for a given team (if any) and make sure the process is fair on its face. No matter what you do, some people will be upset, even angry, about the changes. If the process is fair and open from the outset, there will be less long-term upset.

4. Determine and publish guidelines for volunteering or selection to teams. Avoid getting into this step until you have actually finished the basic design.

5. When the recommendations are accepted, have pairs of design team members go out to every group to explain the design and answer questions.

Remember, no matter what is done, there could be, and very likely will be, some people who will not like the design. Some may even be angry about it. Do the best you can to design a workplace which will delight the customer, be less stressful, and make the organization function more smoothly. Don't let the fact that *some people* will not like the design prevent the design team from doing what is best for most people and for the customer.

That is what Whitmore, Vaughan, and the five other members of their design team did. They tried hard to walk the line between functioning in an open manner and not tantalizing anyone with premature descriptions of what options they were considering—although people did ask! This team had the added burden of a hectic schedule of design meetings in addition to their own workloads. Because they only had time to meet on-site, design team members were often interrupted by the work they left behind. Add to that the challenge of asking people for detailed information about their jobs, while looking at a way to restructure those jobs. Their task was not a simple one.

They did not even have a permanent place to meet, or to keep the myriads of lists, notes, and materials they began collecting. Having felt a constant lack of time and space, both Vaughan and Whitmore would tell anyone that a design team needs both! And when that redesign was complete and presented to the 74 potential team members, what was the outcome? It will be revealed, as promised; but just not yet.

Design Characteristics. Certain principles of redesign generally apply, despite the differences between organizations, and successful redesigns tend to have certain characteristics in common. Therefore, the list of design characteristics that follows is another useful strategic tool for all design teams to closely examine, and follow whenever appropriate.

1. The design should intentionally cross traditional functional lines and force closer internal customer-supplier relationships.

2. A work team should be responsible for a whole process if at all possible. This ensures that the team controls all or most of the components of the work. This increases ownership of the whole job.

3. Team developers can and should eventually develop more than one team. Design for multiple teams per team developer if possible.

4. One of the main goals of self-directed work teams is to reduce the need to "manage people" and to push decision making down to the lowest appropriate level. The design of the work can encourage or discourage decision making and problem solving.

5. Where possible, specialization should be reduced and cross-functional work encouraged.

6. Creative, "out of the box" ways of thinking are required to gain good solutions.

7. Begin by asking how this organization would be designed if it were started from scratch today.

8. There are no sacred cows. Don't let traditions or potential legal issues tie up the team. Whatever ideas you finally end up with may need to be approved by other levels or groups, but don't limit yourselves early in the design process or you will end up with something much less than is possible.

9. Try to find the best configuration to serve the customer. Look at the design as if you were a customer.

10. Look at the design from the internal customer's view as well. Ask, "Who will this team serve internally?" Can any of these "external" functions be brought into the team to make it more whole?

11. Don't worry about making it perfect. Do your best. We do not know enough about our system to make it perfect. Settle for a good 80 percent solution. In 12 to 18 months the organization will come back and do another redesign with the knowledge and experience we have gained.

Suggested Guidelines for the Design Team. Design teams are likely to function more easily and effectively if they heed the following guidelines.

- Persons on the design team *do not* represent their respective work areas. They represent the unit as a whole.

- Use consensus to make decisions. *Consensus* defined: a decision made that all can live with, despite varying degrees of enthusiasm or commitment. Consensus means the decision gets generally 80 percent agreement on most of the details of the proposal.

- Use problem-solving techniques rather than arguing. These techniques include the affinity diagram, brainstorming, flow-chart analysis, the Ishikowa fishbone, the interrelationship digraph; a consultant or your Human Resources Department can help with the specific technique. Which one you choose is less important than remembering that your job is problem solving, *not* arguing.

- Use data analysis techniques: line and bar graphs, histograms, pareto charts, etc. Again, there are resources available to address the need for specific and useful information that the design team must generate.

- Rotate facilitators each meeting or every hour. Chapter 2 featured a more detailed discussion of leadership rotation, which keeps involvement, motivation, and group ownership of the process high.

- Designate a recorder and timekeeper for each meeting and let the group decide if these tasks may, or may not, rotate.

- Set the Code of Conduct as early as possible. Participant expectations are managed more effectively in this way.

- Set a firm date for completion and for recommendations given to the Steering Committee, and plan from the beginning how to keep on that schedule.

- Invite resource people to the meetings as needed, and then, politely and respectfully, get rid of them. To be kinder and gentler about it: The design team will need input that is sometimes best obtained by inviting someone to address the group. But an audience of even one is far more than any design team should have!

- Do your homework before each meeting. Collect data carefully when required and be ready to present it as scheduled. To be ill-prepared is inconvenient, a time-waster, and sends a message of disrespect to your design team colleagues.

- Summarize results at the end of each session and distribute meeting notes to all members as soon as possible. This will accomplish more effective communications and operations for the design team.

- Consider these questions as a final guideline for defining the scope of the design team's explorations:

How will the physical layout be changed for teams?

Where will be teams be located?

What policies need to be reexamined or rewritten?

What union contract issues need to be monitored in the process?

How will team members be assigned?

How will we make the transition to teams and keep up production?

Who will be team developers?

How many team developers will be needed?

What jobs will the former managers have if they are not selected to be team developers?

What resources will be needed to make the transition?

The local structure at the worker level needs redesigning before the full team structure can be put in place. To better understand their workplace, the design team may do data collection in unfamiliar ways: interview workers and management at length; take tours of other, uninvolved sections of the company, or visit other companies; read books and articles on workplace redesign. As we've heard from Allen Fulford, which people become leaders in this process, and the things people become willing to do, often come as a surprise, especially to local managers. However, it is to be expected that design team members will take their work very seriously. This includes the ones willing to "bite the bullet" and make hard recommendations which make business sense but break sharply with past traditions and practices. It is their own house they are designing, and they are the ones who will have to live in it.

It is also important to note that any given design team cannot create a perfect design the first time. That is why the goal that the design team get it 80 percent right is fair and useful. Next year, another design team will be convened to clean up those areas which the first team did not anticipate. As the Wolferman's experience illustrates, a second design team, and subsequent ad hoc teams, can be formed as necessary. If an organization is able to convene the first redesign and go from there, the environment will be open and trusting enough that the need for subsequent redesign will be obvious and widely supported.

Some companies create a design team which functions full time for the duration of their assignment. This is not as effective or productive as a part-time assignment. The design team should stay in close touch with the workplace and the workers. This can only be done if the members are also working their regular jobs at least part of the time. The job of redesign will actually get done better and faster if the design team is a part-time, temporary assignment.

Again, it must be a balancing act. As the Bell Atlantic Collection Center design team found out, the demands of the day-to-day work on the job create added stress on the design team as they perform their task. Because there is no blueprint, management should be willing to listen to the design team and support all reasonable requests.

A Key Task: Examining the Role of Specialists. One of the design team's key tasks is to reexamine the role of specialists. At the Collection Center there are three main categories of collection work. Traditionally, the system has operated with collectors trained in only one area, who are unable to accomplish work of the other two types. The team design calls for each collector to be trained in all three areas.

Bell Atlantic has been typical of American corporations, which have typically used highly segmented work with job descriptions for each job which carefully outlined its duties and level of responsibility. Most line jobs had narrow responsibilities. Government and large corporations have been especially enamored of this approach. Smaller companies and organizations have often been denied the luxury. Many small businesses function more or less as teams by virtue of their size, and this has fostered flexibility. It is also true that many small businesses follow a top-down model, despite the small distance from the top to the bottom.

Specialization was developed 100 years ago and championed by the famous industrial engineer Frederick Taylor. A narrow job design made it easy to train people for the work, or replace them. Specialization also facilitated central control by the supervisor. This is true of both low-skill and high-skill jobs. The more narrowly the job is defined, the more the workers are dependent upon the supervisor to coordinate the work flow and parcel out resources. Such narrow definition creates a whole class of people who are pseudo-specialists. At SMP (a UAW plant), the custodial group had eight job descriptions for a twelve-person department. The actual skill differences between jobs were negligible, yet each of these people thought of themselves as a specialist. Moreover, they clearly talked like they owned their job. Declarations such as "That's not my job" or "That's Fred's job" were often heard.

This system of narrow job duties has always been found to create frustration for management and drive up the cost of doing business over time. The supervisors complained that there was a job to get done but they could never get the right people on the job at the right time. "We are always playing catch-up," one supervisor complained in a private interview. When the transition to a team structure was concluded, one broad job description was created and everyone was cross-trained to do all jobs. It took less than three months to cross-train everyone, with an immediate improvement in productivity. With redesign, the team's job is to keep the common areas clean and safe—that is everyone's job. Job ownership now falls to the team, not individuals. In addition, the custodial team has tried to make cleanliness and safety the whole organization's concern. They have enlisted help from other teams, placed signs around the facility to encourage cleanliness, and routinely visited other teams to brief them on housekeeping issues. The efforts of this team have made a great difference in how the whole plant viewed cleanliness. Now, instead of playing catch-up, this team is generally ahead of its assignments.

In highly skilled work teams, the design is more complex. An oil exploration group had about 60 people including geologists, geophysicists, geochemists, landmen, technicians, and clerical support. The company reengineered the process by breaking up the old specialty groups and putting different specialties together in work groups. Once this was accomplished, the groups were trained to do their own team redesign. One team studied their processes in such detail that their flow chart filled a 20- × 7-foot sheet of paper. When they were finished they found they were able to cut out 30 percent of the work activity. In the past, technicians and clerical support people had complained that they felt they were not being used to their fullest in the new groups. In the task analysis, the teams discovered that up to 40 percent of a geologist's time was taken up doing lower-skilled tasks. As a result, they began cross-training all support and technical staff to do many of these tasks. This immediately freed the geologist to do those things which required her specialized training, and also gave the technical and clerical people much greater responsibility and more interesting work. Subsequently, several of the technicians found a number of ways to automate much of the routine map drawing, leading to even greater time savings. Through their own efforts, the teams were able to cut as much as 50 percent of the time it took to prepare and recommend a site for exploratory drilling.

Asking two simple questions can help in understanding how a team with specialists should be redesigned. The first is "What is the level of specialization required to do the job?" The second is "What is the necessary level of interdependence to do the job?"

In most cases, specialization is the enemy of efficiency. That is, the more people specialize, the less valuable they may actually be to an organization. *Specialization* is defined as a cluster of skills and knowledge requiring such a high level of training and/or education that cross-training is not practical or there are legal or license requirements which would preclude cross-training. In an oil exploration team it would not be practical to cross-train a technician to be a geophysicist. In a medical office it would not be legal to cross-train a nurse's aide to write prescriptions. Yet even in these specialties there is room for "downloading" of skills, as illustrated in the example of the oil exploration team.

The questions to be answered by the design team are: *What level of specialization is really necessary to get the job done properly? And what level of cross-training is practical in our environment?* Whitmore, Vaughan, and the Bell Atlantic collections office design team found that the three existing specialties—which had traditionally created lines collectors could not cross—took a few months training at most to learn. As a result, the design team recommended that all associates receive full cross-training within the first year, with the expectation that everyone would do all jobs. There were decreases in errors and miscommunications, along with much less conflict in the office. The Collector Job Wheel shown in Fig. 7-1 is taken from Bell Atlantic's team-training materials and illustrates the design team's solution to redesigning the

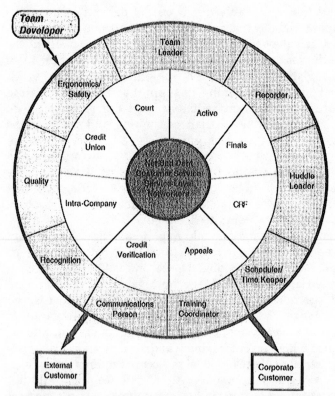

Figure 7-1 Collector Job Wheel. (Thanks to the design team of Bell Atlantic's South Virginia Collection Center for this design.)

collection center's work. (In Chap. 10 the wheel concept will be detailed. For now, examine the middle circle most closely to see what the design team came up with.)

Self-directed teams must have all the skills necessary to do the work and be able to shift significant work from one person to another. Unnecessary specialization creates an environment where one or more persons have a literal veto over getting the work done. Elaine Vaughan was the only person at the Virginia Beach center who was trained in all three specialty areas. With more than 26 years service, she was willing from the outset of the transition to teams to share what she knew. She echoes the primary question: What is absolutely necessary and what is not? That which is not can be cross-trained to others on the team. Our rule of thumb is that every task on the team be able to be done by at least three persons on the team. The Bell Atlantic Collection Center design team felt all team members could, over time, be trained in all areas. Whatever the final design, the team will be assured that a resignation, sickness, vacation, or promotion will not stop the work. Well-trained teams easily pick up the excess workload for short periods of time until the person returns or can be replaced.

So what was the result at the Bell Atlantic Collection Center? Manager Allen Fulford says that he would have been thrilled beyond expectation if two-thirds of the 74 people who had the choice picked the transition to teams. Whitmore and Vaughan hoped for high numbers each time they hung a list of what a job entailed. They worked hard to listen to the feedback each list yielded, while honoring the design team's commitment to deflect the constant repetitions of "What's it going to be? When are we going to know?"

This was a design team which found a way to listen to the many voices of its organization. Their presentation was put on videotape for those who missed it or came along later. Apparently it was a presentation worthy of preservation. Out of the 74 people eligible to choose a team, 72 people did just that. The number speaks to this design team's success.

8

The Role of the Team Developer

From Cop to Coach

There is a useful parallel between traditional attempts to manage people as objects, and the version of croquet played on the Red Queen's croquet ground, as described by Lewis Carroll in *Alice in Wonderland*.

> Alice thought she had never seen such a curious croquet-ground in her life: it was all ridges and furrows; the croquet-balls were live hedgehogs, and the mallets live flamingoes, and the soldiers had to double themselves up and stand on their hands and feet to make the arches.
>
> The chief difficulty Alice found at first was in managing her flamingo: she succeeded in getting its body tucked away, comfortably enough, under her arm, with its legs hanging down, but generally, just as she had got its neck nicely straightened out, and was going to give the hedgehog a blow with its head, it would twist itself round and look up into her face, with such a puzzled expression that she could not help bursting out laughing: and when she had got its head down, and was going to begin again, it was very provoking to find that the hedgehog had unrolled itself, and was in the act of crawling away: besides all this, there was generally a ridge or a furrow in the way wherever she wanted to send the hedgehog to, and, as the doubled-up soldiers were always getting up and walking off to other parts of the ground, Alice soon came to the conclusion that it was a very difficult game indeed.
>
> The players all played at once without waiting for turns, arguing all the while, and fighting for the hedgehogs; and in a very short time the Queen was in a furious passion, and went stamping about, and shouting, "Off with his head!" or "Off with her head!" about once a minute.

The parallel between traditional organizational structure and Carroll's croquet with the Red Queen is quite striking: substitute supervisors for Alice, and the President, CEO, and/or upper management for the Red Queen. All the supervisors are playing at the same time, trying to get their work done by managing the resources, depicted by the furrow-filled croquet field. The employees—represented by hedgehogs and flamingoes—sometimes operate as instructed, but sometimes look up with "a puzzled expression." Supervisors, like Alice, operate without properly coordinating efforts. Imagine if Alice was only one of many players joining the Queen in this chaotic game! Imagine all the Alices functioning on this field, using the instruments and agents given by edict of the Queen, completely oblivious to the inefficiencies of a poorly designed workplace. Add to that the pressure of the only consistent feedback from the top of the organization: *"Off with their heads!"*

In the transition to high-performance teams, managers must change their behavior from that of cop to that of coach. Because names have such a powerful influence on behavior, it is important to change not only the functions but the titles of those who will be charged with developing the teams. The word *supervisor* reinforces the behavior of overseeing other people. At the same time, the various nomenclature that means *manager* implies human beings can be "managed." Both terms are undesirable in a team-based structure because they do not accurately describe the role in a high-performance environment.

The notion that people need a supervisor, or need to be managed, is suspect. Examine again the fable from the Introduction to dispel this notion. As a reminder, look as far, or as close, as the homes and families and total lives of your employees. Employees need no supervisor to raise their children, buy a house or car, plan a vacation, allocate family resources. They do all of these quite well without "supervision." They also serve as presidents of local clubs, as officers, directors, and deacons in a host of religious, civic, and fraternal organizations, as players and coaches on teams. It would be naive to proffer the position that everyone, everywhere, can do everything. But employees who clearly have little or no say in their work environment are in charge of creating and operating in a broad range of environments outside of their jobs.

Why do people function well in these environments? Because they have ownership of these systems. People who have ownership need information, training, consultation, knowledge; they do not need supervision. Hired *hands* need supervision. As discussed in the previous chapter, narrow job definitions and management control over all the resources, assignments, and strategies are a time-honored tradition. But the times *must* be changing. Tom Whitmore, Bell Atlantic's team developer, describes his work environment prior to the transition to teams: "Here's what we need done. Do it!" Since the transition, a process has been put in place that will make the "Do it!" come from the team, not from a manager, supervisor, or "boss."

Organizations must pay a price when people are prevented from enjoying psychological ownership; that price is supervision. People who have ownership do not need to be watched over, controlled, or managed; their commitment to that which they claim is rarely questioned. People who do not have ownership often display contempt, benign neglect, or a commitment based solely on what the organization can do for them. They have little concern for the impact of their behaviors on the organization as a whole. The need for supervision is a sign that there is no effective system to encourage and develop psychological and material ownership.

Psychological ownership comes from involvement in planning, executing, and seeing the results of work. Material ownership comes from a system of compensation which is tied to performance of the team in some meaningful way. Material ownership does not mean ownership of stock necessarily, though that can be a part of the package, if possible and appropriate. (Compensation will be looked at more closely in Chap. 14.) However it is structured, ownership means having a personal stake in the activities of which one is a part.

For the last century, managers have labored under the illusion that humans can be managed. The reality is this: one manages things; one must lead people. Like Alice's flamingos, hedgehogs, and soldiers, humans are "cybernetic systems" with their own feedback loops, many of which are not related to the workplace. (The concept of cybernetic systems will be detailed in the next chapter.) There exists a vast range of human endeavor, enterprise, and potential. There are goals and dreams about homes, children, families, friends, retirement, betterments in life, amusements and leisure activities, social action projects on behalf of schools, communities, and the planet. Human beings will always work for *their* goals first. To the extent that the organization's goals help employees meet their own goals, they will work harder. When the corporation makes it difficult for people to realize their personal goals—or when their personal goals are actually hindered by the organization—fear, frustration, and inefficiency rapidly take over. In many companies and agencies these become the unfortunate facts of life.

Valerie Byrd goes directly and enthusiastically to the point: "The strict 10-hour days of people acting like robots are over. People have the ability to think for themselves. We just have to listen." She knows that her organization is far better off with a team structure and is confident that is how things will remain. As a team developer at Leader

National Insurance, Byrd says learning to listen to, and actually hear, what people are saying, was the toughest part for her in becoming a team developer.

At the beginning of her team developer career in May of 1992, Byrd admits she spent a great deal of time, "biting her tongue." She knew then she had to teach herself to keep from giving people an answer, her answer. She knew that what teams need is not supervision; what they need are systems which help workers understand their direct impact on the business. To this end, the role of the team developer is to teach, train, and coach team members in the many skills required to become self-managed.

When making the move away from traditional structures, organizations need to ask, "Why are there supervisors?" The answer; the supervisory function was (and is) developed to gain control over the line workers because the organization did (and does) not trust them, nor would the organization train them in how to do the work. It simply seemed easier to hire someone who already had much of the technical knowledge to oversee the work. With the low level of organizational investment or commitment to the worker, workers become interchangeable parts, easily replaced. In a stable economic environment this system, with all its inefficiencies, worked well enough to get by. In today's fast-moving and highly competitive market, this system is far too dependent upon the supervisor and managers. If people behaved mechanically, like the "robots" Valerie Byrd referred to, this would be an effective way to manage. But people behave more like hedgehogs, flamingoes, and soldiers, each having a mind of its own.

The transition to self-directed teams can be demanding for the team developer and team members alike. Most often, team developers are those who have been managers, assistant managers, and supervisors. They, and team members, find the new role much less clearly defined. The old system seems to have clear lines of accountability. Most often, however, this is only an illusion of accountability that grows more from a "chain of command" that could be used to assess blame when a real problem occurred. Self-managed teams build a system that uses and encourages the team to creatively find solutions to the organization's varied challenges. Under the traditional systems, workers who have felt little ownership in the command chain see the supervisor as accountable.

This point is made quite dramatically by an employee interviewed several years ago in a medical laboratory. He said this:

> If the supervisor did not tell me I did not do it. If she was gone for
> the morning, I did what I was told until I was finished then I went

out and had a cigarette. As long as we met our quota it really didn't matter what other groups were going through. I remember one week when we had almost no work because of a front office screwup, the department next door was screaming for help because a new test had become very popular. We mentioned to our supervisor that we could help. She explained to us that we were not trained to do their work and if the other supervisor found out we could help, they would be *borrowing* us all the time and not planning their own work properly. Above all, helping them would make us look like we did not have enough work to do and that would be a direct reflection on her.

The transition, especially for supervisors, is difficult because of their natural fears, including fears about job security, loss of perceived control, and decreased ego gratification. The drive to contribute at a perceived higher level is what motivates many managers to try and continue to move up the organizational ladder. Keep in mind, this upward mobility exists because the organization's design, and systems which support it, bolster the top-down structure. Managers and supervisors have been known to take pay cuts when they were promoted, especially when being salaried meant they could no longer earn overtime. Why would someone promote into a lower-paying and/or harder-working and more vulnerable command chain position? The motivation for many managers could be to gain the satisfaction that comes from contributing at a higher level, to feel the achievement of a product completed with their direction, to have a wider and more interesting range of tasks, to have more control over their own time and be released from the hassles and drudgery of daily production. All these, and more, are sought by the supervisor because they make her life more fulfilling and interesting.

With the arrival of the team concept, the supervisor is asked to relinquish much of these aforementioned motivators. The team may take them over, because the team gets motivation from these same activities. To that, add the productivity gains and efficiencies from, for example, not having to seek out a supervisor to make a decision, or from team-based decisions that empower the team and the organization. When an entire organization is opened up, the entire organization benefits.

In the transition to true teams, little will be left of the old control paradigm of management. With the transformation to teams, the team developer's raison d'être must change from gratification through control to gratification through development. Much as a parent gains satisfaction and pride from the development of his child, the team developer now must find inner gratification from watching teams grow and develop in the business. The successful team developer is a person who can at once challenge a team and help it develop a team to new heights of performance, without taking primary ownership for that achievement.

When a child leaves home and succeeds in the world, the parent can take credit for laying the foundation, but cannot take credit for the child's achievement. The stronger the foundation, the greater the team's potential for achievement. The team developer's role is to lay the foundation. The team developer's function is not to control anything, but rather to support everything team related: to help the team build interpersonal skills, manage conflict, use feedback effectively, learn quality tools, allocate resources, manage time effectively, and set goals.

The change from supervisor or manager to effective team developer is like the process of the team transition itself—a controlled, studied, supported, and encouraged evolution. It cannot occur overnight. But if it drags on too long, it will likely flounder and die. Generally, in approximately the first 12 to 18 months of the transition to teams, the team developer will have far more interaction and coaching duties than later, when the team is mature. In the evolution of team developers the first 18 months involve a good deal of coaching and counseling. Once the teams have reached a level of maturity, immediate and ongoing development needs will be more predictable and less critical. The team developer will change focus as the teams acquire skills in value-added activities such as long-range planning, developing organizationwide initiatives, software development or refinement, marketing, and a host of other activities. The team developer will spend 80 percent of her time with team issues early in the process, and as little as 30 percent after three years. As teams mature they have less and less need for the team developer, just as children have less need for the parent as they grow older. This course of events carries with it a potential emotional threat: "What happens when the teams no longer need me?"

The skills and talents which team developers bring to the table are essential in maintaining the process, as well as moving it forward. The role of the team developer in the second year and beyond is much closer to that of a staff support person for the team than that of a more active developer. Two years of experience as a team developer gives far more skill and knowledge to the team developer than the same two years as a supervisor. That skill and knowledge should be, and can be, harnessed to ensure the long-term health of the organization. An organization that considers eliminating the team developers as a result of productivity gains has fallen back into the more traditional "short-term gains" mentality. It is true that the ranks of the team developers may shrink through attrition, promotion, or transfer, and these positions do not need to be filled. Many organizations get along fine with half to one-third as many team developers as they did supervisors—after three years. Those who remain as team developers can now begin adding value to the organization in new ways. It is important to discuss this openly with the team developers and to begin planning for the transition early in the process. In this way the team developers see a clear path to success in the organization and will be strong and valuable assets to it, in both the short term and the long term.

Remember, the transition to teams is a process which builds on itself. Management must become more open and trusting at the outset (see the discussion of the trust-building structures in Chap. 4). Once that behavior is modeled by management, the process gains credibility. This creates an environment where openness, trust, and the commitment to truly include everyone in the organization's work occur. As steering committees and design teams are selected, trained, and put in place, the team developers are also selected and begin their important work. Each of these needs the strength and support of the others, all in an effort to create a new human infrastructure that will support the new and true teams.

Who Should Be a Team Developer?

As you might assume from the discussion above, the characteristics which make a good supervisor do not necessarily make a good team developer. In over 10 years of working with this process and with hundreds of team developers, the following numbers seem to be generally accurate and useful:

- Fifty percent of former supervisors can make the transition, if they have proper support and training.
- Thirty percent require a good deal of coaching, training, and close support before they can fully make the transition.
- Twenty percent do not seem to make the transition at all. For them, it is best to take on different duties or transfer to another supervisory position outside the team environment. Some simply retire early or resign.

It is difficult, if not impossible, to predict who will or will not make the transition from manager to developer, from supervisor to educator, from cop to coach. Valerie Byrd assumed she would make the transition to team developer easily. She had been a certified facilitator, and in this role, as she says, "I was a friend to the teams, a support." As a facilitator she had been trained to be an unbiased helper in the team's feedback process (see Chap. 13 for discussion of the feedback process). The team developer she was called upon to replace never had enough time to do the job appropriately. Other duties kept him on the road, and after 10 months Byrd took over the job.

"The team was excited at having a developer who would be there all the time. We all thought I would just step in," Byrd says. She did, but as she said earlier, it involved a lot of "tongue biting." "I was always wanting to say `Do it this way!' But I had to force myself to listen, to hear what people were actually saying." Byrd has become a successful team developer, but she expected the process would be easier for her. She worked hard to be able to overcome her impulse to supply *her* answer. Byrd trained herself to listen to team members and to support their efforts to reach their own conclusions. And she will tell you that her training process is ongoing, even though she is now comfortable in the role.

Surprisingly, it often happens that autocratic, dictatorial supervisors become highly effective, adaptable, and flexible team developers. One supervisor, Steve, was by his own admission, known as a "hard" supervisor. In initial readiness assessment interviews for the company, many employees openly stated that Steve was one supervisor who would never make it in the new team environment. Two years later those same employees gave Steve, the team developer, a surprise birthday party with cake, decorations, and true appreciation of his transformation. Steve said it was doubly gratifying for him because he knew what they thought of him as a supervisor. Steve is an excellent team developer, partly because he, too, was dissatisfied with how people perceived him. With the advent of the team concept, he got "permission" to make a change. He also discovered he became part of a system that now values a more comfortable set of behaviors.

"You will always be surprised about some of the people that will step forward. People you would never expect will step up and take leadership positions when making the transition to teams." Allen Fulford of Bell Atlantic and Joe Forlenza of Standard Motor Products, Inc. (SMP), each used just about those same words. The two men have never met, but they have their commitment to self-directed teams in common. Fulford's work has been discussed directly. Indirectly, you were introduced to Joe Forlenza; he was the one who brought teams to SMP. (Chapter 5 profiled the Steering Committee he served on with Tom Norbury and Ernest Lewis.) Both men know that management must model behaviors, including opening up the organization's man-

The Role of the Team Developer

agement processes. Opportunities for growth and development must be given freely to all those who do step forward. They know that it is difficult to predict who will flounder and who will flourish as the team transition is instituted. But both men know that with the proper training and support, any organization will find people stepping forward to do jobs no one would have expected of them.

Few people bring to the job the full complement of skills required to do this new and innovative task of team development. What are the qualifications for a team developer? Less important are the skills; more important is the willingness to develop personally and professionally, and to learn new techniques, as well as finding ways to share them. Ultimately, the whole organization is learning and developing as well as learning a process to continue growth and development as a way of organizational life. Like Fulford, Forlenza, and other leaders who have taken an active role in making this transition, team developers must model their own development. Cultivating a team environment goes together with personal development; both kinds of "cultivation" must be seen as positive forces in the organization, which they will be if demonstrated by organizational leaders and team developers.

Valerie Byrd was not a supervisor; Thomas Whitmore was an assistant manager; both became successful team developers. It has been mentioned that a few former managers and supervisors may not find a comfortable place in the team-structured organization, either as team developers, consultants to teams in their areas of expertise, or in any other useful and appropriate position. Out of that approximately 20 percent who cannot adjust, for whatever reason, there will always be those who can find no alternative; they find work in the organization outside the team structures, or transfer, retire, or resign and move on.

But the failure of the few to adjust must be seen in the perspective of what the true-team structure does for the organization as a whole. Herb Tuttle of Wolferman's can tell you about the bakery manager who left after teams became the way of life at Wolferman's. Tuttle readily admits that this individual had skills in bakery operation that many felt were key to running the place. It was also clear that this individual could have carved out a position that would have kept him a major contributor in running the operation. However, he could not accept that everyone would be asked to contribute their own expertise to operating the entire company. But at the same time that this one key individual felt he could not stay, dramatic changes were taking place. In two years the entire plant went from one shift five days per week to operating round the clock, seven days per week. Turnover, especially among part-time seasonal workers, went from 300 percent to below 15 percent. Tuttle explains that the last year in which management hired the seasonal workers was the year when they saw the 300 percent turnover. The next season, when the teams hired their own seasonal help, they saw turnover drop 20 times! Yes, some will be compelled to get away, rather than get along with the team transition. But the number tends to be small and the gains to the many outweigh the losses to these few.

And in the last few years it seems that an increasing number of companies are advertising for individuals with team facilitation skills, perhaps indicating a trend in American business toward developing managers who will be effective in a team environment. Many companies now insist a new team developer have strong experience in employee empowerment processes, if not in a fully self-directed environment. However, higher education seems to be farther behind in supporting the new human infrastructure. The typical M.B.A. is among the most poorly equipped to take on the task of team development. Management programs may give some small amount of attention to employee empowerment, but rarely are the systems knowledge and specific techniques to make employee empowerment work part of the curriculum. After all, M.B.A. programs are most often geared to creating increased specialization by putting successful graduates in positions to make organizational decisions on their own. Strong signals are often given to students to climb the ladder of corporate America without regard to the voices of the people who make their promotions possible. They forget Isaac Newton's famous observation, "If I see farther than other men it is because I stand on the shoulders of giants." It is encouraging to see a few universities teaching courses on employee empowerment and even some courses on self-directed work teams, but much work is still required. There are a few programs which put people in teams and give them the opportunity to experience this way of working. Again, their own development models that of the team. As individuals and team members, a successful training program (either for a degree or an organization) teaches people team-supportive ways to work and behave.

How Should the Team Developer Behave?

In team meetings the team developer functions as an often silent conscience. Modeling of behavior is critical, and it begins with the first team meeting. The team developer must not lecture, give answers, or criticize the ideas tendered by team members, and absolutely must not argue with team members.

What the team developer should be doing at meetings to insure personal and team success begins with asking questions about team goals and measurements. In asking the questions and serving as the team's conscience, it is important for the team developer to draw all team members into the discussions by asking for opinions and experiences, while being sensitive to the fact that there may be discomfort about the discussions, especially at the outset. For many employees, this will be the first time anyone has ever asked them these questions, and many find it takes time to participate in talking about the work they do. Recognizing and praising people may be different and even difficult for the new team developer, just as it may be new for team members to hear. But here again, modeling behavior is a key to making the transition work.

The real work of the team developer is done before and after the team meeting. Before the team meeting the team developer meets with the key players in the meeting to make sure they have a well-developed agenda and know what they want to accomplish. After the meeting, the team developer might meet with the team leader to do some coaching and discuss how the meeting went. The team developer might meet with others who had key roles in the meeting and coach them as well. This will be an important role until the team gets used to the process, i.e., for approximately the first year.

Outside the meetings, the team developer will provide administrative support to the team while teaching the team how to take over its own administrative duties. Things like timekeeping, administering overtime, developing work schedules, tracking quality and productivity; these, and most other management functions, will be taught to the team over time. The successful team developer looks for every appropriate opportunity to teach some new task to team members. Wherever and whenever possible the successful developer turns over more and more growth opportunities and responsibility to the team. Just as team developers will want team members to seek them out for coaching and learning opportunities, developers must seek these same experiences for themselves. Modeling builds skills and credibility at the same time.

Many team developers, especially those who have been the manager, or "the boss," will be viewed as authority figures until proven not to be. The most common response to authority figures is either dependence and submissiveness or behaviors that are in opposition to what the authority figure says and does. Neither of these responses is helpful to the team process. Add to this defensiveness, and you have a recipe for team developer failure. The comfort of the new team as members learn trust, communication, and real empowerment must be a primary concern to the successful team developer. Without a level of emotional maturity and an ego that can be kept under control, the developer will be prone to reprisals, unconscious discrimination, and negative reactions to feedback from team members. The group will recognize these behaviors and either withdraw or feel a need to fight back. The successful team developer can separate who they are from what they do as they work with the team to empower them to take charge of their work.

The Team Developer's Tasks

Now let's look at the major tasks of the team developer. The three tasks of the team developer are to help the team stay focused on goals, help manage the boundaries, and help with training and team-building activities.

Focusing on Goals. The team developer teaches the team how to measure and set goals. The team developer should have strong training in using quality tools. Throughout the process the team developer emphasizes the use of tools for analysis and problem solving. On a monthly or quarterly basis the team reviews its performance against goals with the team developer. When problems are encountered, the team developer has an opportunity to teach the team skills in problem solving, work-flow analysis, and process improvement.

Keeping the team focused on goals requires meeting regularly with the team leader and the quality leader to coach and teach them. Helping the team chart the team measurements and interfacing with management about cross-team problems aid in keeping the focus on team goals. Just as each organization, steering committee, and design team will help define what the goals and measures will be for that environment, the team developer becomes the messenger of the team process to the team. (Subsequent chapters will look at more specifics of team structures and systems, all of which team developers will use in their team-building work.)

Managing Boundaries. Early in any team's development they will easily stray into territory which is "out of bounds." Teams often say, "You said we are empowered, but you won't let us do anything." The team developer, with the help of the Steering Committee and the levels of empowerment (see Chap. 5), shows the team the road map toward full empowerment. Empowerment is a developmental process. At each level the team tests its muscle and group intellect before moving on to the next level.

One company did not fully appreciate this tendency of teams to try too hard in the early stages, and had two different teams develop plans for changing the corporate sick leave policy and the compensation system. While these needed modification eventually, they should be out of bounds for a young team. It is enough that they learn how to set and track their own goals and processes without trying to change the entire company.

There are two different types of boundaries. First are the organizational boundaries of responsibility and accountability. Teams often try to solve other teams' problems rather than look at themselves. A new insurance-processing team may want to work on a problem they see with underwriting while not facing the fact that their own team has an unacceptably high error rate. The team developer's role is to ask, "Why is the team working on an underwriting problem when we have so much to do in our own house?" The team developer needs to be aware of the boundaries of responsibility and accountability, and has to ask the "embarrassing questions" when the team steps outside them.

The second type of boundary is related to the maturity level of the team. A three-month-old team is not ready to begin hiring and disciplining its own members. This is a task for a very mature and knowledgeable team (12–18 months). The team may participate in some meaningful way in these activities. But they need to know they cannot own these processes until they have been fully trained. In each organization, and perhaps for each team, that will mean learning a new set of skills. In addition to specific criteria for the position to be filled, team members will need to learn such personnel information as EEOC guidelines and legal bounds of job interviews, as well as interviewing methods. It is through this training that the work of managers and supervisors is actually distributed to the teams.

Training and Team Building. Early in the life of the team, the team developer should emphasize building the team. Brief (10- to 15-minute) getting acquainted exercises are very important. Even people who have worked with each other for years may know surprisingly little about each other. The object is to help the team members know each other well enough to begin trusting and working out differences.

Teams are not equipped to handle both close interdependence and demands of the business. The team developer must take up the slack here while helping to educate the team. During team meetings, mini-training courses should be given to the team on various business issues: budgeting, marketing, hiring, cross-selling, understanding the compensation system, quality, discipline, scheduling, problem-solving skills, work-flow analysis. These mini-courses keep the team informed, increase their skills, and reinforce the learning they do in the formal classroom sessions on many of these topics. (In the Bibliography there is a list of additional training resources, as well as relevant titles from the entire gamut of team readings.)

In a start-up mode, when no one really has the skills, team developers will be able to develop two teams (6 to 10 persons) each if they have proper training and guidance. As teams mature, the number can increase to three or even four teams. The mature team needs less guidance than the new team, and the new team members need more coaching than the senior team members. Since team members will come and go, and teams may form or reform to meet business needs, four teams is a maximum for one team developer. If a team consists of 6 to 10 people, this would be about one team developer for every 32 individuals. But the critical factor is the number of teams, not the number of people on the team. Four teams of any reasonable size is all one person can handle effectively.

Depending on the other expectations of the team developers, the number of teams may never go beyond three per team developer. If a team developer is expected to conduct training sessions, provide technical consultation, lead or participate in cross-department task forces, and develop software or test marketing or customer service initiatives, that developer will need something less than four teams. These are general guidelines; each organization must find its own levels, numbers, and assignments.

Evaluating the Team Developers

Evaluation of a team developer must reflect changes in the systems throughout the organization. A key system change is always in the performance appraisal system. A new system will need to be designed to evaluate the skills and performance of the team developer. The key principle in team developer appraisal, as well as manager appraisal, is to ensure that each person is appraised by their internal or external customers. Unless the system itself rewards and recognizes this type of behavior, other behaviors will prevail which may not be compatible with the goals of the team concept.

The team developer's performance should first be tied to the development of the team in accordance with the levels of empowerment set out by the Steering Committee. If a team progresses well along these levels they will be acquiring the skills to improve their performance and their interpersonal functioning. A team which does not progress does not improve in skills and will not improve in performance. This aspect of performance might be 30 percent of the team developer's appraisal, and would be directly tied to the Steering Committee's appraisal of a team's development. This appraisal component will weigh more heavily in the first two years, since teams require less and less of this type of behavior as they reach maturity.

Second, the team developer's performance appraisal should be tied to the team's own evaluation of the team developer. The team developer must see the team as a customer, or she will be tempted to revert back to old supervisory behaviors. A system of team performance appraisal should be developed to give team developers feedback on their work from the team's perspective. This aspect of appraisal might be 30 percent of the evaluation. It would be based upon a "performance contract" between the team and the team developer in which both spell out their expectations and criteria for assessment.

A team developer's performance on specially assigned projects and as a member of the team of team developers might comprise another 30 to 40 percent. This portion of the appraisal would be done by the other project members or other team developers.

Without redesigning the appraisal system, as well as the compensation system, team developers will never be able to fulfill their new role. More than one company, in implementing the transition to teams, has failed to find the political will to change its systems. The result is upper-management behavior which continues to treat team developers as line supervisors. If upper management continues to recognize, reward, and appraise team developers as if they are line supervisors, team developers will continue treating the teams as subordinates. They do this because they feel they are being held accountable for the team's results, *not* the team's development. This leads to micromanagement on the part of both team developers and management. It is not a process built on modeled behaviors and systems which support empowered employees.

Organizations have begun the team transition with very strong growth in individual teams only to see that growth slowly erode as the teams, and team developers, were strangled by the noose of micromanagement. One of the most difficult tendencies to spot and deal with is "management creep." In the first two years, management sees great gains in team performance over the traditional top-down structures. This leads to management's expectation of continued gains at an accelerated pace. When teams hit the two-year plateau, management tends to panic and step in to put pressure on the teams. This is a time when management should be giving training and providing compensation incentives for performance to both the team developers and the teams. The more management tries to pressure the team developers and teams, the more poorly they perform, which leads management to increase the pressure in a very traditional way. This negative cycle leads to employee turnover and increased training costs.

Joe Forlenza advises, "As much as you think you know, there is always more to be learned. This process takes a major commitment for training. It is a process which never ends. A timeless process where implicit trust and development must occur over time." Forlenza knows the pressure management can apply, especially when early gains in productivity spur them to fall into old behaviors. There is a tendency among management to push for more—rather than pushing for the process to take the course set by the Steering Committee, design teams, team developers, and pushing to get all the resources needed to get them trained and in place. Forlenza had to be aware of what the corporate reaction would be to the changes he was making. But he got the support he needed to make self-managed teams the new way of life at SMP in Kansas. After more than four years, Forlenza now spends one week per month in Kansas; the rest of the time he is at other SMP locations, spreading the team process. His commitment to team development is spreading; he is a successful developer of teams.

How Do the Team Developers Develop?

Training is the foundation for the teams and is just as important for the team developers. Team developers initially should get comprehensive training in group process, conflict mediation, problem solving, data analysis, and facilitation. While training is essential, the real task of developing team developers is done in the team developer team. The team developers should be considered a team in themselves; this team may span more than one department if the number of team developers is small in a given area. The primary purpose of a team developer team is to provide a support and training group for the crucial self-development. Traditional managers and supervisors are largely left to their own devices and to the haphazard development efforts of *their* managers. This system does not develop uniform skills and is not suitable for the team developer role. The structure of the team developer team should be designed to provide team developers a forum for discussing their issues and problems in developing teams and the new human infrastructure to support them.

At SMP in Kansas, all team developers and all managers at the entire plant have attended a team developer team meeting every month since introduction of the team concept. They convene their meetings at a local restaurant where they have a 60- to 90-minute meeting and meal. During this time they *do not* solve problems; rather they encourage problem sharing and idea gathering. Team developers are encouraged to share their concerns and frustrations as well as their successes and effective techniques. The net effect of this process is to encourage strong, uniform skill development. If team developers are having problems, they can get ideas and feedback in this safe, friendly, and cooperative forum. If they have had a success, they can share this as well.

The team developer team need not meet every week, though this may be desirable in some organizations. The meeting can be held once a month with the members rotating team leadership responsibilities just as the teams do. In addition, in the spirit of open meetings (Chap. 4), two or more nonmanagers should be invited to the meeting to see the process and take their observations back to the teams. Other educational activities may be planned such as case studies, reports from other efforts in the team concept, or training in new skills. Other duties the team developer team may perform could include cross-department coordination, training courses for teams, discovering and dealing with cross-team problems, troubleshooting, and process improvement.

As Forlenza states, this is a training process that will change over time as the organization, and its individuals, transform to true teams. What Forlenza calls "a timeless process where implicit trust and development must occur over time" is brought from upper management through the Steering Committee and design teams to the organization and its teams. As the process continues, keep in mind that the main messenger of this change is the team developer.

9

Understanding Group Process

The Mechanistic Model vs. the Cybernetic

One of the best kept secrets of self-directed work teams is the process by which teams grow and develop. The less successful approach to teams generally bypasses this basic process of building effective groups. Some of the best team intentions of management have led to tragic results. By leaving out the process of growth and development for the team itself, organizational leaders have done the equivalent of sending teams out on the high seas in a rowboat.

Without a supportive organization, teams will flounder and fail about 80 percent of the time. The other 20 percent will do well for up to two years, but the organization will slowly close in around them and restrict their movement until they can no longer function as a true team. The new human infrastructure must be in place as a framework to support team growth. When management trains only itself in team process and fails to construct a supportive and team-friendly infrastructure, teams cannot survive. The obstacles teams encounter will, over time, subvert the success of any and all teams. Time after time, companies with functioning self-directed teams which were designated as pilot programs or test groups have exhibited the same pattern. These groups start out with a good deal of enthusiasm and rapidly discover that if they are to do anything, they will have to do it on their own. Management has neither the skill nor the inclination to facilitate their development. This leads to an elite mentality on the part of the team members, as they see an ambivalent and unsupportive organization all around them. Other groups develop hostility towards them and supervisors see them as a threat to the rest of the organization's way of life. As the lone team experiences success in accomplishing its work, despite these odds, members gain a strong feeling of group identity. The group personality includes the sense that it is special in many ways. Unfortunately, the team sees the rest of the organization as quite hostile—if not an actual enemy.

These groups often do surprisingly well, despite the odds, in the same way that an elite and dedicated fighting force may rally and hold off an enemy of overwhelming size. The long-term effect, however, is the polarization of the workplace and strong negative feelings throughout the organization. After about two years, it becomes very difficult for the team to maintain itself against the larger organization. Its members often have learned valuable skills and shine in the organization. This allows them to transfer or be promoted to better jobs outside the team. Then the team is left in a weakened position. It now has to integrate new members who have not experienced the bonding of the original team and who are not prepared to stand up to the larger system. In some ways, new members become Trojan horses to this isolated self-directed team. They are not as dedicated to the team and often have ties and loyalties to the old system and the rest of the organization. This, then, is the beginning of the end of the team. It may take another two years for it to become reabsorbed into the organization, but eventually it will be nothing more than an "experiment that failed." This scenario can be prevented only if the larger culture changes radically, becoming more friendly toward employee empowerment, which is in turn the basis for successful teams. (The case against pilot programs is also discussed in Chap. 4.)

Traditional organizations and management structures use a mechanistic model of group process; team-based organizations use a cybernetic model. The mechanistic model assumes that people can be managed as inanimate objects. That is, tell people to do something and they do it just the way you intended. Like machine parts, designed to fulfill a particular function in a prescribed manner, people are placed in the mechanical model to accomplish predictable tasks. It is possible, and even a usual occurrence, for a work unit to be comfortable with and function well with their manager; her style will appear to work in this mechanistic way. Work that is routine and is easily organized by one central figure often appears to work this way. These groups are often made up of individuals who like structure and routine. They can get vast amounts of work done and are easily directed by a strong central authority figure. If the work they do, and the pressure on that work, changes little from day to day or year to year, this can be seen as a successful system. Only small changes in routine, however, can upset such groups completely. And in the contemporary work environment, change is becoming the only reliable constant. Implementation of a team approach with cross-training and process improvement requirements can throw an organization working on the mechanistic model into prolonged chaos.

Many organizational leaders believe in the mechanistic model, despite the vast amount of evidence that it is not effective in the fast-moving global economy now emerging. Listening to their language reveals their zeal, no matter how unreasonable, for the mechanical approach, both in and out of the work setting.

"I told him to do it this way and he messed it up!"

"I gave them specific instructions a dozen times and they still don't get it!"

"If you would read the memo, you would know how it's supposed to be done."

"I told my daughter if she cleaned her room by noon we would go shopping, and she did."

"I gave my husband a dozen roses so he would forgive me for having forgotten our anniversary."

Implicit in all these is the belief that "my actions can, and should, cause a specific and predictable effect." When the expected effect fails to materialize, the human tendency is to find the fault in the person, just as one would find fault in a machine part which broke. If the people in a mechanistic system do not behave as desired, they are obviously "broken." The system is geared toward fixing or replacing the broken part or person. A mechanistic view of the world says that people respond in specific, predictable ways. (This may remind you of Alice, as a metaphor for management, in the previous chapter.)

This is the predominant view of the world held by most workers, but it is particularly troublesome that most managers hold it as well. A typical manager's outburst reveals the frustration it often engenders: "I have told them a hundred times to check these boxes against the packing slip before shipping them, yet they still let bad product go out! When I turn the key to my car, it starts properly; why don't people respond as reliably; after all they are supposedly smarter than my car. They must be stupid [broken] or they would not do things like this."

The underlying assumption is clear: "When I tell someone to do something, they should do it just as I intend." Those in charge of any organization structure and order work for their greatest comfort, as do their employees as much as is possible. The work progresses smoothly enough, and, at the end of the day, instructions have been carried out, work was accomplished, and the books balance. People feel good and the manager can go home feeling like something concrete was accomplished.

This approach hides a multitude of sins, problems, and challenges while it assumes that processes which work smoothly are also the most efficient. This fundamental assumption by all, or at least most, in the organization allows for the perpetuation of an illusion of efficiency. In order to move forward in work-process improvement, this stable routine must be disrupted, often to the chagrin of all. The goal is to refine processes continually and ensure that everything possible is being done to serve the customers of the team. This cannot be done if routines—the mechanics of operations—take precedence over the customer's wishes or needs. When disruptions to the "normal routine" occur, because of new customer demands or other required changes, interpersonal processes will suddenly surface which were not evident before. People will suddenly become easily disturbed, deadlines will be missed, work will become less efficient while large amounts of emotional energy will be focused on what is wrong with the whole process. For those wedded to a mechanistic model, the threat of its disruption, or its actual demise, can cause a real personal crisis.

There are some personalities which do not seem capable of the transition to self-directed teams. These people may well leave the organization. They can often be people who were very high producers in the old system, whose success depended heavily on structured routine and on the stability of the system. Like the bakery manager at Wolferman's described by Herb Tuttle in Chap. 8, key people in the existing structure may have great difficulty in the transition to teams. Before Wolferman's began the transition to teams, this highly placed individual was considered a successful professional. But the organization as a whole found a way to be better even though this individual could not be part of the new team-based structure.

In a volatile environment the mechanistic model can only fail. As more and more organizations either choose, or are forced to be, more responsive to customer need, the cybernetic model replaces the mechanical. The main component of all cybernetic designs is the feedback loop, which allows for self-correction. Simple cybernetic systems include thermostats and automotive cruise control. All organisms are cybernetic. From protozoans to humans, all living organisms have the ability to receive and act upon information relevant to the tasks they perform. At the Red Queen's croquet ground, Alice is seen using the flamingo to strike the hedgehog and knock it through the arc of the soldier. As Alice swung, the flamingo lifted its head, the hedgehog crawled away, and the soldier moved about. Each of these organisms received feedback on their position in this mad sport and did their utmost to remain safe. (They were more experienced than Alice, and knew they only had to hold her off long enough for the Queen to render her ubiquitous instruction, "Off with her head!")

The team process makes use of the cybernetic systems model; it can seek and use feedback for self-correction. In the mechanistic model, the accepted routine provides the illusion of security, but also prevents adaptation to current and ever changing conditions. By blocking the use of self-correcting feedback, the mechanistic model leaves a work group able to rely on its routine only, and unable to adapt to almost any change. In the team approach, the security needs of individuals are not met by the structure of a routine. Instead, security needs are met through stronger interpersonal relationships, which provide a trusting environment in which to work. This new team environment allows for rapid change. The sharing of the psychological burden of rapid change in response to market conditions across the entire team replaces the security once found in the predictable, conventional, unresponsive, and ineffective routine. Understanding group processes is a key to instituting the cybernetic systems which support the true-team structure. This view of groups and how they function will complete the examination of design issues in making the transition to a self-directed team-based organization.

The Anthropological Context of Teams

Humans seek, even crave, security—especially emotional security. In the past, corporations promised security through wage and salary plans, benefit packages, health insurance, bonus payments, commissions, and all kinds of compensation. These have been a substitute in many ways for a more fundamental guarantee—interpersonal security.

Looking back in human history, anthropological evidence for well over a million years shows that human ancestors were highly social creatures. Long before the industrial age, before farming or herding, these hunter-and-gatherer ancestors accomplished the tasks of day-to-day survival in groups. Groups provided security for the individual members of the clan. When wild animals, forces of nature, or other clans threatened, there was strength in numbers. No one person could survive easily alone, so human genetic survival was dependent upon the protection of individuals by the group. The very immature and dependent young were especially needy of the group's protection.

The roots of individualism are only a few hundred years old in human civilization; the roots of interdependence are a million years old. Within this genetic heritage of interdependence is found the fundamental building block of self-directed teams. While humans in most contemporary societies desire financial security, people have always craved the emotional security which comes from a group working together to survive. This basic drive to survive through cooperation, while stifled by much of our culture, is still fundamentally intact within the human psyche. But, as in prehistoric tribal culture, cooperation comes only within a context of trust. The cultural system and its leaders must find ways to support, nurture, and build the sense of trust in the group.

While we are not proposing a transition to a contemporary tribal system, people can work more effectively if they tie into the basic drive to cooperate for survival. In order to accomplish this, the leaders and the cultural milieu must be believable and trustworthy. A corporate culture that only pays lip service to the principles of cooperation for survival will earn the disdain of the work force. A leader who does not live these values will be equally disdained.

Western and Asian notions of hierarchical structures have advanced knowledge, economic well-being, and political security for many. But it would be foolish to think that this is the only way to organize humans into productive groups. While hierarchical organizational approaches have brought great benefit to humanity, they have also inhibited equally beneficial talents. How little work is, at present, accomplished in true-team environments? How much time and productivity are wasted? What societal talents have been lost through hierarchical (mechanical) approaches:

- The ability to focus on a problem without regard to rank or position and find the best solution.

- The ability to work closely together with a common purpose for a common good.

- The ability to teach others the norms of the culture in a positive manner, congruent with the purposes of the larger organization.

- The ability to subordinate individual good to that of the group, trusting that one's own needs and desires will be met eventually.

- The ability to share the profits of labor in an equitable fashion, meeting everyone's needs to a large degree.

- The ability to trust the leadership to make equally hard sacrifices as the workers.

These other abilities can be made available to the organization through teams. Teams recreate much of the social climate of earlier societies, allowing people to feel more emotionally secure and able to devote more of their energy to productivity and creativity in the workplace. Hierarchical organizational structures do not satisfy the natural human need for emotional security. Individuals spend an inordinate amount of energy trying to create conditions of emotional security. They create work friendships, cliques, and emotional alliances with others in the workplace. The less secure a person feels, the more energy he puts into trying to make emotional alliances with others. Gossip, personal conflicts, office politics, posturing for position, and a host of other activities that have little to do with accomplishing work are the result. These endeavors take up tremendous amounts of time in phone calls, meetings, discussions, interventions, ineffective trainings that absorb time without yielding benefit to the customers. The cost in economic terms is enormous.

In virtually all cultures where the basic unit is a clan or extended family group, the leader has both privileges and obligations to the group. The leader is obligated to perform certain rituals to protect the group, to ensure fertility of the soil or a profitable hunt. The leader is also called upon to provide wisdom and sit in judgment, and leaders are held accountable by the clan for their decisions. In no traditional culture is the leader allowed to rule the group with impunity or without consulting the other elders, priests, shaman, or warriors. This aboriginal system of decision making, while unfamiliar to modern Western culture, was the rule of humanity for thousands of generations before modern hierarchical structures became more popular, about six thousand years ago. Much of humanity lived in nonhierarchical cultures until less than three hundred years ago. Much of Africa, South America, North America, and large parts of Asia and Oceania were populated with cultures which had very little or no hierarchy until the last few generations. This means that the nature of leadership has changed radically in only the very recent past.

To repeat, the move toward autocratic, top-down-only, "the boss knows best" leadership is a relatively new phenomenon. This type of leadership largely ignores, or tries to suppress, the more fundamental cooperative and group-oriented nature of people. By centering decisions on an arbitrarily appointed leader, called a "supervisor" or "manager," and by ignoring the need for humans to team up, much energy, effort, and experience are wasted—wasted as people try to create a human group which will provide them with emotional and interpersonal security. If this natural tendency is respected, providing the cultural vehicle to nurture and maintain groups, they can produce high-quality products and services while the individuals in them feel very good about one another because they are secure in their emotional environment.

A number of conditions affect a group's ability to develop and mature. The size of the team, the membership, the selection procedure, and the group's interpersonal processes have a strong influence on the success of a team-based organization.

Size of the Team

One of the key functions in team development is the number of interactions required of a group to learn to work together and trust one another, as well as preserve an effective and efficient work team. Take these scenarios:

- Consider that it can require 15 to 30 minutes of contact per day between two people over a period of six months for them to understand each other's styles and expectations and to adjust to working cooperatively together. This is an investment of 65 hours over six months for two people to learn to work together. During this time mistakes and misunderstandings will occur which can hurt productivity, even when working toward a cooperative team-based organization.

- Consider the addition of a third person; the investment of time must increase immensely. Where two people required 65 hours, three people may require 195 hours to accomplish the same contact time.

- Consider the addition of another, now the fourth person. Now, something truly statistically significant happens. The amount of time required for four people to share the same amount of contact as the initial two increases to 390 hours. With five it becomes 650 hours.

The overhead in time and energy increases dramatically with group size. This explains in large measure why smaller teams tend to mature faster than larger teams and why there seem to be optimal sizes for teams. Teams with more than 10 to 12 members require a good deal of time to mature and pay a higher price in "interpersonal overhead." On the other hand, if a team is too small it may not have the ability to take advantage of cross-training and job sharing, which are a basic tenets of the true-team organizational structure. Size also plays an important role in the stability of teams, both new and mature. A group of three to four people is less able to adjust to the temporary or permanent loss of a member than a larger team.

Type of work and degree of specialization should also be considered in determining team size. A "corporate complaints" team functioned quite well for several years with only four persons, partly because the work was not highly structured or time-sensitive, an absence was less devastating to this team than it might have been to many others. The team did "borrow" people from other larger teams occasionally to maintain its workload. This design was the choice of upper management, who wanted customer complaints placed in the hands of a few highly trained, experienced, and accountable people.

A look at the structures of sports teams can also shed light on the question of team size. In every major sport, there are no more than 12 persons from a team playing actively at any time, with the exception of rugby with 15. A basketball team fields 5 players at a time, American football 11, Canadian football 12, soccer 11, baseball 9, and so on. (Those on the bench waiting to be sent into the game are often organized in team units within the team, like offense, defense, and second string.) It would seem that this consistency of size says something about the natural size of effective human groups.

Size of the local organization is influential in the maturation process. Large organizations tend to have greater difficulty implementing because of their more complex bureaucracy. When an organization breaks down into units of 150 persons or fewer, the process can move forward faster than when the organization remains one large administrative unit. Joe Forlenza, Ernest Lewis, and Tom Norbury described how Standard Motor Products, Inc. (SMP), has benefited from smaller business units. By splitting into four units of no more than 150 people each, SMP made a successful transition to teams. Forlenza and his colleagues learned the efficacy of a more reasonable and substantial focus on their organization's work. The smaller units, with 15 to 20 teams each, are much more responsive to their internal and external customers.

At Bell Atlantic's corporate Human Resources Department, Margaret Sears is one of two organizational development consultants who has been working to bring team-based structure to this corporate giant. Managers like Allen Fulford had been calling Sears and her colleague Janie Payne asking "How do we get teams?" Fulford's was one of several work units chosen as initial application areas. After 72 of 74 eligible workers asked to be assigned to teams, the design team at the Residential Collection Center chose a reasonable size format: the 72 employees were divided into nine teams. Sears and Payne knew that in a company as large as Bell Atlantic, finding appropriate units to begin the team process was a way to "have a focus to begin looking at the larger system."

The Bell Atlantic design team that Elaine Vaughan and Tom Whitmore served on addressed the team size for the Residential Collections Center with many cups to juggle, literally. Team size could not be the only factor. They had to balance functions, as most of the collectors were trained in only one of three categories the center, therefore the groups, would have to process. Also, the agreement with the union maintained seniority, as well as requiring each team to be balanced by job function experience. (It is planned that cross-training over time will give team members the training to accomplish all three of the collection functions.)

Once they knew that 72 out of 74 eligible employees had opted for the team structure (see Chap. 7), eight teams of nine people each made sense, given the environment and type of work. So they put people's names in cups according to seniority and function and drew names from the cups. More important than exactly who was in each team, was the size of the team. However, each team had to be assured of its balance of the crucial criteria: in this case, function and seniority as defined by the design team. The "cup method" gave the design team a simple, unbiased way to make their team assignments.

Team Membership and Selection

As demonstrated by the Bell Atlantic example above, more than size must be considered in forming groups. Group membership may also be a factor in team maturation, especially when specific issues of the environment must be addressed, such as union and function criteria at Bell Atlantic's collection center. However, membership criteria have often been given too much attention. Some organizations go to great lengths to test and place "the right" people on a team. While this may work well in a pilot program or for isolated teams, it is not practical in other situations, nor is there evidence that it greatly improves efficiency. If the organization has the resources to test and place people, it may shorten start-up time, but beyond start-up, there may be little effect from these placement efforts.

The real test of self-directed work teams is to use the people already employed in the organization and teach them the skills needed to work effectively in teams. Selection is a luxury which may not be worth the cost, unless already a part of the culture or when, as noted, specific criteria are crucial to accomplishing the work. Often, the criteria of the local environment dictate teams formed from the people already in that work area without any selection process. The design team proposes a structure which builds many team assignments directly into the structure itself. The process (or lack of) works quite well.

The primary effect of an elaborate selection process within an established organization is to increase the Hawthorne effect. (As described in Chap. 4, the term *Hawthorne effect* refers to research done in the 1930s at the Westinghouse Hawthorne plant, in which researchers noticed that simply paying special attention to workers can get strong positive production results.) Making people feel chosen or special will increase their commitment to the process. In the absence of meaningful criteria, selection can have its own reward, even if minimal.

A team's probability of success is enhanced if it is well chosen from the beginning, to be sure. But it is far more enhanced if it is well trained and effectively led. All too often, management uses selection as a substitute for training. It is a myth that any company can hire already trained employees. The differences between two companies in the exact same business can be tremendous. Hiring a well-trained person from one company to work in another does not negate the need for extensive training in the new company's methods, especially any system of team management; no matter how competent an individual is in the work, everyone needs some amount of training in working together. Valerie Byrd freely admits she was wrong when she thought she would be ready to make the switch from facilitator to team developer. She also admits that while she has vastly improved in her new role over time, she also knows that working in the self-managed team structure is a process that requires considerable—and constant—training. From the leaders who begin the process, to the Steering Committee, design team, and teams, it is use of a process that grows teams to efficiency and success.

Once the team process is well established, the best method of screening is a system of team interviews where teams screen, interview, and hire their own members. The results at Wolferman's (see Chap. 8) were a decrease to 15 percent turnover in seasonal help from 300 percent when teams took over the interview and selection process from management. While this may be a dramatic example, teams will always do a better job of finding and keeping other team members than any other selection process an organization can adopt. A team which hires its own members takes a great deal more interest and pride in training the individual. In traditional top-down management structures the selection and hiring is done at a level, or several levels, removed from the employees. So colleagues are being selected by managers and other administrators who assign them. Groups feel "stuck with" the person management selected. If the person does not work well in the group, the group blames management. If the person does succeed, management of course takes the credit for finding this gifted individual, even though much of the day-to-day training of that individual was done by the work group, not management.

With proper training in the technical aspects of the interview and selection process, teams will do a better job of hiring than traditional managers. In addition, teams have a strong commitment to making the process work and training the new person properly. This alone leads to a much higher probability of individual success and a greater degree of long-term group cohesiveness.

Interpersonal Processes in Teams

There are two components to managing the relationships within the team: the first is managing the interpersonal processes; the second is organizing and maintaining goal focus. These are easily identified as "task" and "process." Both must be developed and maintained if the team is to mature. Traditional organizations often overlook this important fact. By not allowing groups to interact, except through a supervisor, and keeping goal setting and organizational development in the hands of managers, teams will lack the most basic aspects of a team-friendly human infrastructure.

In recent years, with the increased volume of the clarion call for total quality management (TQM), organizations have begun to seriously examine the need to teach groups the tools of organization and goal setting. Many of the "quality" initiatives have been focused on teaching work groups to measure their progress, set goals, and problem-solve their own processes. This is a very positive step in moving away from the unresponsive, stifling, top-down management structures. But the human infrastructure is rarely sufficiently developed to support the new behaviors which TQM encourages; therefore, these initiatives alone do not bring dramatic changes to the bottom line. The human infrastructure, which must include an emphasis on interpersonal processes, is the essential second ingredient. Teaching teams to get along, to work together, to respect each other, and to trust one another creates an environment in which organization and goal setting can thrive.

Like success in so many other mortal enterprises, success in managing team relationships requires balance. Overemphasis on either the task or process side of the team equation will result in ineffective development. The task side of teams deals with goal setting, timeliness, meeting deadlines, and refining work flow. *Task* is similar to the engine in your car—it is the equipment with which work is done. *Process* emphasizes human emotion and interpersonal relations—it is the oil and gasoline which lubricates and fuels the engine. One cannot work without the other. Instituting TQM without sufficient attention to human process is like running the engine without oil or gas. It takes a tremendous amount of energy to get results which do not last. At the other extreme, companies which overemphasize interpersonal processes are pouring oil and gasoline into an antiquated engine. People may feel good and be highly motivated, but the engine breaks down frequently. Task functions include initiating, information seeking, information giving, consensus testing, and consensus evaluation. Process functions include harmonizing, gate keeping, encouraging, supporting, collaborating, and compromising.

Successful self-directed work teams must have the appropriate tools or they are doomed to spin their wheels on the overflowing oil. Organizations which emphasize TQM without training in interpersonal skills, conflict resolution, and redesigning the human infrastructure will find the friction soon overcomes even the modest results of poorly motivated individuals. In the rush to get results from all manner of quality initiatives, organizations, and their management, disregard the human side of the equation. *Quality* is a word with a range of meanings; bracketing it with the words *total* and *management* does not bestow techniques, strategies, and processes that will enhance an organization's ability to accomplish work. The tools in Part 3 will.

Gary Henrie knew he had to find a better way to run the South Central Counseling Center. When he took over as executive director, he knew this rural all-purpose social service agency was racked with bad morale and crisis mentality. Explains Henrie, "Total quality management sounded good. But how did you do it? I could not find the right answer for how to make it work." When he found a system for working toward self-managed teams, he found a framework and the tools to use it. He found the tasks and the processes to make the remarkable turnaround profiled in Chap. 4. We saw that his agency was able to grow—to serve more clients, increase its programs, add to its staff, and be ahead of state mandates for care and certification. Henrie found a way to build an organization that has the systems and capabilities to deliver total quality; he accomplished this by making the transition to a self-directed team-based organization.

In addition to task and process, there are other general principles of group behavior of which everyone should be aware as they begin learning the skills and techniques of successful teams. By looking at these issues in general here, the specific skills detailed in Part 3 will gain a more useful context and perspective.

All groups have natural internal difficulties. Psychologically, groups engage in behaviors related to perceived authority figures, especially in organizations where top-down authority has been the cultural norm. If a team perceives management or the team developer to be overbearing and nonparticipative from the start of the team transition, some members of the group will engage in dependent behavior. They will say things like "I just do what I am told. Management may say they want my ideas but I also know how to keep my mouth shut and do my work." Dependent behavior is acquiescent and complying; individuals do not show assertiveness or independence of thought.

Dependent behavior will also take the form of waiting to be told what to do. Early in the life cycle of the team, dependent members will expect to be told what to do, and when to do it, and how to do it—it is what they have learned to be comfortable with. They will participate in goal setting and other team activities, but they will seem helpless when faced with acting on those goals or taking initiative. Instead they will consult managers, talk with supervisors and other team members, but will not take any action on their own. These are normal behaviors of the dependent team members. It can even be the behavior of the entire team. This conduct stems from the fear of failure and its traditional consequences. In the past, when employees took initiative, management took credit for things done well and doled out punishments for decisions perceived as poor. This type of treatment over a period of many years creates a condition called "learned helplessness."

To overcome this learned helplessness, management must realize it is the main cause of the behavior. Team members find it difficult to believe that management will behave supportively if they should make a bad choice while working toward a team-based organization. Management continues to contribute to the doubt and fear by panicking or treating team members in top-down or patronizing ways when the team does not behave as management expects. Dependency stems from workers' long established patterns of waiting to be told and from disempowering behaviors in managers or team developers.

Ron Williams is a manager who started developing a team in a newly designed cellular manufacturing unit at Standard Motor Products, Inc., when that company had begun the process of transition to teams. He found it very difficult to stay out of the supervisor's role. As a supervisor, Ron was known as a very fair and positive person. Ron is a large man with a pleasant disposition and a way of talking to people that makes them believe he cares. But early on in team meetings he would hear things he did not like or knew could not be done. He often found himself stepping in and telling the team they could not do something or that to do it required further decisions by management. This angered and frustrated team members. Sometimes they would just give up and leave the meeting feeling like the team could not really do anything despite the promised new team environment. They expressed frustration and feelings of helplessness.

As time passed Ron received feedback from the group that his style was getting in the way. (Part 3 will discuss the specific feedback skills and techniques that Ron, his team, and his company used.) It took the team members a long time to gain the courage to tell him; when they finally did, Ron could see how his behavior was hindering the team's growth. Ron began changing his behavior. Because of his high level of training in manufacturing and process analysis, he could see and hear problems in a way that the team could not. Instead of telling the team they could not do something, Ron began finding opportunities to teach the team to analyze problems and make solid decisions which were in line with business goals.

Especially in an established work force, newly converted teams experience frustration, even anger, because their perception is that management is not "doing its job." It is common for team members to say that a certain task is management's job, not theirs, and management is mistreating them by asking them to do "management's work." Like Ron's team before he began to act on honest feedback from the team, several things happen to teams feeling this frustration:

> First, while the team may desire the freedom of empowerment, they fear the loss of the security they had when the supervisor was "in charge."

> Second, neither the team nor the team developer has enough knowledge and experience to know how to behave in this new situation. The team fears that mistakes it will make will be treated in a punitive way by the manager.

> Third, the team developer fears that the team will not act rationally, but the team developer also fears she has fewer tools for addressing problems. At the same time, the team developer is not sure she can trust upper management to act in a problem solving rather than a blaming mode.

The general lack of trust at all levels leads to greater caution and a stifling of growth and development. Groups at all levels will continue risk-aversive behavior until all gain enough experience with one another to begin trusting.

Fundamental to the dynamics of teams is trust. It may take many months, if not years, for teams to gain enough experience with upper management to feel they can trust them to act responsibly without acrimony or capriciousness. Both past history and the way the transition is handled will have an effect on the outcome. The speed with which the self-directed system replaces the traditional system is largely a function of how consistently management behaves in an empowering fashion.

Ned Hamson, editor of the *Journal for Quality and Participation,* once had a team send him an article on some simple problem-solving groups. He was not impressed with its work and put it on the back burner. When he finally got around to talking with the team he asked, "Why did it take you four years to get some pretty basic problem solving going and see results?" The team replied, "It took us four years to finally trust management."

Said Hamson, "I've been working in the quality area for years. That one incident taught me just how hard this quality stuff is."

It will take 12 to 18 months of training and experience for team developers to overcome the old habits of supervision and learn how to lead problem-solving sessions and mediate interpersonal conflicts. Teams themselves will require 12 to 18 months of work together to learn to trust one another and work in harmony. These time estimates, while generally coterminous, seem like a very long time for the system to develop. But the task of making a fundamental change in patterns of behavior which pervade the entire organization is formidable. Consider that these patterns have been in place in our corporate national culture for a century, and *formidable* may seem too tame a term.

The leadership of the team falls to the team itself, not to a preselected person. (This will be covered in Chap. 10.) The rotation of leadership within the team provides for greater skill development as discussed earlier, but it also accomplishes another major objective. In the transition from traditional systems to self-directed teams, old patterns must be unlearned and new patterns established. In a traditional organization, leadership was often haphazard. And outside the formal structures was the "counterleadership," which was hidden in the underground of informal communications. Many of the most effective leaders in the workplace are those who can rally people against management decisions and effectively scuttle those decisions through poor-quality work or inaction. These leaders are in position because they voice the concerns and know the fears of the work force. They are neither good nor bad, though management would like to think so. They are a bellwether, an indicator of how well management has communicated and listened to the fears and needs of the work force.

In the self-directed environment informal leaders can have a huge positive or negative influence on the process. A system of rotation keeps the group on its collective toes (see Chap. 10), and ensures that all team members have a chance to learn and establish leadership skills. This creates a very strong and positive system of informal leadership in the teams. More leaders surface as people learn assertiveness and business skills. They learn to articulate their ideas, concerns, and fears as well as or better than the old leadership. A system of leadership sharing grows people into more effective leaders rapidly. The challenge for management is to be able to respond and provide leadership to these more assertive and knowledgeable people. As the psychologist Abraham Maslow noted, "Both the exploited and the exploiter are impelled to regard knowledge as incompatible with being a good, nice, well adjusted slave."

The development of knowledge and leadership in the teams requires a fundamental change in management. Failure to understand and adjust to this development has led to the demise of many self-directed efforts at or around their second year of development.

As management, employees, developers, and teams contemplate and make the transition to true teams, increasing trust in work relationships is a crucial component. Some basic blocks to trust are "resistance" and "hidden agenda." Resistance serves to protect the group from distraction and threat, and was in all likelihood a viable survival skill in a top-down hierarchy. In fact, resistance is often lifesaving, as when a body resists an infection. To blame the group for resistance is like blaming the body for a natural reaction. Until the group feels comfortable with the transformation, all efforts to change will be resisted.

Hidden agendas can also retard the growth and success of teams. As groups are moving to accomplish their work, group members' aspirations, attitudes, and values affect the way they react to that work. The undisclosed needs and motives of group members have a greater effect on teams that are not yet ready to trust the team as a cohesive and viable work unit. Hidden agendas, operating beneath the surface, are related to personal needs: for self-worth, belonging, the need to be liked, to feel powerful, to be accepted, to achieve, to be recognized, to feel safe. Hidden agendas must be addressed. Effective team development means an investment in finding, facing, and processing the hidden agendas of the group.

By dealing with resistance, hidden agendas, and team leadership, it is possible to move toward building trust in people's working relationships. The biggest issue in building trust is directly related to fear. People are fearful of change—and for good reasons. These fears should be openly discussed by everyone in the organization. In gearing up to make the change to self-directed teams, it is crucial to all other group processes to deal with any and all fears. Ask groups to write out the fears they have and give them opportunities to talk about them. There are four categories of fears found to be endemic to the transition to a team-based organization. The most common fears voiced in each category are catalogued below as cautious counsel in moving people past what they fear to what they can accomplish. The catalogue takes the form of a series of questions and answers.

1. What are the fears of the team developers as they change from being supervisors?
   - Afraid of job loss.
   - Fear loss of control while still being held accountable.
   - Afraid management will continue to behave traditionally while expecting us to change.
   - Afraid new role might not be liked.
   - Afraid management will continue to reward for results over which employees have less control.
   - Afraid there might be an increase in work.
   - Fear of not belonging.
   - Fear of losing touch with the actual work and becoming technical experts.
   - What happens if top management changes? Will the whole process be dumped and all the work go down the drain?
   - How will evaluations be accomplished?
2. What are the fears of associates as the teams are being formed?
   - Afraid peers might be too controlling.
   - Afraid of making a mistake.
   - How will team handle it when other team members aren't carrying their weight?
   - This may be just another fad. They will pull the rug out from under this, too, if it doesn't work.
   - There may be a drastic conflict between union and management.
   - How can teams handle the discipline?
   - Fear of gossip throughout the company.
   - If management changes, will new leaders be as committed to this as our current manager?
3. What are the fears of the union?
   - Is this another way for management to do an end run on the union?
   - Is this a way for management to show there is no need for the union?
   - Could the union lose members?
   - If there is more efficiency, will jobs be lost?
   - Will this weaken the union's position?
   - How will the individual be valued when so much emphasis is being placed on teams?

- Will this increase the number of grievances?
- How will discipline be handled?
- Will this be a partnership of convenience for management? Will they back out or change the rules if it doesn't go management's way all the time?
- How will any conflicts between local issues related to the team transition and the desires of the national or international be handled? Will the local president get in trouble with the national president if he or she goes along with this process?
- If this doesn't work out, will union officials be vulnerable in the next election?
- Is this a permanent change or will it change again when top management changes?

4. What are the fears of top management?
   - Will it lose control or power?
   - Will teams make bad decisions for which it will be held accountable?
   - Will the stockholders, board members, or other stakeholders allow the time and flexibility to make this happen?
   - Will there be a decrease in quality or customer satisfaction as it gets started?
   - Will compensation costs get out of hand?
   - Will the union use this as a way to hold management hostage to union demands?
   - How will management be able to maintain control?

Once these fears have been openly talked about, the process of planning begins to minimize the possibility that the fears might come true. Knowledge of group processes used positively will maximize the success of the transition to teams. Placing these fears in front of the organization and talking openly about them begins the process of trust building and planning for the challenges ahead.

PART 3

A System for Self-Directed Work Teams

10

Organizing the Self-Directed Work Team

The Book's Most Important Sentence

Without goals which can be measured there is no team.

The above sentence is the single most important statement in this book. Teams have a hard time focusing on goals. At the beginning of the team process, this is even a bigger challenge. People throughout any organization can lose sight of the goals involved in meeting customer needs. The journey to becoming an efficient and effective team needs the boundaries of goals to keep members on a constant course. The goals serve as the beacon showing the way. The measures make the goals credible and usable. Whatever system is used to attain true teams, goals must be defined and measured; goals must be used to inspire, motivate, and guide the team and the organization. (There will be more on goals and teams later in this chapter and section.)

The goal of the balance of this book is to detail the system that author Darrel Ray uses in implementing the transition to self-directed work teams. Part 3 will detail the information, techniques, and strategies that comprise this system. Use any of the ideas here; we hope it will make your organization a better and more efficient place for work to be accomplished.

Leadership and the Team

Teams can perform almost all tasks a supervisor once performed. To succeed, teams must be responsible for setting their own goals. But the positive power unleashed by teams extends to teams measuring their own progress, representing themselves in management meetings, providing information to the larger organization, corresponding with customers, dealing with suppliers, evaluating equipment, providing basic maintenance on machinery, and even hiring new employees and being responsible for some levels of self-discipline. The limits to team duties are set only by the organizational top leadership, the Steering Committee, or union contract. The more teams are empowered to achieve, the less management involvement and interference there will be, which ultimately is non-value-added activity. When those who do the work manage the work, it can be done much more efficiently.

Team leadership, especially as teams are learning, is the key to making teams thrive. There are many approaches to formal team leadership. Teams can elect their own leadership, management can designate the leadership, or leadership can be rotated. If management designates the leadership, it is likely that the appointed leaders will always be viewed as another form of manager. This is not employee empowerment; it says management is still trying to maintain control. Many companies try designated leadership only to find that teams seem to stop maturing fairly early in the process. It is possible for a well-trained designated leader to develop and nurture the skills of the team very effectively. But, eventually, fully empowered teams must be allowed to develop their own leadership.

The two most successful approaches to team leadership are *leadership rotation* and *elected leadership*. Each of these systems has its strengths and weaknesses.

Electing team leaders has the advantage of forcing the leadership issue on the team early. Teams learn from the beginning to deal with their own leadership; this advances, often more quickly, to strong ownership in the team. There is one big drawback to the election system—it does not encourage leadership development of less dominant people. Those who are already most dominant in work relationships, those who seem to possess a high level of interpersonal skills, are those most likely to be elected. This will provide development opportunities for those elected; but it will arrest development for others. Most people have tremendous leadership capabilities, but many do not believe this. Lack of opportunity has left many unaware of their own ability to lead. Recall what Joe Forlenza and others have admonished: Do not be surprised by those who will step forward when given the chance!

A properly structured system of leadership sharing will encourage development of these raw skills in everyone. Some teams elect leaders periodically (every six months or so), with the option of retaining each leader for no more than two terms. This system works best in a mature team which has demonstrated consistency in practicing management skills. Early in the life of a team may be too soon to expect reasonable resolution of leadership issues. The election of leadership can create unnecessary turmoil and interpersonal conflict, especially at a time when skills for dealing with these challenges are limited. The election system is best used after the teams have had a couple of years experience in the team process.

Regardless of the details used to build the system of leadership selection, it is most effective when members share leadership and team members' duties change periodically. While slowing the development of any one person, this actually facilitates the rapid development of the whole team, and, thereby, the organization. Whether an election or rotation system is chosen, the key is to structure assignments and share leadership.

The Wheel Concept

The *wheel concept* as presented here was designed and developed by one of the authors (Darrel Ray); it is used exclusively with client organizations, and is a proprietary system. The wheel is used to structure leadership and other team tasks in a way that eliminates many of the struggles and difficulties around power and influence. In Chap. 7, the wheel was mentioned during the discussion of the Bell Atlantic design team's effort, where it was used as a means of assigning work to team members. The same principle applies in each use of the wheel. The wheel is designed to keep every member involved in the team's processes most of the time. It increases ownership of management tasks and encourages accountability and skill development by all team members, not just those who are elected or selected. Every team member is routinely responsible for some part of the management process. Everyone soon realizes that power struggles are of little use. The rotation of team jobs means that team members rapidly learn "to walk in one another's shoes," reducing the blaming and infighting which often occupy young teams.

The wheel concept is based upon these principles:

1. Most members hold a team job at any given time.
2. All members must perform a team job when it falls to them.
3. No one may refuse to do their team job.
4. Everyone will serve in every team job once before the rotation begins again.

The wheel concept requires the close attention of, and substantial training for, the team developer. Even if the organization is providing training for the team jobs, team members will still need a good deal of encouragement and coaching. Organizations often try to tailor the leadership system for the convenience and control of managers or team developers. This is the predominant way things have been done; it is what people know. But it inhibits team development and creates a dependency relationship between team and management. If team developers are effective in coaching during the first 18 months, the need for intense attention will decrease rapidly. If team developers are not effective, they will find themselves constantly having to train, and retrain, team members. The wheel gives structure and fair distribution to training requirements and saves time and effort in the long run. A reasonable question may be, "If it is that much trouble, why not simply use the election system every six months?" The most team-supportive answer: elections from the beginning actually lengthen the time it takes for the team to learn about self-management and create opportunities for interpersonal conflict over leadership issues. These can be avoided with the wheel, but at the cost of intensive work at the outset.

Benefits of the Wheel Concept

1. Increases work efficiency.
2. Integrates the social and technical aspects of the job.
3. Emphasizes measurable goals and self-appraisal.
4. Increases commitment to quality and customer satisfaction.

Mechanics of the Wheel

1. Each person has two jobs: the task job and the team job.
2. All members learn to do each of the task and team jobs.
3. All team jobs are rotated at least once a quarter.
4. All members will be cross-trained in each of the other skills within a given period of time (18 to 24 months).
5. The team is in charge of certifying a team member on the skills of the team.

Figure 10-1 The wheel concept.

Once a team is accustomed to rotation, it becomes second nature: training requirements decline dramatically, individuals continue to stay in closer touch with management and other teams, and the benefits of the team structure become more and more significant. Transfer to other teams is much easier, since members already know the basic team jobs and can fit right into the rotation. The entire organization finds new and more effective ways to communicate about the work it does and how it can best be accomplished. Figure 10-1 describes the benefits of the wheel concept, and the mechanics of the approach.

The wheel has three major components, as the sample wheel in Fig. 10-2 shows. At the nucleus are the team's goals, measurements, and self-discipline; these drive the team and help track its progress. The "hub" of the wheel enables members to keep their eyes on the

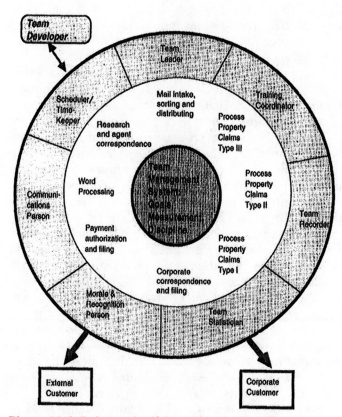

Figure 10-2 Redesigned self-directed work team wheel.

target—the activities of the group. Second are the core jobs (seen in the second concentric circle) that define the specific tasks the team performs to accomplish its goals. These are the production tasks of the team: processing claims, taking orders, manufacturing or assembling, cleaning, maintaining, word processing. If these jobs are rotated, it is according to the design of the work and the functions the team must perform. As with the different job functions on the Bell Atlantic Collection Center's wheel (see Fig. 7-1), rotation in this second circle is not the same as for the team management jobs. More will be said on core-job rotation later.

The outer circle represents the team leadership jobs. Each of these tasks was traditionally performed by the supervisor; they now become the work of the team. Members rotate clockwise on the wheel once every three or four months. This rotation allows sufficient time to learn the task and practice it well. Longer rotation carries a twofold risk: that individuals will feel stuck with a job they don't like or that they will like the job so much they begin to think of it as their own. Either will reduce the effectiveness of the individual's development, as well as the team's. Shorter rotation does not allow for skill mastery, decreasing team effectiveness.

Since teams and management must be able to communicate effectively with one another, it is important to synchronize several parts of the wheel across an entire unit. First, wheel rotations should be synchronized for all teams in a unit. For example, all teams rotate January 1, April 1, July 1, and October 1. Synchronization like this allows training to be easily coordinated. It also makes it possible for the Steering Committee to publish lists of the players on any given team at any given time. This ensures that anyone can go directly to the person with whom they need to communicate. A team leader from Team A could quickly look up the quality leader on Team B to discuss an issue.

The titles for the key team jobs like *Team Leader*, *Quality Leader*, *Communicator*, and others should be the same for all teams throughout the organization. If each team has different names for similar positions, it leads to confusion about roles and functions throughout the organization. It will also lead to increased difficulty in team-to-team communication. Consistency in team roles across the organization makes it much easier for people to move in and out of teams. In union shops, where team members may bid out of a team or a shift, this consistency means people can go from one team to another with a clear understanding of what the roles will be in their new team. In nonunion environments, consistency provides the same stability across the organization.

Training of team members in their wheel jobs falls initially to team developers, managers, or trainers. Each organization will need to address early on the training needs of team members. Each position team members will be asked to fill will require some type of training, whether informal instruction or a more formal training experience. The organization, through developers, managers, and trainers, will need to develop a series of mini-courses such as "How to Run a Team Meeting," for team leaders; "How to Chart Team Measures," for quality leaders; and "How to Keep the Team Book," for recorders.

As team members learn the various duties and gain experience in carrying them out, more sophisticated training will be needed in such things as statistical process control, quality concepts, team administration, and problem-solving methods. At the same time, each team member is responsible for training and coaching the person who next takes his or her current wheel position. Through this system, team members become more and more sophisticated in the enterprise of running the team as a business. The process builds and strengthens itself.

Rotation can be done by team jobs or core jobs (either of the two outer circles). Core-job rotation should be done on a rational basis, according to the needs of the team and the organization. If the team design calls for all team members to learn all core jobs, then rotation on a daily, weekly, or monthly basis might be appropriate, once everyone has been trained. If the design calls for limited cross-training, core-job rotation may be much more limited. A team with marketers, planners, purchasers, and accountants would not rotate but might have some form of job sharing or cross-training for higher effectiveness and customer responsiveness. An organization should decide on a specific number of wheel jobs which all teams will have. If a team wants additional jobs, these can be added. Having specific wheel jobs which every team shares makes the job of training and coordination much more manageable. The Steering Committee will be able to put out a quarterly list of people who hold wheel positions. Having the positions rotate at the same time in all or most teams throughout the organization will allow for a list to be updated and maintained for the whole organization. As with so many other building blocks of the team process, customer needs dictate choices; jobs must be rotated, but the system of rotation must be developed by the organization to serve its customers most effectively.

Wheel Positions—A List of Suggestions

The following list is designed to give you an understanding of the positions discussed, but is not comprehensive. As we have said many times before, each organization must design, develop, and use its own system. An organization may very well require positions not listed here to meet its teams' and customers' needs. Positions listed here may need to be designed differently, or rotations made using a schedule or scheme not mentioned here. This list is not prescriptive, but another tool to aid in understanding the process.

Team Leader

This person leads the team meetings, is responsible for the meeting agenda, and provides administrative support for the team. The team leader represents the team to management and other segments of the organization. The team leader may distribute work and coordinate work with other teams. In some organizations, the team leader attends a departmentwide "huddle," or brief planning meeting, each day to coordinate workloads between teams and plan production. The team leader may also be involved in budgeting and planning for the team.

Since a majority of the team leader's time will be spent organizing, running, and following up on the results of meetings, the guidelines below are given. Any team leader would also be well-served by studying Chap. 4 and the trust-building structures, especially the 59:59 Rule.

Team Leader Guidelines for Conducting Effective Meetings

- Effective meetings require work.
- Prepare for the meeting in advance.
- Start on time, end on time.
- Stick to the agenda.
- Stress effective communication and listening to one another.
- Keep discussion moving.
- Do not let a few members dominate.
- Maximize participation.
- Strive toward group-centered leadership.
- Rotate and share responsibilities.
- Do not make decisions for the group.
- Do not accept solutions quickly without adequate discussion.
- Do not mistake silence for agreement.
- Encourage minority viewpoints.

- Give frequent summaries.
- Evaluate meetings prior to adjournment; ask "How did we do?"

Quality Leader

This position is responsible for tracking all team measures and for helping the team problem-solve quality issues. Quality leaders mark the charts for the team and keep the team informed about team, departmental, and organizational measures of quality and production. This person should receive extensive training in the quality philosophy of the organization. In traditional organizations, everyone is given training in quality principles but very little opportunity to use them. On the wheel, only the quality leader is given training and is expected to lead the team in this area. When the positions rotate, the next person receives the training. As time goes on, many people on the team will receive the training and will eventually have extensive experience in applying the principles for the whole team. Thus the team becomes more conscious of quality issues at the same time as its training level rises.

Communicator

Sometimes referred to as "scout" or "spy," the person in this position visits other teams, departments, or management meetings to gather intelligence about what is going on in the rest of the organization. Communicators are expected to report to the team on their findings. As they visit other areas, they will hear of good ideas which can be shared, challenges which can be avoided or solved as other teams did, and can spread their own team's good ideas as well. This position is most valuable in helping foster healthy competition between teams. When the scout attends another team's meeting, both teams have an opportunity to compare their team with another. They often find that their own team is not as sophisticated or mature in some way as the other team, and are spurred to increase their own skills and knowledge.

The communicator is also responsible for disseminating all relevant and appropriate information to the team. If management wants to make an announcement, a meeting of the communicators might be called to brief them so communicators can in turn inform the teams. They are also expected to communicate with other teams, departments, or segments within the organization. It is up to the communicators to coordinate announcements and facilitate the flow of information throughout the organization. In many companies, the communicator is also responsible for working with the newsletter editor to provide team stories or examples.

As the process proceeds and teams mature into high-performance work groups, they tend to isolate themselves and think of themselves as superior. This is destructive competition and elitism. Having regular contact and communication with the organization is crucial to help teams remain grounded in the reality of their own strengths and weaknesses. The communicator position helps prevent elitism from developing by keeping information moving.

Recognizer

This person is charged with celebrating the team's successes and recognizing team members' performance. Morale is the medium in which this position functions. In the past, management was expected to do all the praising, recognizing, and morale building. In fact, management rarely knows what is really going on in the ranks of the line worker. Team members know much better who is doing an outstanding job, who deserves special recognition, and who could benefit most from some public recognition of efforts made on behalf of the team.

The morale person also recognizes birthdays, organizes team social functions like picnics or baby showers, buys get well and sympathy cards, and attends to the social needs of the group. While this job might appear frivolous, over and over again it has proven to be a key to the success or failure of a team. Teams who share both fun and human concerns for one another generally are more productive than teams who seem less solicitous of team members' basic social needs. As with all other parts of the team-based process, nothing should be left to happenstance. Activities of the team require the attention of someone on that team. It is the recognizer who takes the lead in making recognition a public part of the process.

In many companies, the recognizer position is taken over by a standing committee, which plans organizationwide activities like the company picnic or charity fund drives. During the floods of 1993, one midwestern company planned flood relief efforts for employees' families who had been stricken. The recognizers organized and coordinated the effort. In another company, the recognizers plan the annual company or winter holiday and summer family event.

As team members serve in this position, they learn more and more about the team members as individuals and the needs of the team as a group. This position, more than any other, brings the team together. As people rotate through the position, each learns the significance of public acknowledgment. Whether it is recognition of a job well done or helping raise money and consciousness for a cause, the recognizer's role is crucial in shaping a team conscience.

Training Coordinator

This position coordinates the cross-training and skill development of the team. The training coordinators are not trainers themselves, but ensure that all members receive the skills and coaching required for the mission of the team. They are in charge of the cross-training plan for the team and work with the training coordinator of the steering committee.

The organization which chooses a team-based structure has made a major commitment to training. Implementing the team process, with its emphasis on cross-training and information sharing, means there will *always* be training to coordinate, and someone has to make the arrangements.

Recorder

The recorder is the archivist for the team, taking minutes and recording team decisions. They are in charge of the Team Book, which holds all the team's current documents such as team agreement, yearly goals, and quarterly objectives. The recorder is responsible for maintaining this book, keeping it up to date, and bringing it to each team meeting. Figure 10-3 shows an example of a Team Book's Contents page. Figure 10-4 shows a recorder's minutes from a team meeting.

Contents

1. Team Goal Statements
2. Mission Statement, Team Agreement
3. PERT Charts on Projects
4. Time Lines for Project Completion
5. Quality Measures
6. Pareto Charts on Problems
7. Birthdays and Special Dates
8. Minutes of Team Meetings

Figure 10-3 Sample contents page from a Team Book.

Minutes for Tigers Team Meeting, June 5, 1992

1. We went over the written premiums and loss ratio for May.

2. We talked about everyone going out into the field with Ed for a week. We need to let Keith know some dates by June 12th.

3. We talked about the new rates in auto and the decrease in applications as a result of it.

4. Theresa showed us the number of phone calls that just came in on Peggy's line from 5-1-92 to 5-26-92. She received 1226 calls. This is about twice the number of calls that the other two teams received.

5. Mary told us of her new hours and told us that we need to schedule a feedback meeting for this month.

6. Terri talked about how the cross-training is going; currently we have 6 certifications for the quarter. We plan on having 10 by the end of the quarter.

7. Terri also discussed how important it is to answer the phones. Recently we have been having some problems with the phones ringing for a long time without anyone answering them. We can't have this problem; it must be resolved!

8. Lori gave us some information from the other team meetings. They are looking to open up N_____ again. But they will be very selective. Nothing is for sure yet though.

9. Theresa told us that we don't know if we can hire someone for Betty's old job. Pete will continue to look at M_____ APP count. If we can't hire someone we will put someone from another team in that position.

10. Kevin S. appreciates all the help he gets verifying coverage. Also there has been an increase in claims lately.

Figure 10-4 Team meeting minutes.

Scheduler/Timekeeper

From scheduling the team meeting room to making appointments for the team, the schedulers and timekeepers make sure the team is explicit in its respect for time. Keeping track of time in the team meetings keeps the meetings effective. As the team moves to higher levels of empowerment, this position may be expected to schedule vacations, overtime, and attendance, and maintain the records that go with these time-tracking tasks.

Huddle Leader

At the beginning of each workday, most teams have a five- to ten-minute "huddle," or brief meeting, to coordinate activities, make adjustments for absent members, review production schedules, and make announcements. The huddle is just that; a brief update of important information. It is not the time to problem-solve! This meeting is the responsibility of the huddle leader. He or she may come in 15 minutes earlier than the rest of the team to prepare for the huddle. The huddle leader might pick up production schedules, check with teams from the previous shift, or attend a departmentwide huddle. The team leader may take on this position.

Other Possible Positions

A reminder: This list is by way of suggestion, not prescription. The process will determine the team makeup, including the positions on the wheel. Other special jobs may be developed by the teams as a myriad of conditions, considerations, and confluences will dictate. Some of these positions could be:

Safety/Ergonomics.   Responsibility for training, monitoring, and charting safety procedures. The person in this position will attend companywide, and even corporationwide, safety meetings, and then report relevant information to team members and all others as appropriate.

Cross-Shift Coordinator.   In organizations where there are multiple shifts, one person may be designated to stay 15 minutes late to talk with the team coming on and share information. Machine difficulties, shipping delays, crashed discs; this cross-shift communication can greatly reduce the natural friction between shifts as they learn to communicate the problems of the previous shift and air their differences.

Budget Committee.   Preparing budgets can be a time-consuming and complicated process. Because the learning curve for this type of work can be long, some teams elect a standing budget committee of two or three people. These folks learn the entire budget process and represent the team on budget issues. The team leaders may or may not be involved in budgeting. This trained standing committee may remain for one or two years and rotate on a staggered basis. This reduces the time taken in learning and ensures continuity of knowledge.

The Rule

Once the wheel is designed and agreed upon, there is only one rule: every team member does each job in turn. To make the wheel concept credible, it must involve all team members, especially for the team jobs represented in the outer circle. Everyone should be expected to do all team management jobs. If one person is allowed to skip a job they do not particularly like, that opens the door for a conflict which can tear the team apart. Once the team is in place, its credibility and success depend on everyone being part of the process. Individual musicians can display all the panache and style of a virtuoso. But when the symphony convenes, its success depends on everybody following the same score. For the team structure to thrive, everyone must follow the precepts of the process. When each team member has "walked in the shoes" of each position on the wheel, it builds a depth, strength, and virtuosity for the team. As a focused unit—and as individuals—the ownership of *all* their tasks makes the teams powerful work groups.

What if someone does not want to serve? Initially there is often fear and resistance on the part of team members:

"I'm afraid of speaking in front of groups!"

"I hate statistics and math."

"I can't write very well—how can I be the recorder?"

But rotation through the team management positions has a profound effect on team members. In team after team, formerly shy and unassuming people turn into skilled business meeting leaders, skilled process analysts, and effective problem solvers. People who saw a job they *knew* they were incapable of accomplishing have had entire new worlds of possibilities open to them. "Do not be surprised who will step up!" It would be naive to assume the great doors of possibility will sweep open for everyone forced to stretch beyond their expectations. In other words, some people who are shy and unassuming before their turn at team leader will remain that way. Many who hate statistics and math before their turn as quality leader will feel the same after tracking and charting the team's work. Whether their assignments are seen as drudgery or revelations, the rule must not be violated; *people must not be allowed to abrogate any team responsibilities.*

Voices will be raised in protest against this rule. It could be argued that this is not the most efficient way to run the team. If people are allowed to do what they do best, then the team would manage itself more efficiently, more quickly. On the face of things, this seems reasonable. In the short term, it probably would yield a smooth-running team more quickly than strict adherence to the "Everyone must play" rule. On closer examination, especially when looking longer-term, it is really another form of false specialization. Allowing people to do what they do best only inhibits the development of other skills and knowledge in the team. It prevents wide sharing of leadership and allows a few to dominate. The reason for switching to a self-directed team-based organization is to involve everyone in operating the organization. Requiring everyone to take their turn protects the integrity of the system itself.

The job wheel is initiated by having team members volunteer for the various positions. Then team members receive training on how to do the job they've volunteered for. Once everyone has a place on the wheel, it then simply rotates. Everyone eventually does each job; eventually, everyone is fully trained in all parts of team management.

The Team Agreement

The "one rule" stated, the team requires additional guidelines for its behavior. Every team needs a mission statement and a team agreement. Teams will make an effort at writing and following these early in their life together. Most teams find it takes several months to refine and modify these to fully fit their situation. Working out the mission statement and team agreement is an important exercise for the team and should be treated as such. The time and effort will be a good investment in learning to work together. Often, a team's mission statement will reflect that of the larger organization. Like all mission statements, it should be a concise summary of the organization and group's major goal. The refinement of its own mission statement and set of guidelines will give the team ownership of its work life. After several months, members will revisit the agreement and put it in a form the team can live with. Developers should encourage the team to discuss its agreement frequently and to check their behavior. When an outsider is present at a team meeting, he or she may be asked to give feedback on how well members adhere to their agreement.

Team agreements often include two types of guidelines: operational guides and interpersonal guides. *Operational guides* cover issues related to the mechanics of running the team. Examples include:

- We will start team meetings on time.
- We agree to attend meetings on time.
- Meetings will last only as long as agreed to in advance.
- A written agenda will be made for each meeting.

- We will provide reasonable notice to the team if we are going to be absent from work.

The second component of the team agreement deals with *interpersonal guides*. Examples include:

- We will actively respect and honor one another's views and opinions.
- We will resolve conflicts directly with team members and will refrain from going to other team members or outside of the team.
- We will praise and actively recognize our fellow team members.
- We will honor our differences in working together.
- When a team member's performance hurts the team, we will coach him/her to improve without judging or blaming.

Goals, Again

At the center of the wheel concept are the goals, the self-discipline of the team. This is where the team actually begins. Once more for emphasis: *Without goals which can be measured there is no team.* Teams have a hard time focusing on goals in the beginning. Without team developers' strong support and encouragement, teams will tend to ignore or downplay their goals. The team developers should be insistent on the new teams setting and tracking goals publicly. Every team should have a large display board, flip chart, or changeable signage in their work area where the team goals are tracked. It is important that these be public and openly available to everyone on the team and to other teams. Any boundary is most useful when it is visible. Objectives which are hidden away in a book are easily ignored. It is difficult for the team, management, or other teams to tell how a team is doing if team goals are tucked out of sight. Public display of goals keeps everyone focused on the work to be accomplished. If the goals are being met, it becomes a meaningful proclamation; if the goals are not being met, there is pressure on the team to identify the source of the problem and get it resolved.

The Steering Committee plays an equally important role in this area. Every three to six months during the first two years of implementation, the Steering Committee should send out audit teams to check on teams and give them specific and detailed feedback on how well they use the process. (Chapter 13 details feedback procedures.) The audit team is usually a pair of individuals who represent the Steering Committee. They use a standardized checklist (see Fig. 10-5), and their own good observational skills, to discuss with team members how well they are adapting

---

Steering Committee Team Audit Report

___ ___ ___ ___ ___

Team   Department   Developer   Date   Time

<u>Yes</u>   . <u>No</u>

I. Meeting Mechanics:
1. Start on time?
2. Members arrive on time?
3. Written agenda in advance?
4. Safety short films?
5. End on time?
6. Team Book up to date?

Comments:

II. Wheel Position Report:
1. Did all positions report, or was there an alternate plan?
2. Were reports brief and well-prepared?

Comments:

III. Performance Indicators (Charts):
1. Safety
2. Productivity
   a. Are trends improving?
3. Quality
   a. Are trends improving?
4. Other: Specify

Comments:

IV. Continuous Improvement Activities:
1. Does team improvement have goals?
2. Are there significant gaps between goals and current performance?
3. If gaps exist, are problem-solving sessions being undertaken?

Figure 10-5 Steering Committee team audit report (designed by Standard Motor Products).

---

4. Are action plans being formulated?

Comments:

V. Levels of Empowerment:
Based on this audit, at what empowerment level
is this team rated?

(Circle one)   1   2   3   4

Recommendations for the team in attaining
levels of empowerment? (Specify)

VI. General Comments:

Figure 10-5 (*Continued*)

to the team-based process. Like the act of establishing the guidelines, accomplishing the audit is a powerful influence on the team focus and development. In the audit process the team developer and the Steering Committee are providing oversight and accountability for the teams.

The Team Name

Human groups have a strong need to develop an identity; witness the logos and insignias which pervade contemporary culture. These names provide the basis upon which to build identity and pride. For choosing a team's name, there are no hard and fast rules except one: the team name is the responsibility of the team—they can change it. It is their name. Once the teams have selected their names, the rest of the organization and management should begin referring to the teams by name, rather than function. This sends the important message that the team's job is larger than a function. No matter what their mission, the name is the center of the team's identity. Teams need to have an identity independent of their mission.

The process of picking the team name is just another of the small steps which comprise the entire team transition. It also provides the team important experience in interpersonal communications. Here is a list of actual team names, with parenthetical commentary:

Genesis

Miracle Workers (a credit/mail-processing team)

CIA (Cells in Action—a manufacturing team)

Tough Enoughs (a pick and pack team)

Wolf Pack (a packaging team)

NE1KAN (an insurance team serving Kansas and Nebraska)

Phone Rangers (customer service team)

Sisters of Mercy (all-female customer service team)

Missouri Tigers (insurance applications team)

Phoenix

Versatiles (support team in insurance company)

Team Design Revisited

As the teams are being organized it makes sense to look at what other designs are available. The design of a team should be built around the team's customers. In most cases everyone would be expected to serve in every team job, but it is also necessary to be flexible enough to respond to special circumstances. Persons who are out of the team, traveling much of the time, may have trouble meeting many of the responsibilities. Drivers on a team who are rarely in the building, except for team meetings, may be unable to perform some of the team jobs. They will still be expected to fully participate in most problem solving, in collecting data, and working on special project groups.

Some teams require redesign based on multiple levels of skills and education. When a team has members who possess advanced degrees, are highly skilled technically, and have legal or regulatory certification requirements, the design of the core jobs will not call for complete rotation of work. Nevertheless, everyone is still expected to perform the team jobs, the outermost circle on the wheel. The important principle is that leadership be shared no matter what the design for the work may be.

Once teams begin to follow through on plans made by the Steering Committee and design team, the question is often asked, "Should a team be larger or smaller?" In Chap. 9 some guidelines for team size were presented. Early in the process it is important to keep teams within the 6- to 10-person size limit. It allows teams to become comfortable with team operations and mature faster, while learning the business quickly as well. If it is difficult to configure a team of this size, it could be that there needs to be a more fundamental rethinking of how the work should be done. However, there are some organizational work designs which are not easily adapted to this size; for these, a team of 18 to 20 might be necessary. Before making larger teams, it is crucial for the design team to look carefully at its own assumptions. It is often a failure of creativity or courage which makes a large-team solution so enticing, when it is potentially disastrous.

The importance of supportive human systems is reiterated here. The way you set up a human system largely dictates the behavior of the humans in that system. If the system is unwieldy and violates some basic principles, the performance will be less than optimal.

The above considered, there are some situations where larger teams may be appropriate. This seems most true for organizations where cross-shift coordination among groups is critical and when a large number of people are expected to service a single group of customers without respect to geographical boundaries or product line. In these situations, large teams can work, but there is always a cost. There will always be a sacrifice in group effectiveness when the size goes much beyond 10. Perhaps larger groups can start as small units until they have some experience in the team approach. Remember, this is a process built on a series of processes. Geographically separated groups are always difficult to develop into teams, and such development may not even be an appropriate application of the team process. The central organizing fact is a common purpose and measurable goals for which the team can be held accountable independent of its individual members. If this is not possible, then neither is a team-based organizational structure.

Another difficult question that comes up as the process begins is this: "How many teams can one individual play on?" In a number of cases it is desirable for one person to serve on more than one team. A person with a unique and sophisticated skill might be expected to serve on multiple teams. There may be only one geophysicist available for three different teams. In a manufacturing plant, the tool and die specialist can serve three teams while being the formal member of one team. When an individual serves on more than one team, accountability becomes a difficult question; however, it is not an insurmountable challenge. It becomes very important to make the expectations clear, and to specify how that person will be assessed by his or her customers. These individuals on more than one team are largely individual contributors rather than strict team players. They still may hold positions on the wheel of their home team, the team with which they spend most time and attend most team meetings. But these individuals may be excused from certain duties or jobs of the team. (If there are rules, there are exceptions!) In some cases, their skills are so valuable that it is best to use their professional expertise, and let others on the team manage the day-to-day functions. In a psychiatric hospital a psychiatrist might serve a half dozen teams. This scarce resource should be used to its fullest; he or she might not serve in any team function, but this structure will allow the greatest numbers of customers—i.e., patients—to be served.

When the process of organizing the teams first begins, the team transition can seem like a daunting change which will never easily be accepted. There will be resistance and challenges. But think of this process as building a new, strong structure, brick by brick. If attention is paid to each step, each brick, the end result will be a strong new structure.

11
Training the Self-Directed Work Team

Training Teams

"Train, train, and train," describes Margaret Sears. As one of two key people in the position of organizational developer working to bring self-managed teams to Bell Atlantic, she backs that statement up with action. In the several units within this communication giant, the transition to teams is under way. As at the Residential Collection Center (worksite for Allen Fulford, Tom Whitmore, and Elaine Vaughan; see Chap. 7), team developers are implementing plans made by each unit's Steering Committee and design team. In reviewing the training schedule Sears has planned for team developers, she stopped counting at 17 days training over several months. These training sessions cover such subjects as group development, group dynamics, leadership issues, and managing cultural diversity in the workplace, and have the added benefit of giving the developers a support network of classmates who are peers.

Joe Forlenza, who is now taking self-directed teams to new locations within his company, Standard Motor Products, Inc., knows what Margaret Sears knows. "This process means a major commitment for training. It never ends, this is a timeless process."

Herb Tuttle at Wolferman's estimates that everyone there spends at least one hour per week in team meetings or training. There is ad hoc training in production changes as needed, and special project teams are assembled all the time. These take at least two hours per week for those involved. Tuttle also knows what Forlenza and Sears discern:

The transition to self-managed teams requires a major commitment of time in training and meetings.

Teams can only perform a task if they have been trained properly for that task. Look back at Chap. 10; there is an entire spectrum of tasks that team members will be asked to do, which have never been expected of workers before. That outer circle of the job wheel reflects the management tasks that will become the responsibility of the team. It is reasonable and right to empower employees; that is the basis of true teams, as has been said, and repeated. It is reasonable that teams will need to be trained in the new and supportive human infrastructure. It would be unreasonable to make the transition to teams without first considering the importance of training in making this process work.

The traditional choice has been to spend the majority of corporate training dollars on managers. According to the Commission on the Skills of the American Workforce, 1990, only 7 percent of the $30 billion spent on training goes to the line worker. From the perspective of the new human infrastructure, the workers who add the most value to products and services have traditionally received the least training. Managers were trained because management was expected to have the highest skills and take primary responsibility for coordination—of everything. Historically, institutional expectations of managers have been quite high, while institutions have always expected little more than compliance from those workers who add the most value and have direct contact with products, services, and customers. In a team environment, the resources dedicated to training must be shifted heavily toward those who can add value.

Team-based organizations are investing in a long-term relationship with their teams. Each team must be given the skills to perform. Use the plant metaphor for teams: training is the food by which teams are nurtured and allowed to grow. Attempt to cultivate teams or plants without providing the proper sustenance, and both will wither and die. In the case of teams, this will leave an organization to deal with disillusionment, frustration, and cynicism among team members.

If the metaphor is too subtle, heed the words of Wolferman's Jack Padavano: "Training dollars are an investment in *future* return and profit. Payback may be one to three years!"

The Learning Team and Its Four Stages

To best understand the self-directed team structure, it is helpful to view the team as an organism, with the capacity to develop and learn as a unit. The knowledge a team has is *not* contained in any one person's head, but in the collective "head" of the whole team. Group knowledge is developed through a system of shared leadership, training, and continuing experience. It takes a team a year or more to develop the knowledge and cohesiveness required to become high-performing.

Using the term *the learning team* helps members and management focus on the importance of the team as the unit of learning, not the individuals. From the outset, management and the Steering Committee develop training and evaluation systems, and eventually compensation systems, which focus on the entire team, not on its individuals. While an individual may have special areas of knowledge or skill, it is the team which supports that person's efforts. Focus on individual skill development detracts from team skill development. Training the group as a whole on a skill set, or training two or more associates at the same time, places the emphasis on team learning. When two persons are given a specific skill, they are expected to train the rest of the team in that skill, when and where appropriate.

Training is central to growth, and the sequence of training is one of the most crucial elements of the ongoing training process. Just as a child must learn multiplication before learning calculus, there should be a sequencing of learning experiences for teams. Just as the Steering Committee must convene before the design team can be assembled, proper progression must be considered throughout the transition process. In fact, a product of team-based organization is an awareness of the importance of sequence.

From the outset, each team follows a sequence in its collective emotional development, moving through fairly predictable stages of development from formation to full maturity. The learning team must know from the get-go that there are stages, in their development as well as in their training. Team members need to learn about these stages to better understand the dynamics of their new way to work. So, before examining the training program, we'll ask you to consider the four stages of team development discussed below.

Stage 1: Forming (Testing or Pseudo-Team)

The first stage, the *forming stage,* marks the transition from focus on individuals to member status. People are cautious, trying to get themselves oriented to the new way to work. People often believe that teams are "just another management program," fad, or hype. Many will take none of this seriously and some will become instant zealots. The range of group behaviors will reflect politeness, uncertainty, anxiety, anticipation, and attempts to define the team's task. There are likely to be complaints about the team tasks or personal time pressures. At the forming stage, large amounts of energy will go toward getting oriented and "testing the waters." Initially, less will get done and questions may be raised about how this new system could possibly be more efficient. Tasks may not be accomplished on time or correctly as people learn to work differently and share responsibilities.

The most common questions heard at this stage:

Why am I here?

Who are these others?

Can they be trusted?

What are we going to do?

What will I be required to do?

Will I be able to contribute?

Will I be accepted and included?

There are interventions which need to be built into training to help the team deal with the issues of the forming stage. There needs to be a focus on members getting to know each other better. In the Bibliography, and through their Human Resource Department, team developers and members can find "getting-to-know-you" games and "self-disclosure" exercises. These experiences may seem to some to be a waste of time. This is a prime example of how the commitment to the process and to support of a new human infrastructure is made. Whatever helps team members know how to work more effectively with each other is a wise investment. Development of the Team Agreement is a good task, which also fosters growth during the forming stage development. For the team to set goals within the first six weeks is also a good target task. This, too, is an example of a positive process which yields a useful resource. The Team Agreement and goals will begin to provide definition, boundaries, and direction.

At this stage, teamwork on a name and logo can also provide positive building blocks. There is a tendency for people to get very focused on seemingly trivial things like designing the logo or team T-shirt. The best way for developers, leaders, and team members to handle this often-frustrating experience: be patient and gentle. This is when members should be reminded of the team's goals.

Training and meeting experience should include discussions on the topic "What do we expect of one another?" The team developer can both lead and model by starting an open discussion on how he or she will be acting. By conferring on what the team can reasonably expect from their developer, from the organization, and from each other, the process will begin to take on meaning. When expectations become explicit and are discussed openly, it may even come as a great relief to some. Like a young child, the new team may ask hundreds of questions, and many of the questions will seem repetitive, even monotonous, to developers and leaders. Each question can best be seen as an opportunity to teach thinking skills and business knowledge. With every response, the organization can reinforce the goals and mission in making the transition to a team-based system of management.

One other valuable resource: Read *Zapp! The Human Lightning of Empowerment* by William C. Byham and Jeff Cox. This allegorical approach to empowerment is engaging but quite precise in its treatment of the concept of true empowerment. After team members have read this book, a discussion of it can be a valuable learning experience.

Stage 2: Storming (Chaos and Conflict)

This second stage is the most difficult in any group's development. As team members get deeper and deeper into the task of self-management, there is a tendency to get in each other's way. Much of the chaos and conflict of the *storming stage* stem from a lack of effective processes and procedures, and lack of experience in working together. Members soon realize that the task is more complex than they had at first thought. People find their peers frustrating. They argue about what to do and how to do it. Consensus still seems a goal and not a reasonable method of reaching solutions. People begin blaming one another and challenging the leader. Scapegoating and headhunting are common problems at this stage. Individuals tend to rely on their own opinions and experiences, rather than cooperating, trusting, and working with team members.

The group behaviors of the storming stage are easy to recognize, but reflect the most difficult obstacles to establishing a true-team environment. Arguing, infighting, establishing cliques, challenging leadership, general conflict, and attempts at resisting or escaping from tasks are common at this stage. The common questions at this stage cluster around three general concerns:

How much influence and control will I have?

How will I be successful?

How will we work together?

The dynamics of the storming stage leave everyone feeling a bit drained. There often seems to be little energy for working toward team goals. This is one more example of why sequence is often crucial. If goals have been established effectively from the outset, they will survive and be more helpful during these difficult storming moments. Having open discussion about conflict and blaming, members will begin to find solutions to the questions surrounding "How will we work together?" As people move through the management jobs on the wheel, the shared experience of leadership and management tasks will begin to pay dividends. Reviewing goals and examining team performance data at every meeting is a crucial component of living with the team process. It is also important to use a feedback system such as the one detailed in Chap. 13. It is critical that monthly feedback sessions be scheduled well in advance and schedules adhered to. The organization as a whole must be seen as reinforcing its own expectations.

Team developers will need to step forward to mediate conflicts. Again, here is an example of training which must be provided for developers, and employees. Chapter 13 will also reference a conflict mediation system. Whatever the system, people need strategies to deal with the natural conflicts arising out of this new way to work.

Often the chaos, conflict, and storming will interfere with charting of goals, as well as inducing a forgetfulness of goals already established. A refocus on these will help counter the blaming and fighting occurring between team members. Problem-solving games which reinforce the power of group solutions over individual ones can serve as valuable training experiences. Reviewing the concept of consensus, and the process of getting to consensus, can be a valuable activity as well.

Stage 3: Norming (Emptying)

During the *norming stage,* the members clarify their roles and expectations. The groundrules for working together have now been worked out. *Emptying* generally takes place early in this stage; this is when team members unload much of what they were hiding from one another. Communication becomes much more direct and honest, with performance feedback becoming more focused on behavior than on personal differences. This releases the pent up emotions brought on by fear. Large amounts of energy are now directed to purely positive places: direct communication and problem solving. More cooperative behaviors toward the task are observed. The group begins to function more smoothly and with much more coordination. Members begin to accept and feel more comfortable with the goals, their own roles, and the tasks the team is accomplishing.

In the norming stage group behavior often reflects more direct communication, performance-based feedback, less defensiveness or intimidation between team members, cooperation, shared confidences, trust, friendships, a common language, and real group cohesion. The questions team members are concerned about at this stage tend to be:

Will I be valued?

Will we be successful?

This is the stage at which teams become very productive and effective. Members now have the process skills, and the experience in working together. Members see their own roles, and the roles of others, more clearly. The energy of the group gets directed toward the team's tasks as it begins to make significant progress toward its goals.

Revisiting the Team Agreement is a useful exercise at this stage. Developing a procedure for orienting and training new team members should be done if it has not been already. If this orientation process is in place, it could be revisited at this stage as well. Reconsideration of how the team is functioning requires reviewing. Brainstorming all the unwritten rules that have developed will be revealing about how far team trust has developed. (Examples of the unwritten rules are "Don't talk to Susie on Monday morning," "Mark charts by 9:00 each morning," "Skip huddles on team meeting day.")

People should be taking larger roles in all of the training. Conducting a mini-course on "How to Coach Another Team Member" is something most members should be able, even willing, to do by this stage.

Stage 4: Performing
(Achievement/Affection)

The team has reached maturity at the *performing stage*. The members perform well together. Relationships, expectations, roles, and processes become solid and effective. Members have genuine feelings of respect for one another and what the group has accomplished. The mature team can solve problems and react to changes quickly. There is real caring for, and appreciation of, one another. The team shows confidence in its abilities and sets "stretch" goals for itself. The group behaviors often reflect confidence, energy, the ability to work through tough group issues, a focus on problems rather than people, and insights into personal and group processes.

This is the "self-" stage: *self-facilitation, self-leadership, self-critique,* and *self-change* describe the way the team functions. High satisfaction with their achievements is illustrated by spontaneous celebrations and individuals accepting identification with, and loyalty to, their team. The questions at this stage are:

What new goals can the team achieve?

Will the team be recognized?

Will the team be broken up?

Can the team improve?

At this stage, the team is a highly effective work unit, with cohesiveness and high performance. There is high commitment to team goals. During the performing stage it is important to try to avoid the insularity, the "circle the wagons" mentality, that high-performance groups can develop. This is the time to emphasize cross-team problem solving. The communicator should be visiting other teams and bringing ideas. Communicators and other teams' members should be attending meetings throughout the organization. Challenging the team to learn more problem-solving skills and more about the business will keep interest high and serve as an outlet for people's energy. The challenge for a true team developer at this stage is to stay out of the way. Learning to serve as a background resource can be a challenge for developers who have been at the forefront of making the team transition.

Teams will experience highs and lows, depending on how quickly they work through the issues in each stage. A good team developer knows that these cycles are normal and tries to assist the team in coping with the issues. The duration and intensity of each stage vary. Some teams develop faster than others, some slower, but the stages cannot, and will not, be skipped. They can only be facilitated by informed, skilled, and trained team developers and team leaders. Understanding the four stages reduces the penchant toward overreacting to normal dynamics or setting unrealistic expectations which could prolong the development period. Team growth will be dictated by many factors—but stages and sequences can be predicted, expected, and therefore, useful.

A Dramatic Example

Before examining the important sequence the team-based organization transition should follow, there is a story to be told. It is the most dramatic example we know of a team living through, and getting over, the first three stages to reach the fourth, mature stage. Although the individuals and their organization remain unnamed, we assure you that the story is a true one.

This is a story about the A Team. It is comprised of 10 account specialists in a unit of about 240 people within a large financial service corporation. From the first moment the team-based management structure was introduced in the unit, this team was in conflict. It almost seemed that the A Team slipped directly from the forming stage to immediate storming. Anxiety and uncertainty turned into infighting and arguing. Tension permeated every interaction. As obvious as it may seem on paper, it took raw courage for Eric, the team developer, to face the major issue straight on. But he did.

The team was made up of five caucasian women and five African-American males. After all the classes, trainings, and process discussions, it was Eric who had to ask the tough and embarrassing questions. He asked the group to face the fact that the men had preconceived notions about the women and the women about the men. The gulfs of gender and race had not been confronted head on, so they became the informal, but powerful, unspoken agenda. Eric convened a team meeting and began by saying, "Let's put the real issue, the unspoken thing, on the table. You women have set ideas about us men; and we have them about you." Two hours later, the team began moving past this conflict. It took Eric's courage to move the team through the storming stage to norming. In the wake of this honest discussion, gossiping decreased and the team's ability to work together soared.

The A Team even found its members meeting informally after work. These sessions led to more and more focus on how their work was being accomplished. They began to realize there was a duplication of effort by their own team and the corporate headquarters. The corporate redo of their chores was leading to their own work slowdowns, inefficiency, and waste. These problems were clearer and clearer to the A Team, but not to headquarters. In the true team spirit, they prepared a detailed report on how the work could be accomplished more efficiently, but with the oversight that headquarters was requiring. The report was an example of superior group accomplishment. It displayed the efficiency in productivity that is the promise of self-directed teams. But the A Team was seized with fear. If they turned in the report, they would be explaining to corporate headquarters how to eliminate half their work; therefore half their jobs would be threatened.

But sitting on this report seemed less and less like something a mature team would do. They mustered the same courage that had let them confront fear and prejudice, and submitted the report to the corporation's top management. They decided it was time to test management and see if the promise not to eliminate people based on productivity savings was on the level. Two members of the team were called to headquarters to present the data in the report.

Headquarters agreed that work was being duplicated and there was a way to reduce by half the A Team's workload. And that is what management did.

They also found a way to reassign work to the A Team that allowed it to remain intact. Further, the corporation found it saved $60,000 to $100,000 in the first year alone when the A Team's recommendations were implemented. The team progressed to the final stage, the performing stage, once they could trust that their good work was valued and supported by the larger organization.

The A Team lived through the four stages of development, followed the training sequence, and in the end, became a prime example of how to become a true team.

The Sequence Is Important

The sequence for implementation of the team transition consists of four steps, which must be accomplished in order:

1. Redesign the organization.
2. Establish the team concept in the work force.
3. Train employees in quality tools.
4. Realign the compensation system.

The sequence is flexible in that the last two can be performed at the same time. But the first two *must* be done in sequence. Organizational redesign must be the starting point, followed by establishing the team concept throughout the work force. Failure to follow this sequence will undermine, even sabotage completely, the entire transition process.

The sample program plan below shows typical implementation activities. The sequence is much more significant than the actual timing. The times have been included because they are the most reliable averages, and should be taken as such.

Sample Program Plan for Conversion to Self-Directed Work Teams

A. Management commitment planning, and work redesign (60 to 90 days)
   1. Top-management training

2. Study groups to identify natural work teams
3. Develop a plan for future work redesign
4. Develop a plan of transition for team managers/team developers
5. Identification of start-up areas/teams

B. Training and problem identification (with middle and line management) (30 days)
1. Identify internal customers and analyze
2. Develop critical measures
3. Identify and train facilitators for teams

C. Training teams in problem solving and team development (90 to 120 days)
1. Train each team in problem solving and team building
2. Develop internal resources for troubleshooting
3. Further develop team developer roles and begin backing off traditional managerial behaviors

D. Implementation of development plans (3 to 12 months)
1. Train teams in statistical and quality methods
2. Full implementation of cross-training programs
3. Completion of work redesign with teams
4. Completion of preliminary compensation program, e.g., gainsharing, pay for knowledge, profit sharing

E. Continued team development and training (2 to 3 years to full maturity)
1. Life with the self-management process

In addition to the sequence of training, an organization must consider the three types of training required: technical, management, and interpersonal skills training. The *technical skills* are those required to accomplish the tasks related to the production and delivery of the team's products and services to customers. *Management training* is giving executives, team developers, and teams themselves the skills they need to accomplish management tasks. The *interpersonal skills* come from the trust- and relationship-building experiences, both formal and experiential. Some training in all three categories may be accomplished in the classroom through formal training sessions and mini-courses. But a surprising amount of training, and learning, will be done on the job every day, the primary trainer being the team developer.

Who Should Do the Training?

The reality is that the training done at the outset is best done by experts who understand self-directed work teams and their pitfalls—especially training for the upper-management team, the Steering Committee, and design team(s), and initial training of team developers. To begin, training must be done by people who have a background in, and perspective on, the entire self-managed team process. Whether done by trained and qualified internal employees or outside consultants (see Chap. 4), those who drive the process at the beginning must know how to operate this vehicle of change. An organization may have hired someone just for this transition—or one may find people in place waiting patiently for the organization to exhibit the desire to change. The resources of internal training, such as Organization Development Departments, can be brought in as soon as the design and planning work has been determined. As teams become more competent, they will take on a remarkable level of training tasks themselves. Team members may volunteer to teach classes or become tutors for other employees in skill development.

The Steering Committee often appoints a Training Committee to keep abreast of training needs. It becomes the responsibility of this committee to manage the training resources and their delivery. Much of the best training is done one on one in the teams themselves. The organization should foster an atmosphere of learning all the time. Employees are incredibly motivated when they feel they are learning new skills and concepts which make them useful and important to the company. The Training Committee can quickly find the resources required get closer and closer to "home." Employees who are challenged to use their minds are among the most motivated and effective teachers. The better the training from the outset, the more effectively the values of training are shared throughout the organization.

Because the team-based organization fosters reduced specialization and increased cooperation, cross-training also escalates dramatically. Once the teams have been established, most begin developing a cross-training chart which guides them in the process of wide skill acquisition. The team itself takes a survey of all the skills required to accomplish its mission. They then list these skills along with the person(s) who currently have these skills. A plan is then developed to train others. The general rule is that every skill on the team should have no less than three backups. That means that if someone is sick or resigns there are always at least three others who could do that task competently. The underlying principle in cross-training within the team is *"No one should have veto over getting work done."* Work should proceed as smoothly without any given person present as with them. While the team may be stretched and challenged if someone is absent, the critical work will still get done. Most important—the customer will never know there was a challenge the team had to meet. The last thing any customer—internal or cash-paying external—wants to hear: "Richard is on vacation this week. Call back next Monday and he can help you." A fully functional team responds this way: "Richard is on vacation this week but I can solve your problem for you."

The initial cross-training period can be difficult. Early in the process, after teams have been formed, the work may have been integrated into a single team, while the skills are still segmented. During the first few months, members are trying to keep production up at the same time they are trying to learn new skills. Team developers should work closely with the teams to develop a cross-training plan and goals that balance the need for production with the need for new skill development. This is a hard task, but pays high dividends in the end when teams learn to distribute work and execute efficiently. A well-functioning team looks like a ballet, with everyone moving gracefully through the work and enjoying themselves as well. This becomes possible when many people can back each other up or complete a task with as few handoffs of the work as possible.

Team members can get discouraged in these first few months and say they cannot perform and cross-train at the same time. While this may be partially true, the team developer must insist on a cross-training plan and on working on that plan a little every day. It will not be long before the team begins seeing the benefits. The cross-training matrix shown in Fig. 11-1 is a sample of how to plan this important aspect of the process.

One of the hurdles teams face concerns highly skilled performers who are reluctant to teach others their skills. The team developer may need to work very closely with these high-ability people and help them address their fears. The team will be viewed as a threat to their position and their status as an expert in the workplace. There is no easy way to work through this, but it must be addressed. The self-managed team concept flattens the organization, giving many people the skills which only a few possessed in the past. Status and power are now devalued, while cooperation and wide skill acquisition are valued.

In teams where different levels of education and expertise exist, the cross-training issue will need to be carefully thought out. Once teams understand the principles of redesign and the benefits they will gain, they are quite capable of developing their own approach to the work and skills needed.

	T	=	Trainer (Highly skilled in this task and able to teach others)
	C	=	Certified (Can do 80% or more of this task)
	NA	=	Not applicable
	TBT	=	To be Trained/Month
	S	=	Support trained

	Task 1	Task 2	Task 3	Task 4	Task 5
Jerry	C	T	C	NA	TBT/4
Sara	TBT/2	C	TBT/?	C	TBT/?
Janie	C	S	TBT/3	NA	T
Margaret	NA	TBT/4	TBT/?	C	C
Althea	C	C	S	T	C
Lisa	T	TBT/2	C	C	NA
Ron	C	TBT/5	T	C	TBT/?
Sandra	TBT/?	TBT/?	C	TBT/?	TBT/4

Figure 11-1 Cross-training matrix, developed and maintained by the training coordinator.

During the discussion of the wheel in Chap. 10, mini-courses in the management tasks on the wheel were discussed. Each quarter, for example, before the teams rotate, short courses of two to four hours should be given to prepare people for their next wheel job. Team developers, especially in the first 12 to 18 months, will need to take responsibility for these courses, whether teaching them or making sure others do. These courses should be offered about two weeks before the job rotation. Examples of useful mini-course topics for various wheel jobs are:

Team Leader: How to run a team meeting

Quality Leader: How to chart and track team goals

Recorder: How to keep minutes of team meetings and decisions

Recognizer: How to recognize team members and have a positive influence on morale

Timekeeper/Scheduler: How to schedule people for work, overtime, vacations, sick time, personal leave, etc.

These courses emphasize good basic skills which everyone on the team needs to possess but which many line workers do not have. They may be given every quarter for the first 18 months or until most team members have been through most of the courses.

Consequences of Training

One of the great fears of management concerns the potential decline in productivity during the training and development phases of the team transition. This is a justifiable fear. However, it is well worth facing this challenge in the short term to reap the dramatic long-term gains of becoming a team-based organization.

In the initial phases, there is a sense of chaos as people search for their new role. This is disconcerting to management and teams alike. Quite surprisingly, the "chaos" does not seem to lead to a downturn in actual productivity. People seem to buckle down and do more. In this early stage, they often report a new sense of purpose, hope, and motivation.

At Standard Motor Products, Inc., Tom Norbury reported a 10 percent improvement in productivity in the first six months of 1991 despite all the training and meetings which accompanied the start of the self-directed work team transition. At Wolferman's, the company experienced record profits during the first year of the transition. At South Central Counseling Center, the organization documented savings of about $60,000 on a $2 million budget in the first year it went to self-management, and $160,000 in the second year. The savings allowed bonuses to be given to all employees, while many other counseling centers across the state cut budgets and staff.

There is no guarantee that productivity will not decline, but whether it does or not is largely a function of how well the process is executed. A well-organized transition strategy, combined with strong training for team developers and employees, allows teams to begin finding ways to improve and cooperate immediately.

South Central Counseling Center Executive Director Gary Henrie has dealt with the struggle between teams and time since first bringing the trust structures to what was a fractured and demoralized organization. Eighteen months later, with a team management process in place, Henrie reported the results of an employee survey. People were asked to list the positive aspects of self-directed work teams; there were more than a dozen that were repeated on most lists. When asked to list the negatives of this new system, one was mentioned unanimously: "Too many meetings!"

Henrie was quick to explain that "people listed too many meetings as a negative. But they also realized the contradiction that it took all these meetings and training to make all the positives possible. People at the counseling center know that there is an investment of time to make teams work."

Managers often express concern about the number of meetings and training sessions. Meetings are a problem only if they are not used as an investment. Using training and meetings properly leads to better knowledge and coordination. Immediate results can often be seen which will show on the bottom line in 12 to 18 months. The reason for poor results, especially in the early stages, is related to mixed signals from management and a poorly executed transition plan. Happily, the Hawthorne effect plays a role in improvement early on as well. As people are given more attention and a new purpose, they tend to perform at higher levels despite a lack of skills. As new skills develop, real problems get addressed and process improvements are realized. The initial act of redesign of an inefficient workplace relieves people of the onerous weight of unnecessary procedures and excessive handoffs. It also helps the work force become better organized and more focused on the core of the business.

For self-directed teams, training is a way of life. Every day holds the potential for skill development or process improvement.

12
Modeling and Communication

"Management Will" and Leadership

The first team in the organization to be formed is the management team. Although a good deal of this book has focused on the line teams, the origination, development, commitment, and leadership of top- and middle-management teams are crucial to making an organization team-based. If the leaders do not model team behavior and function as teams, the line workers cannot be expected to do so. Management must communicate, in word and deed, that the new organizational structure has upper-level support.

At the earliest stages, even before the team process is begun, the top-management team must begin the redesign of itself and the organization for maximum customer impact. This almost always means despecialization of the top-management group and a broadening of responsibilities across old functional boundaries. In many companies, upper managers have a tradition of rotation into different functional areas for career development within the traditional hierarchical organizational structure. This rotation is an excellent place to start despecialization and plant the seeds of the new human infrastructure. Managers must learn to let go of their "territories" and see the organization as a whole. The trust-building structures described in Chap. 4 begin the process of sharing leadership, responsibility, and accountability; this is also a good beginning of true teams.

Gary Henrie described in Chap. 4 how he began with the trust-building structures at a time when his social service agency and its almost 50 employees were in a state of chaos. By convening open meetings and skip-level meetings, and introducing leadership rotation, a strong foundation was put in place for the transition to teams. When Henrie took the job at the helm of the agency, he found himself constantly wondering why. In less than two years, with a firm team-based management structure in place, Henrie smiled, saying sincerely, "I have the best job in the world!" This change came after he made the commitment to bring a new way to work to his organization.

To repeat: It is vital for managers, owners, presidents, and CEOs to make a full and wholehearted commitment to the process. To do anything less is to invite failure. If senior managers cannot display an honest dedication to fully implementing the team process, we would advise that an organization not proceed toward teams.

In order to discuss and assess "management's *will*" to support this new way to work, we use the following list of actions that "management will" take to implement the team concept:

- Management will, by adopting the team concept, pledge to no longer behave capriciously. It will not make arbitrary changes when things do not go as it wants.

- Management will itself behave like a team member.

- Management will agree to stick to its own standards, not interfering with the application of those standards—e.g., by making quality, hiring, and policy exceptions.

- Management will think of teams as partners in the business with an interest in the goals of the business.

- Management will ask the teams to assist in developing plans to meet business needs and will ensure that teams are represented when plans are being made which might affect them.

- Recognizing that behavior is strongly influenced by what behavior is rewarded, management will support the teams with appropriate group incentives. If individual effort is rewarded, then teamwork will rapidly become secondary, inviting inappropriate competition between individuals to the detriment of the team.

- Management will support teams with training and coaching so they may make effective decisions and solve problems.

- Management will hold the teams responsible for setting and meeting their own goals.

- Management will insist on the teams measuring their own performance.

The principles expounded above are important in virtually all aspects of the team process—and the process can only begin with *management*. And the person at the top, like the CEO in the Introduction's fable, is often the key individual in bringing the commitment to team to the organization. In all cases, the transition to teams requires a firm and insistent hand from the president or CEO. Without clear direction and an insistence on shared responsibility and accountability, there will only be bickering and territorial disputes at the top. This infighting and squabbling rapidly permeate the entire organization and render the team process impotent. When upper management continues to fight turf battles, the remainder of the organization will follow that destructive model. The first role of management must be to provide leadership and focus for the company. The second role is providing teams with the tools and knowledge to perform to their full potential.

How do managers and executives provide leadership? They begin by communicating a mission and coherent set of values to everyone in the organization, by developing clearly stated business objectives, and by communicating those objectives. Further, they begin rewarding teams for achievement of the objectives. There is a reliable test to assess how meaningful the objectives are to the organization: ask a random sample of line workers. Their agreement with what the objectives are indicates management's ability to focus and communicate the organizational objectives. It is not enough for the management team to be focused on objectives. These objectives must be translated into the goals and objectives of every team. The final stage of organizational assessment (see Chap. 6), private interviews, often reveals contradictory interpretations of corporate goals. Sometimes the contradictions expose ideas which are diametrically opposed. It takes very little time for such inconsistency to work its way through the entire organization. Consistency, on the other hand, pays benefits slowly and steadily.

One corporate giant in the financial services industry uses a variety of very creative and effective ways to communicate the corporate mission and values. Of course, the mission is posted throughout the organization, as are a set of nine key corporate values. This corporation takes the notion of values a step farther than most companies. Instead of an "Employee of the Month" this savvy corporation highlights a "Value of the Month" and attempts to catch people in the act of living it. When someone is caught living the "Value of Customer Responsiveness," her picture is posted throughout the building, along with a short description of her customer-responsive exploits. She may receive a small bonus. An entire team may be recognized in this manner as well. The effect of this process is to recognize and reward behaviors directly related to the values which are important to the company. This linking ties the individual or team to the corporate goals and enhances the communication benefit.

In traditional Employee of the Month programs there is no cognitive link between the organization's mission and the attention to the individual. These types of programs are not merely a waste of time, they are certainly counterproductive to the team-based organization and can become a destructive force by creating barriers between employees. Recognition is a powerful force, but it must be focused to advance the values of the organization.

Positive recognition of the team concept is part of how an organization builds new communication structures. These structures should emphasize direct contact between the management team and line teams. As the organization matures, developers should have less and less responsibility to provide the communication link between management and teams. The objective is to eliminate this intermediary function and let teams take over much of this communication. This eliminates much misunderstanding and allows teams to be held directly accountable for their own communication throughout the empowered organization. Management must pay attention to building the new human infrastructure by providing the training, coaching, and support needed to help the teams mature.

Teams and Unions

Unions have made some quiet but dramatic gains in the last five years. In the next century, labor leaders may look back at the 1990s as a time when labor redefined itself and created a new and important role in the American economy. Labor has become a true partner in companies throughout North America including USX, Ford, and GM's Saturn, as well as many smaller companies. This new role has been developed through farsighted and committed leaders who recognize that the fate of the worker and the union lies in the health of the company. To be an effective partner in the self-directed team process, union leadership must learn as much as possible about the business in which the workers live. Union leaders must learn to work with management to make strategic decisions and educate their membership.

The responsibility of creating viable self-directed work teams must be shared between management and the unions. In organizations without unions, employees' voices are no less significant. The union is, however, an institution which must be brought into the process early and often!

Unions, by their nature, exert political pressure on their organizations. Whether progressive or conservative, union officials are elected.

Officers attain their positions from the groups they serve. To be elected and maintain a position, leaders must constantly weigh the needs, desires, and dreams of the membership. At the same time, leadership requires something more: the ability to see ahead, understand the problems of the future, and sell the membership on a course of action they may not be inclined to readily accept. The history of adversarial union-management relations is a long one. And even in nonunion environments, the convention is about the same: management and employees must argue, battle, conflict, and confront in order to determine how the organization will operate. When self-managed teams are first mentioned, it is difficult for workers to believe that management is serious about change. Union officials must help to tear down old adversarial approaches. At the same time, a healthy skepticism is appropriate and reasonable to supply the checks and balances needed to ensure that promises are kept and progress is made.

For any leader, whether elected through the union or chosen by informal mandate of peers, this is a tough road to travel. Employees sometimes lose sight of the fact that management also has a great deal on the line in considering a team-based structure. Both sides must carefully build strong bridges of trust through effective and frequent communication. Union focus will need to change from an exclusive focus on grievance and contract issues to a broader view of the business world. Union leaders should use the Steering Committee and other forums to listen to management and learn about the business. Those who do not understand the market position of a company, who do not know the level of customer satisfaction, who do not have the current quality figures on the tip of their tongue will have great difficulty in understanding and participating in the difficult decisions the company must make. Regardless of the organization's structure, the above items tend to be significant concerns of management, while union officers often have had a more limited scope. It is far more common for union representatives to be occupied with filing grievances and disputing contract issues than thinking ahead and planning for the future. But no longer do unions have the luxury of letting management alone worry about the company's survival and profitability. If both employees and bosses are not involved in planning and working for the future, those at another company will be. Union officials must be closely involved in work redesign, in work-rule reduction, in work-flow analysis and process improvement. There will always be a need for grievances and contract concerns, but these are a fundamental component of the old top-down tradition. The new human infrastructure supports efforts and systems which look at root causes and solve problems before they reach the grievance stage. This requires forward thinking.

Most shop stewards will privately admit that a large percentage of grievances come from a small number of people. These are often creative, but dissatisfied, individuals who have a great deal of energy. The union can make life easier for all by helping these individuals find ways to use their energy and creativity positively. This is not to say that these grievances, and the people who raise them, do not deserve to be represented in the new human infrastructure. Rather, common sense and education are imperative in proceeding with grievances in the team environment. Neither the union nor the company is served by frivolous grievances which have the effect of paralyzing both, creating an atmosphere of fear and mistrust. Negotiating and settling grievances at the base level, while listening to those who do not have grievances, is the most team-supportive strategy. Too often the old axiom rings true: The squeaky wheel gets the grease. Often, union officials and informal leaders are cowed by particularly intimidating and vocal members. These few loud "voices" literally browbeat leaders into taking stands on issues which are actually hurtful to the membership in the long run. It is sometimes appropriate to counsel members that their grievance is inappropriate and even harmful to the interests of others. Some union officials may recoil at this thought, thinking it is antithetical to their mandate. But those same officials find it fitting to counsel a junior employee not to file a grievance on a seniority issue because it might upset more powerful members. The issue is not whether or not to represent a member, but how the larger membership is represented. If a series of grievances undermines the very objectives the union is striving for, a strong leader needs to shed light on and extinguish these flames of failure.

If the grievance procedure is used wisely, it can be a valuable vehicle for identifying entrenched problems and developing permanent solutions. Grievances can often bring to light problems in policy or procedure which could not have been anticipated by anyone. Consider the following example: A union-management team worked months on an overtime policy. Within a month after it was implemented, a grievance was filed which brought to light an important and unanticipated problem. Both managers and union officials initially expressed a sense of dismay, even betrayal, when the issue was raised. But they put these feelings aside and worked out a revised policy. When finished, the committee agreed it had a much better policy and owed the employee who brought the grievance a word of thanks.

Organizational leaders must look closely at work rules and seniority issues. Many of the work and seniority rules in force today were developed 50 to 70 years ago for a different time and place. They remain in the contract because neither side alone has the power or courage to change them. Management doesn't want a crippling work stoppage over a rule change, and the union doesn't want to face angry workers who are being asked to learn more skills and relax inefficient seniority rules. Narrow work rules and seniority lists can run up a company's costs rapidly. There is a need for work rules and for seniority in most shops, but they should be minimized and follow common sense with respect to the goals of the business. Rules which create overtime for a senior employee while others have too little to do increase the cost of products or services while decreasing the company's competitiveness. Many of these types of rules greatly increase labor costs. It is possible to successfully change rules while still providing reasonable protection to workers. No one is protected if the organization goes out of business or relocates. Holding on to antiquated rules may have short-term benefits, but will have devastating consequences in the future for everyone.

Union leaders need to be aware that the team concept initially causes anxiety and uncertainty among the work force. There is no doubt that there will be accusations by a vocal minority of union leaders "selling out to management." Even the most successful implementations of self-directed teams have had 10 to 20 percent of the work force who did not like teams and would rather go back to the old way of working. When discouraged, remember that there were a lot more than 20 percent who did not like the old system. Change is simply difficult, and it is as difficult for the union membership as it is for the leadership or management.

Both management and union, executives and workers—in fact, everyone in an organization—has a great deal to gain by learning to cooperate closely, and much to lose if they don't. The adversarial tradition gives each side a clear position to cling to, regardless of the true nature of a situation. The team-based system of cooperation, problem solving, and dedication to serving customer needs breaks down the adherence to such positions. Partisanship is replaced by the focus on accomplishing work as efficiently and effectively as possible. *Both* sides need to remember that *neither* side has a monopoly on virtue and that both will make mistakes.

The Use of Symbols

An effective leader is a mistress of symbolism. What many top managers fail to understand is that their every action has some symbolic impact. When an important meeting is closed to the union, that is symbolic. When management fails to share financial information, that is symbolic. A manager who insists on open meetings which involve everybody is leading through symbols. The failure to manage symbols is one of the major downfalls of managers. Managers who do attempt to use symbols often fail to use them appropriately or mix the message up by presenting other contradictory symbols at the same time. Careful thought, and some skill, is required to make symbols powerful tools.

The best leaders recognize that "things can be managed, but people must be led." As Alice's croquet game in Wonderland illustrated, the failure to recognize this fact leads to bizarre outcomes. Symbols are the primary tool by which people are led. Symbolic acts on the part of top managers must be sincere, appropriate in the context, and congruent with the values the leader espouses. When Lee Iacocca took a $1 salary as he was trying to bring Chrysler out of bankruptcy, he was presenting a context-appropriate symbol. As bad as Chrysler's financial position was and as large as Iacocca's salary could have been, his voluntary reduction could not have had a significant effect on the bottom line. But the symbolic act had power. It was certainly appropriate in the cost-cutting environment he was trying to foster. It was congruent with his stated value, "Everyone puts something on the line." When the UAW was given a seat on the Chrysler Board of Directors, it was a powerful symbol of the formation of a partnership to save the company.

The flip side: While Roger Smith was espousing cost cutting and "right sizing" for General Motors in the late 1980s, many of GM's top managers were given bonuses at a time when the company was losing record sums. Such behavior has profound negative symbolic value.

Strong leaders understand symbolism and find ways to use every symbol available to communicate the values of the company. They create signs which say volumes about the company to the customers and employees. Chapter 4 referenced a top-management group who could have taken a cruise, but chose to let a committee find a way to use the trip money to benefit everyone. The money was used to give a companywide weekend party. This has had profound, long-lasting symbolic value in this company. It is a chapter in the company's history which speaks to employees, new and old alike.

A corporate vice president made a policy of meeting every quarter and going over the financial status of the company in great detail with the entire company. It takes six long meetings across three shifts to accomplish this. Employees do not necessarily understand what is discussed, but over the course of the last several years they have become much more sophisticated in their understanding of the business. Their understanding does not come from this once a quarter meeting. The symbol-savvy leader is telegraphing to the entire company his expectation that every employee will learn as much as he or she can.

Jack Padovano, vice president at Wolferman's, Inc., has a strong sense of everyone sharing the load. He is the manager who described the traditional manufacturing setting as a dictatorship, and was a driving force in the success of teams at this specialty bakery. During their busy Christmas season he can often be found in the Customer Service Department answering phones and taking orders. No one believes for a minute that this makes a major difference in the number of customers served, but everyone knows that Jack expects all to pitch in no matter what their job description to satisfy the customer. Jack's behavioral symbol is unmistakable and speaks loud and clear about the company's value of impeccable customer service.

Ordinary daily behavioral symbols are probably more important than such grand gestures. In the case of Leader National Insurance, Vice President Peter Worth is present at team meetings on a frequent basis. At Champ Service Line (a division of Standard Motor Products, Inc.), the managers participate in the feedback process which will be outlined in Chap. 14. At South Central Counseling, Gary Henrie is religious about conducting skip-level meetings with all areas frequently. When employees see these behavioral symbols, it brings the values the manager preaches to life.

An insurance company president was fond of saying, "I have an open door policy. Anyone can come into my office and talk about anything they think is important to the business." As the organizational assessment of his company was being conducted, he asked us to specifically inquire about his "open door policy." In more than twenty-five interviews only four people said they had ever taken advantage of this "open door." All four said they had tried to go in and talk with him about problems, but found him to be defensive, even angry. Each of them claimed they would never attempt to talk with him again. Not surprisingly, many of the others we interviewed were very aware of the experience these four had had. Almost all vowed to stay away from his office based on the experience of others. Failing to use the symbol of the open door properly caused this executive and his organization immeasurable damage and prevented him from receiving important information.

Performance appraisal systems carry strong symbols. (And will be detailed in Chap. 13.) A *Fortune* 500 company contracted with one of the authors (Darrel Ray) to conduct an extensive and expensive training course for a large segment of middle and upper managers on giving and receiving feedback. During the course of the organizational assessment it was learned that none of the direct reports to the president had received any type of formal feedback, nor had any of the vice presidents given performance feedback to their subordinates in the last two years. As the contracted program was being put together, questions were raised about the company's commitment to the new feedback process. The entire upper-management group vowed it would start modeling feedback and require everyone to give effective performance feedback. A two-year follow-up disclosed that virtually none of the training had been used. All the vice presidents reported that they had had no feedback since the training, and only a handful of directors, who reported to the vice presidents, had received formal feedback. The negative symbolic value is clearly conveyed to all levels of the organization:

1. We do not value feedback.

2. Training is for others, not for management.

3. Management expects others to practice what it will not practice itself.

4. Continuous improvement through feedback is not important.

Conceivably the most destructive symbol to the team concept is presented by the top manager who espouses teamwork, but runs his or her own group in an autocratic manner and fails to use team skills. Symbolic significance is found in the daily or weekly schedule of managers, the president, or the CEO. A vice president who holds regular weekly meetings with the union president and a monthly meeting with the local union officers displays symbolic and practical support of employee empowerment. A manager who schedules himself weekly attendance at different team meetings throughout the plant is saying that teams and meetings are important to him and the organization. In the course of a year he is able to visit most teams. The vice president who takes a group of line workers to a two-hour lunch each week and really listens during luncheon conversation is speaking loudly with her actions.

The symbols embedded in these behaviors have far-reaching consequences for the organization. They convey upper management's commitment to the work force and build a model for middle management to follow. Of course, it is also important what behaviors accompany the symbolic efforts. It does little good to attend a team meeting if the manager becomes defensive or angry when the team asks a hard question. Damage results when a manager goes to lunch with a group and uses the information gathered to punish or blame.

Throughout this book the focus has been on developing the new and empowering human infrastructure. It is a demanding and a complicated process, but the skills needed to implement it are still only a fraction of the skills required of a top manager. Along with all the skills described here for making the transition to teams, there is a fundamental need for basic business skills. There is no substitute for the

leadership and focus a boss can bring to the table. To think strategical-
ly, to focus the company on important goals, to educate the teams in
business realities is the duty of every member of an organization.

Finances: A Special Symbol

Perhaps the most powerful symbolic act a leader can perform is to
open the books of the company or division. And opening the books is
not only a powerful symbolic act, it is a practical step. Teams that
understand company goals and objectives are much more committed
to these goals. Secrecy is the death knell of the team concept. The manager who cannot open the books sends the signal that workers cannot
be trusted. This is one reason why privately held companies, especially family businesses, have such difficulty effectively implementing
self-directed teams. They often have long and deeply felt traditions of
financial secrecy. Financial secrecy is a clear sign of mistrust. Fears not
dealt with will consume enormous amounts of energy, little of it spent
in positive ways.

Managers withhold financial information from teams for many reasons: they don't want to worry teams with information over which
they have no control; they are afraid teams may misuse the information or disclose it to someone outside the company or use it against the
company. These are all based on false assumptions.

First, if employees have no influence over the bottom line, why are
they employed? Team members are the primary movers in fulfilling
the organization's mission; they should be given all the information
possible to help them understand that mission, and how it can be
accomplished. Employees should be worried about the bottom line—
just as worried as management. No one in an organization should be,
or needs to be, protected from the realities of business. It is a holdover
of the old patriarchal system which says that those in authority are
there for a reason and must know what they are doing, like the "Father
knows best" attitude, which implies employees are too immature or
childlike to understand. Issues of company finance are kept from
employees to serve a misperceived notion of what is good and right.

Second, management cannot prevent information from getting to
competitors even if it wanted. Management fools no one but itself in
believing its financial information is a secret. If people want it badly
enough, they can get most information on company finances, even
from a privately held company.

Third, management's belief that workers will use financial information against the company may be more paranoid than practical. It may

also be self-defeating. To paraphrase the management fear: "They might use the profit and loss statement to get more money in the next contract negotiations." In fact, labor often has a very inflated view of profits and a poor understanding of business processes. Union presidents have not been trained in how to read financial records any more than other employees. There is little training, except for management, in issues of overhead, marketing, price structures, taxes, and so forth. The more secrets kept about finances, the bigger the fantasies workers have about company profits. The biggest favor management can do itself is to carefully train every team member in how to read and understand the company financial statement, or a summary of that statement, published every quarter.

In the course of his consulting work, Bradford Ray (brother and associate of Darrel Ray) has developed a game called The Lemonade Stand. The game was developed in response to a startling discovery made over the years: Most team members have no idea how money is made. Even well-educated, sophisticated employees often harbor misguided notions about company finances and profits. Intended to demonstrate business principles, the game takes about an hour and a half to play, during which several lemonade stands compete to make a profit. Of the hundreds who have played this game, only about 20 percent could make a profit and keep their stand going. The person who holds the record for the highest profit in the game to date is Dennis Johnson, a member of the housekeeping team called the Road Runners at Standard Motor Products. (The fact that Johnson was The Lemonade Stand star was not lost on the managers playing the same game that particular day.)

The North American worker has been sheltered from the day-to-day worries of business for too long. Organizations have kept employees in the dark, feeling they could not handle the truth or understand the numbers. When things do go wrong and layoffs are announced, it comes as a big surprise to the work force. In effect, workers have been denied an opportunity to do anything about their fate because management has withheld the bad news about corporate performance. Executives often say that management does this to protect the worker, but in fact it is to protect itself from having to answer questions. Management chooses not to deal with the difficult and disquieting queries about its operation of the organization, or why it avoided bringing workers into the decision-making process, that it would face if it were open with those workers. This creates a pervasive sense of mistrust between management and employees.

Without proper information, teams will not reach their potential, nor will they trust management. Finances are the lifeblood of any organization. If that information cannot be shared, then the company cannot truly empower its employees.

In sharing financial information, it is important to understand that people will display a broad range of comprehension levels. This puts even more pressure on the integrity of the information presented. Especially at the beginning, there will be inconsistencies in financial comprehension. Management will have to conduct mini-courses in finance and use every opportunity to teach budget concepts to the teams. It will take several years of continual, focused effort for teams to grasp the full import of the numbers. But what a breakthrough! Once teams do understand, they can go so much deeper into understanding the organization. With proper design, the financial statements can reflect teams' contribution to the bottom line. Teams will be able to take an active and knowledgeable role in controlling costs, evaluating equipment acquisitions, negotiating with vendors, and a host of other activities. When it comes to issues of trust and expanding the organizational brain trust, financial disclosure is the last bastion of top-down communication. Full disclosure of the organization's money matters is the last difficult step to true employee empowerment.

Communicating Values via the Newsletter

Once the management team has achieved a clear focus and consensus on its corporate objectives and has begun modeling behavior which supports them, a program of corporatewide communication can begin. One of the primary methods of communicating values and goals can be through the newsletter. Unfortunately, many corporate newsletters are unfocused and without purpose, except perhaps as vague attempts to make people feel good. The best purpose a newsletter can serve is to teach and encourage the goals and values of the organization, especially when making the transition to teams. To that end, here is a sample mission statement and a set of guidelines for organizational newsletters. The guidelines are designed to help develop and reinforce the team process throughout the organization.

Mission of the Newsletter Staff. To provide a communication vehicle through which the values of the team concept and the company can be taught. We are committed to a high quality of content, and to producing a publication which we would be proud to give to any customer or to corporate management.

Eight Guidelines for Newsletter Development

1. Articles should be team-focused. Highlight what a whole team has accomplished, and how.

2. Twenty to thirty names should appear in the body text of each newsletter, with many direct quotes from those named. Let people brag about themselves.

3. Two to four team pictures, or pictures with more than one person in them, should be featured in each issue. No individual pictures should appear the first six months, or managers' pictures the first four months; photographs should be taken up close using tight head and face pictures.

4. Each article should teach one principle each month, using examples of the teams' successes. Each issue can have a theme. For example,

   October: Quality improvements, examples in our teams
   November: Team leadership roles and how they are being used
   December: The role of the union
   January: The role of the team developer and how some team developers interact with teams and their expectations
   February: Measures and charts and how we use them
   March: Living by our code of conduct

5. Articles should be written from the perspective of the team, *not* the editor, management, or interviewer. Write in "active" language, with three to five direct quotes from team members in each story.

6. Charts, statistics, or measures should be used in every article to document and reinforce the idea that measurement is important.

7. Three people, besides the editor, should be on the newsletter staff. These can be rotated every six to nine months. The editor should be the same for one year, with a new one brought onto the staff at the nine-month point for training. The team communicators can be called upon to provide information, though they should not be expected to write more than a very rough draft.

8. The newsletter should be written with the organization and its customers in mind. Each story should tell what is being done and how. Does it give the kind of information that would convince someone the organization is truly committed to the team concept and quality service?

Reporter

Nov./Dec.   **Volume 25**

Spotlight on The Hit and Run Team

In the front office the 2 Customer Service teams merged in October. Hit And Run has members from both the TROUBLESHOOTERS and Xceller8ers. Debbie Smith explained, "Hit And Run is not about accidents. It's like a baseball team-RBIs, hit the ball, and run to make points and score."

EDP, Customer Service, and the Distribution administrators were arbitrarily broken in half to ensure phone coverage. But people who sat side by side and worked together every day were on different teams. They decided to combine based on a team member's suggestion during a problem solving session. They solved the coverage problem by having a team meeting at 7:00 am before the switch board opens up. It means a mandatory hour of overtime for everyone but no lost working hours during the week.

"There's more communication. Everybody hears things first hand instead of second hand and that prevents confusion. People on the free spaces on the team wheel are on a

Hit and Run Team Meeting

task force. I'm on the task force now. We have little meetings to write up proposals to bring to the team meeting. It saves a lot of time during the regular team meeting. We are working on self-assessment. We had self-assessment before but we are changing the questions to make it more effective," said Linda Fulkerson. Another job for the Hit And Run task force is to come up with a new team wheel. They are considering a baseball diamond.

"Coverage and communications have improved. Coverage is better because the team meeting is before work. Hit And Run is a good team and Customer Service is a good department", feels Nancy Gilliam. ♠

C2Q Passes Safety Milestone

C2Q team achieved 365 working days without recordable accidents on October 21, 1993. C2Q, the Wire and Cable support team is keeping track of working days and not calendar days. The team celebrated with a pizza party on November 8, 1993.

Some people might not appreciate this accomplishment of an office team. However, C2Q had a member report a severe case of carpel tunnel in 1991. Otherwise the team would have exceeded 500 days without an accident. While safety risks might be reduced in the office, risks are not eliminated. Eye strain, back problems, and repetitive motion disorders are all hazards in extensive CRT and computer use. Congratulations are in order for C2Q. ♠

Figure 12-1 Sample newsletter.

The Art of Getting Along

Sooner or later a man, if he is wise, discovers that life is a mixture of good days and bad, victory and defeat, give and take.

He learns that it doesn't pay to be a sensitive soul - that he should let some things go over his head like water off a duck's back.

He learns that he who loses his temper usually loses.

He learns that all men have burnt toast for breakfast now and then, and that he shouldn't take the other fellow's grouch too seriously. He learns that carrying a chip on his shoulder is the easiest way to get into a fight.

He learns that the quickest way to become unpopular is to carry tales and gossip about others.

He learns that most of the other fellows are as ambitious as he is, that they have brains that are as good or better, and that hard work, and not cleverness, is the secret of success.

He learns that it doesn't matter so much who gets the credit so long as the business shows a profit.

He comes to realize that the business could run perfectly without him.

He learns to sympathize with the youngsters coming into the business, because he remembers how bewildered he was when he first started out.

He learns not to worry when he does not make a hit EVERY time, because experience has shown if he always gives his best, his average will break pretty well.

He learns that no man ever got to first base alone and that it is only through cooperative effort that we move on to better things.

He learns that the fellows are not any harder to get along with in one place than another, and that "getting along" depends about 98 percent on himself. ✝

Submitted by Mark Jones

October 1993 Results	
Lines Shipped:	385,889
Dollars Shipped:	$8,677,386
Fill Level For:	
Champ	92.3%
Hygrade	93.5%
Standard	96.1%
Total	94.2%

Future UNION Meeting

Wednesday, December 29, 1993

2:45 p.m.
Second and Third Shift
Employees

3:45 p.m.
First Shift Employees

*Commercial Bank in
Bonner Springs*

Please Note: The Union Meetings are changing to the fourth Wednesday of the month at the Commercial Bank in Bonner Springs. In the past, the meetings were in the third Wednesday of the month in the Camp North upstairs conference room.

-2-

Figure 12-1 (*Continued*)

Light Days Pilot Program

The Distribution Business Unit has undertaken a 6 month pilot program called Light Days. Steve DeBusk suggested giving Distribution employees the opportunity to leave work early if there was not enough orders to give people work for an entire day. A committee was formed consisting of Marsha Berry from Personnel, John DeArmond of Standard Distribution, Ernest Lewis as Union Steward , Jim Miller of the Gain Sharing Committee, and Drew Vincent of Champ Distribution. Bob Howard chaired the task force. The task force met once a week for two months to work out the issues. They are continuing to meet to consider questions that arise during the trial period.

John DeArmond, Bob Howard, Marsha Berry, Ernest Lewis, Jim Miller, Drew Vincent

The mission statement of the task force: "The purpose of the Light Day Program has been designed to give the employees "voluntarily" the opportunity to reduce the labor cost, increase productivity as it relates to the gain sharing payout, enhance morale and improve attendance."

The Light Day Program has modified the way Distribution workers operate during the course of every day. At the 6:00 a.m. team huddles employees volunteering for a light day inform the team scheduler. Those employees that choose to stay the entire day are provided work. At 9:00 a.m. the team schedulers meet and analyze the lines to be processed that day to meet the carry over minimums and to compile a list of employees wishing to leave early. Movement of employees between teams take place then to balance the labor requirements for the day. At 11:30 a.m. the team schedulers meet and post the results toward the minimum carry over goals. The decision to release employees, and at what time, is decided after reviewing the order status. All the employees who volunteer are released at the time designated by the team schedulers. The team developers and Human Resources Department are given a list of those employees excused on this program by the end of each day.

All newly hired employees are not eligible until completing 45 working days. Employees who arrive to work late are not eligible for the light day program that particular day.

The employees do not endanger their percentage of payout as it relates to the gain sharing program for hours missed due to light day. The hours an employee misses due to light duty only affects the number of hours paid out in gain sharing (only hours actually worked), but not the percentage of pay out.

Bob Howard, Chairman of the Light Days Task Force feels, "So far it has been a success. We have had a few stumbling blocks with not getting the work done and having to work overtime. But overall people are positive. The program has created an atmosphere where people work together in harmony." ✝

Thank You

Words alone are not enough to express our gratitude to each and everyone of you who came through to make this a little bit merrier Christmas for some deserving Angels.

We adopted 51 Angels from the Salvation Army. The Franklin Center met us with another 100 children who needed help. We came through again. We also adopted out 7 families.

The very best wishes for the Holidays from Betty Kusler, Toni Cisneros, and all those that were helped.

(The CRO Reporter wants to thank Betty and all those who helped organize this special holiday event. They have made it easy for us to contribute during this season.) ✝

Figure 12-1 *(Continued)*

The Five CRO Commandments

1. SAFETY IS PRIORITY #1
It is my responsibility to make our work place as safe as possible for everyone.

2. HIGH PRODUCTIVITY IS IMPORTANT
I will strive to ensure that Champ/SMP makes a lot of automotive products to ship. I will strive to keep a high fill level to achieve my own job security.

3. GOOD QUALITY IS IMPORTANT
I do not want to make or sell a product I would not put on my own car. I do not want to ship an order I would not receive and accept.

4. PERSONAL PRODUCTIVITY IS IMPORTANT
I will strive for excellence in my

own job. I will try to do efficient, productive, and good quality work. I want to do my part to keep the organization running well.

5. GOOD TEAM MEMBER
I want to be a good team mate to the Champ organization. I want to make my co-workers' job as easy as possible. ✝

What Is Your Team Proud Of?

The second anniversary of the Midwestern Distribution Center's switch to a Customer Responsive Organization and team concept is just around the corner. Think about what small or big successes that your team has accomplished in the last 21 months. Talk about the subject in your team meeting. Then write a short description of

one or two sentences each and submit them to John Seymour, Hope Piuck, or Sue Ferguson of the CRO Reporter staff.

We want to publish an anniversary edition of the Reporter. We want to know what Accomplishments Your Team Is Proud Of! ✝

November 1993 Results	
Lines Shipped:	480,614
Dollars Shipped:	$9,921,493
Fill Level For:	
Champ	92.5%
Hygrade	94.4%
Standard	96.3%
Total	95.4%

Letter From the Editor: Fear Of Failure

The path of continuous improvement is a path of change. And change is hard. Along with the prospect for improvement and success is the risk of failure. Many people fear failure so much that they would rather do nothing than change.

Motorola, an electronics manufactuer, is famous for their innovation. A Motorola motto is "We celebrate noble failure." Motorola celebrates failure because they recognize that there must be failures on the path way

to big successes.

We have to recognize that to improve we must make changes. Monitor the results. If the changes don't succeed, we need to recognize that fact. Then analyze why and fix the problem. The fix might be going back to the old way or trying something else different. At Progressive Insurance, "We never punish failure. We only punish sloppy execution and the failure to recognize reality," says COO Bruce Marlow.

Harley Davidson, makers of

motorcycles, has had an enormous turn around in their business practices and business achievements. "Each change effort that we go through sets the stage for the next one. Rather than look at things that we don't do well at first as failures, I'd rather ask myself, 'What are we able to do today that we couldn't do yesterday, and how do those things allow us to become better tomorrow?," said Richard Teerlink, CEO of Harley. ✝

| **CRO REPORTER** |
| Editor: Hope Piuck |
| Advisor: John Seymour |
| Photographer: Carol Myrick |

-4-

Figure 12-1 (*Continued*)

The newsletter is a powerful vehicle for recognition and for communication of values and goals. This dear space should not be wasted on the traditional "newsletter gossip." This includes birthdays, anniversaries, innocuous management messages, or "feel good" fluff pieces. If the story does not teach or demonstrate one or more of the corporate values, then it does not belong in the newsletter. Recognition of birthdays or anniversaries does have a place, but it does not belong in a newsletter aimed at strengthening a team-based organization. Look at the two newsletter stories below. Which will convey the value of teamwork and systematic problem solving on the line?

> Joseph Employee had a great 20th anniversary party last week. Thirty-five people attended a noon lunch and Joe received his twenty-year diamond pin. Sandra Miller, Vice President of our division, gave a brief speech. She has known Joe for fifteen years.

> Joseph Employee, along with Sally Mae and Jeri Sandhill, and the Customer Service Team completed a three-month study and two-month trial of the new customer order and fulfillment process. They identified four key areas in which processes could be eliminated or reduced. This has led to a reduction in errors of over 45 percent and has reduced our turnaround time on orders from three days to 24 hours. Congratulations to the team on a fantastic job. Special congratulations are in order for Joe, who will be celebrating his 20th anniversary next week at a noon luncheon.

The first story teaches no values and highlights an individual apart from his team. The second story focuses on several important values: process improvement, problem solving, measuring results, and working together. Joe still gets his party and a mention in the newsletter, but the fact of his being here for 20 years teaches little of value, and no values, to the reader.

To repeat: Newsletters should be designed to teach and to recognize the values and goals of the organization. Figure 12-1 shows a newsletter dedicated to the team concept.

From the newsletter to each leadership decision, every action, statement, and behavior communicates something. The faster and more effectively team values are modeled and communicated, the quicker the organization will truly team up and make the transition to being self-directed and team-based.

13

Teaching Teams
to Communicate

Tradition and "Aboutism"

A customer service team struggles to get its performance and quality indicators up. In the lunchroom, three team members complain bitterly about two fellow members who have not been doing their share. The same two folks can be heard two hours later in the break room complaining that their efforts to help the team improve its performance have been undermined by the first three. Another member overhears the complaining and gossip and calls a team feedback session facilitated by a trained person from outside the team. The session lasts 60 minutes with the whole team. In the course of the feedback session the individuals share their perceptions and hear the perceptions of others. The facilitator keeps the team on task by holding to a tightly constructed set of rules, which protect all concerned and help get the issues discussed openly. At the end of the meeting, the facilitator asks for a problem-solving group to meet and construct a solution to the team's performance problem and to report back in three days. Within one week the team has not only solved its performance problem but hit upon an idea which is soon adopted by the 12 other teams in the service unit. In addition, the two informally convened subgroups, who were so upset at one another, learn an important lesson in direct communication: *It is better to talk to each other than about each other.*

This scenario illustrates an important segment of the new human infrastructure. People in a team-based organization must have comfort with and trust in a feedback process. And consultants in the field generally realize early in their team-building work just how critical the issues of effective feedback can be. Before closely examining this feedback system, it is important to look at the traditional ways feedback has been handled in organizations, and society at large.

The team in the scenario above had a process to implement at the first signs of conflict, a process which was specifically engineered to prevent conflicts from overwhelming and killing teams. But what happens when there is no process in place?

The simple truth about traditional organizational communication patterns is this: people talk about one another far more often than they talk to each other about problems, conflicts, complaints, and even good feelings about each other's work. Peers all too often go behind one another's backs to try and meet their needs and avoid conflicts. In short, they gossip to each other and to people outside the work group. Typically, this approach has a high cost to the organization. In the case of an organization attempting the transition to self-management, ignoring these destructive patterns of communication means the organization will rarely benefit from the synergies which have been so widely touted in the team literature.

Most communication in conventional corporate life is based upon hidden systems. These systems have many names: "the grapevine," "the gossip column," or "the unofficial chain of command." There are elaborate, unwritten rules in companies about how to handle communications and conflict, how to register a complaint, how to deal with the poor performance of a peer, and how to deal with information which the boss may not want to hear. This hidden system is very powerful because it is based upon fear of direct, open, and honest communication. The customary gossip system holds the key to information flow in any organization.

What happens in an organization when:

- Someone tells a peer about a performance issue related to her work?
- Someone tells the boss the latest initiative is causing major problems in getting the work done?
- An individual talks to a group about how its gossiping is hurting the group's morale?
- News of corporate policy changes is heard through the grapevine before it comes out officially?
- An employee hears about a mistake he made through the grapevine, but not directly from his supervisor?
- Workers sit around and talk about the boss's performance without passing the information on to the boss?

What happens in most organizations is that there are two kinds of responses to all of the above. Within every organization are two cultures:

the formal and the informal culture. The *formal culture* is visible and structured by management. The *informal culture* is largely invisible to management and is structured by the employees. There is a response from each of these cultures to any situation, including those listed above. The conflicts between the formal and informal systems are usually felt as an undercurrent that everyone in the organization learns to live with.

Often, management is oblivious to the power and influence of the informal culture, if aware of its existence at all. The downfall of most employee involvement processes is that they change the formal culture without changing the informal culture. The only effective way to begin the process of changing the informal culture is to change the communication patterns of both cultures. Teams cannot develop and mature unless they change the patterns of communication which have prevailed for decades in the traditional organization.

In the field of team building the important aspect of performance feedback has been routinely ignored or put off. In most courses, a few minutes teaching time, or a brief module, is devoted to this subject, but little else. The issue of feedback is often left up to communications courses to cover. But courses do not make fundamental changes in the informal culture, and so are doomed to fail.

The single biggest killer of teams is the lack of clear and honest communication between the team members. Teams who do not communicate effectively do not do well. After the initial start-up of a team effort there is enthusiasm, excitement, and energy. But within a few weeks or months, the enthusiasm begins to get drained off by infighting and mistrust in the team. Energy is lost as gossiping increases. As enthusiasm and energy wane, excitement turns to gloom, and worse, cynicism toward the team process. While this may be normal behavior, it is not necessary. It severely retards the team's development and prevents team synergies from developing.

The largest problem fostered and fed by the informal culture is the "disease of aboutism." The term *aboutism* was coined by the psychiatrist Fritz Perls; stated simply the "aboutist" attitude is *"I/we will talk about you, but not to you."* Aboutism and its standing in the informal communication system are insidious and deeply embedded in most corporate cultures, and until this changes it is very difficult for teams to mature into high performers. Everyone acknowledges that gossip is destructive to trust and teamwork, but what people need to realize is that its worst manifestations are not inevitable. They can be effectively combatted using a powerful tool for communication and productivity. With effective feedback systems in place, many of the difficulties related to aboutism can be avoided. Effective feedback is the lifeblood of the new human infrastructure.

The CRAY Feedback System

The CRAY Feedback System draws upon common principles of communication and human-systems theory. One of the authors (Darrel Ray) developed the system with a colleague, Cheryl Highwarden. The system also owes a good deal to the theories and techniques of Dan Dana, who pioneered a revolutionary system for corporate conflict mediation, and to the upward feedback model developed by Dennis and Dianne LaMountain. (See the Bibliography, where related materials are listed.)

High-performing teams have well-structured internal systems for giving performance feedback. Team members are able to do this without getting egos involved or creating interpersonal conflicts. Communication is most often clear and direct in nature. At the same time, team members do not engage in interpersonal guerrilla warfare by talking behind one another's backs. While there may be a formal, written evaluation system in place, much of the important communication takes place in real time directly between team members.

The CRAY system is a communications model which structures the method of communication but *not* the content. It is designed to open up communication channels which have traditionally been closed, while at the same time controlling the flow of information and protecting the participants. Its primary purpose is to take the fear out of communicating important information. As Edwards Deming has said, "A fearful workplace creates bad data." Managers cannot manage and teams cannot grow if they do not have access to accurate data. The CRAY system is not a panacea, but we think it is an 80 percent solution. Although there will always be some difficulties that will need a different and more situation-specific approach, we feel that most of the problems and fears related to interpersonal communications can be solved using this system.

The CRAY system is designed to first destroy the traditional hidden communication system, then replace it with an approach that is both visible and effective. With its successful implementation, old patterns of gossip, hidden agendas, and competition will be exposed for what they are: destructive processes which prevent teamwork.

The CRAY system depends on a trained facilitator who is not a member or manager of the team. It also depends upon the team being trained in the process. A set of well-defined rules is given to the team during the training. Management's task is to model the process at their own level and hold teams accountable for using the process. When management becomes aware of a problem, the first question asked is "Has this been handled in the feedback process?" The CRAY system places responsibility on the teams to solve their problems rather than drag management in as mediator or arbitrator. The system works as well between teams as within teams. In many cases, where management once felt obligated to intervene, the new human infrastructure offers an alternative that asks teams to be responsible. Management must insist on the team trying the feedback process first, before calling in management.

Team members must learn that they have the tools to take responsibility for themselves. As seen in the scenario that opened this chapter, any individual may call a feedback session. Most important, feedback sessions are also scheduled monthly. Teaching people how to give feedback, while necessary, is not sufficient to develop an open and maturing feedback environment. There must be a system in place to give members an opportunity to examine their communications and exchange information in a protected environment. Without these conditions, the feedback process never gets off the ground and does not become a part of the culture.

The CRAY system calls for a team meeting once a month at a time set aside strictly for feedback. A facilitator is scheduled to be at the feedback meeting, and all team members are present, including the manager or team developer. During the process, *anyone* may receive *appreciative feedback* or *improvement feedback*, including the manager. The terms *constructive feedback* and *negative feedback* are deliberately not used; these terms have been overused, and their meaning is vague. The focus of feedback should be on continuous improvement, and to that end the linguistic emphasis is on improvement processes. By focusing on improvement, the CRAY system gives direction to changes in performance, which is the real point of feedback.

Team members are encouraged to use the traditional communications skills like "I" messages, making eye contact, and paraphrasing what they have heard. Each person is asked to write out his or her appreciative comments first. The facilitator opens the session to comments on what people have written. Members share what they like and appreciate about how others are doing their jobs. It is important to emphasize throughout this process that the facilitator is following a carefully prescribed set of behaviors in managing each feedback opportunity. The meeting's initial emphasis on sharing positive comments is part of the prescription. By focusing on the affirmative, the meeting is less likely to become bogged down at the start. Every person's behavior is primarily positive, but she or he rarely gets recognized for it. Learn to take responsibility for giving positive feedback and not always expect it to be given by management. True empowerment means teaching self-discipline and self-reinforcement.

When the positive feedback is complete, the facilitator asks team members to write down their improvement feedback. After the time allotted for this, the floor is opened for improvement feedback. Since facilitators receive training prior to their first meeting, they will be able to judge when it is time to shift the focus of the meeting. Team members may speak to anyone, but must follow the rules of giving feedback. The receiver must also follow the rules of receiving feedback. These are explicitly outlined in the training and are enforced by the facilitator.

The principles of the CRAY system are as follows:

1. Feedback should be direct and between the concerned parties.
2. Positive feedback is always separated from improvement feedback.
3. Feedback is always separated from commitments to change.
4. Feedback is separated from problem solving.
5. Feedback is given to one person at a time, not the team in general or several members simultaneously.
6. The facilitator is in charge of the process; team members are responsible for the content.
7. No team member may censor or otherwise prevent another team member from giving feedback.
8. Teams should have regular group opportunities for feedback under the facilitation and protection of a trained facilitator.
9. Private, real-time feedback is encouraged and expected to develop as teams gain skill and trust.

In the initial stages, when the team is first learning how to give feedback, it strongly objects to doing the improvement segment. Team members often say management should do it, or it should be done privately. In an ideal world, these concerns might be met with agreement. Unfortunately, management frequently does not address a problem until it is entirely out of control. At the same time, members, while they say they would rather give improvement feedback in private, rarely do so. What might be good feedback information degrades into aboutism when people do not feel it is safe to communicate. Finally, without this type of process, there is no safe way to talk directly to the manager about her or his behavior.

As teams get used to the system and learn how to give feedback in the sessions, they become more and more comfortable giving it privately. So, in time, much of the feedback that was done in the meeting gets taken care of privately and in a much more timely fashion. This is the ultimate goal, but one that requires the foundation of something like the CRAY system. When team members finally realize that they will get or give the feedback in a structured session, they begin to do it at the time they see the problem. The CRAY system builds certain expectations: that feedback can be given immediately if the person feels safe and skilled enough, or can be given later in the group process with the security and guidance of a trained facilitator. The feedback process provides a safe place in which to practice good communication skills. Without this regular, real-life practice, teams rapidly revert to their old habits of gossip and aboutism, leading eventually to the disruption of the team process.

During the formal team feedback meetings, certain rules are followed to promote the sharing of information without creating defensiveness. As mentioned, the practice of always paraphrasing what was said is a key technique. Another rule is that the receiver may not respond or defend, only say "thank you" and then paraphrase. While it seems unnatural not to allow responses or explanations, once a group allows such rebuttal the feedback process stops cold. The group spends all its time debating and never gets the feedback task accomplished. The purpose of the feedback session is only to share information and perceptions, not to evaluate them. This is done later in a problem-solving format or in smaller group or one-on-one negotiation sessions, which may or may not be formally facilitated.

The complete set of rules for the formal feedback meeting is given below; it is followed by the list of rules team members are asked to follow when giving feedback in the meeting.

Rules for Feedback Meeting

1. Use the "I" message model.
2. Do not interrupt or interpret.
3. Keep the focus on the behavior of the people in the room.
4. People cannot receive two pieces of feedback in a row or give to someone from whom they have just received.
5. Start with appreciative exchange session and complete it before going to improvement.
6. Write it down first.
7. Look at the person and talk to her or him, not the group. Give feedback to only one person at a time.
8. No editorial comments, no apologies, and no commitment to change in the feedback session.

9. Respondent acknowledges and then repeats what he or she heard.

10. If respondent is unclear, he or she may ask for more—e.g., "Thank you, can you tell me more?"

11. No problem-solving in the feedback session. This should take place at a separate meeting.

12. Facilitator will act only as a traffic cop, does not give or receive feedback, remains neutral, and will enforce the rules.

13. No one is required to give feedback, but as a member of the team you may not refuse feedback. All persons have a right to air their views.

14. You may ask for feedback in a specific area if you wish.

15. *This last item is essential!* Respect team confidentiality. To talk about group feedback outside of the team meeting is a violation of team trust.

Eleven Rules for Giving Feedback

1. *Be behavior-oriented:* Describe the behavior, do not evaluate the person.

2. *Use examples:* Be specific, with clear behavioral examples.

3. *Helpful versus venting:* The feedback meeting is an opportunity to support someone else, not to get something off your chest.

4. *Be receiver-oriented:* Pay attention to the receiver's capacity to take it in. Wait rather than overload.

5. *Be timely:* Give feedback as soon after the event as possible.

6. *Give feedback on items within receiver control:* Comment about something within the control of the receiver.

7. *Impact versus motive:* Describe impact of the receiver's actions; do not speculate on intention.

8. *Check for clarity:* Be clear. Check to ensure your message is being heard the way you mean it.

9. *Communicate feeling:* Speak directly to the receiver, with real feeling.

10. *Group sharing:* Give feedback that can be checked for accuracy and validity, if necessary, by others.

11. Ask the person "May I coach you?" and use constructions like "You could be more effective if...."

Once all teams have been trained and a core group of facilitators certified, the process can proceed rapidly and efficiently. With systematic implementation of the process, the maturation time for teams is reduced by as much as 50 percent in some cases. More importantly, as the skills improve and are practiced in the environment, management begins to get better data and more reliable information about the processes. The CRAY system rapidly undermines the old aboutism and creates an environment where direct communication is valued and *feedback* is not a dirty word.

One of the greatest dangers to the implementation of any system is the creative energy teams can muster toward undermining it. No sooner are they trained than they start trying to change the rules to avoid what they perceive as threatening or negative. The facilitator is trained to prevent this and hold the team accountable in the process. Therefore, the facilitator's role is an indispensable one in the CRAY system. But others, including team developers, also have a role in the process. Team developers will find the following set of reminders and guidelines useful.

Feedback and the Team Developer

- Teams will do almost anything to avoid being honest with each other.
- Especially during the first year, the team developer will have to take the lead in scheduling the feedback sessions.
- Remember, the more the team practices feedback in the meeting, the more it begins practicing outside the meeting as well.
- Model and use the communication skills of feedback everyday.
- Be very careful to model receiving improvement feedback. Ask for coaching, and model receiving it well.

The CRAY Feedback System is certainly not the only system. We believe it is a workable one that, like any well-engineered product, does what it was designed to do. You cannot put a high-performance car together with one piston from a Chevy, one from a Honda, a transmission from a Mack truck, and a suspension system from a Lincoln. Well-engineered systems are designed so that each component works in harmony with all others. For this reason, the system must be taught and implemented as a whole.

To skillfully implement the process, management's commitment must be strong and it must model the required behavior. The top-management group is often the first to be trained. This process has worked equally well in a wide variety of environments, from production to research to service. It is a system for human communication, and so will work wherever humans wish to communicate effectively.

Facilitators and CRAY

The facilitator serves two functions in administering the CRAY Feedback System:

1. To protect the team and its members
2. To enforce the rules of the system and prevent behaviors which would inhibit the sharing of information

The facilitator may not be a member of the team. He may be the team leader of another unit, an outside quality facilitator, or simply a well-trained person from another team. The rule that the facilitator must come from outside the team is based on the principle summarized in such axioms as "One hundred percent of all brain surgeons who do brain surgery on themselves die" and "A lawyer who defends himself has a fool for a client." No one can be objective about her own team no matter how well intentioned or well trained. The facilitator has no interpretive role, nor is he present to direct the flow of information. The role *looks* simple, but *is* difficult, because of the natural human tendency to want to get involved, solve problems, and interpret information. The facilitator is there to manage the feedback exchange process, nothing else.

Implementing the system requires a twofold approach. First, facilitators receive initial training, then teams receive training. During the team-training phase, the facilitators-in-training are supervised by the trainer. Facilitators are like operators of a mammoth machine; they must be carefully trained in the necessary skills and supervised until they achieve certification. Anything less than high proficiency in the skills risks damage to the system, the teams, and the organization, rather than creating high performance. Not all facilitator candidates are certified. Up to 20 percent have not developed sufficient proficiency in the process, oftentimes because they do not have enough confidence in themselves or lack the assertiveness skills to control the team and the process.

The guidelines listed below set goals and boundaries for facilitators.

Facilitator Guidelines for Feedback

1. Control process and protect people.

2. Reinforce everything on process sheet and model appropriately.

3. Facilitator may not send or receive feedback. Facilitator must remain neutral.

4. Facilitator needs to be from outside the group. "The eye cannot see itself."

5. *Always* start with positive feedback.

6. Insist on people repeating what they heard in their own words. No one is required to give feedback, but as a member of the team he or she may not refuse feedback.

7. Keep it simple and basic—stick to the fundamentals.

8. Push for specificity of feelings, examples of behavior.

9. Do not interrupt or interpret statements. Intervene if you hear editorial statements, apologies, commitments, or violations of rules.

10. Facilitator or others may ask for clarification. (Try to limit others' need for clarification.)

11. If there are issues for problem solving, interested parties should make time for a separate meeting later. Facilitator may offer his or her services.

12. Insist on adherence to the rule of the feedback sequence and the back-to-back rule (see item 4 of the Rules for Feedback Meeting).

13. Anyone (especially the facilitator) may ask if others have concurred with the feedback or have observed the behavior described in the feedback.

14. Praise participants both for their specificity and how they give and receive feedback. Give participants feedback on how they gave feedback, focusing on the positive.

15. Stay positive and nondefensive.

16. Facilitator may allow another person to help in giving feedback if the first person is having difficulty. Keep this *very* limited.

17. If trouble occurs, just go back to the model.

Any training of facilitators must give them tools to manage the team as it learns to share feedback within the new human infrastructure. Here is one other technique that is extremely useful in formal feedback sessions, and in any other meeting where honesty is a key element:

The Honesty Check

1. Give everyone a card or piece of paper.

2. Have them draw a line vertically down the middle.

3. Ask them to answer this question on the left-hand side: On a scale of 1 to 10 (most honest), "How honest was I with the team in this feedback session?"

4. Ask them to answer this question on the right-hand side: On a scale of 1 to 10 (most honest), "How honest do you believe other team members were with the team today?"

5. Have them pass the cards or papers in to you without their name or any identification.

6. Tabulate the answers to each question and write the average scores down on a flip chart or whiteboard.

7. If there is a discrepancy between the two averages—for example, the average for personal honesty is 8.9 but the average for team honesty is only 6.5—lead a discussion of reasons why the team may be reluctant to be direct and honest with one another.

In the beginning, there will be resistance to the Honesty Check, just as there is likely to be toward the entire CRAY system. Facilitators will generally get answers like:

We already are honest with each other.

We talk out our differences before we come to the meeting.

We don't think it is right to say things in front of the whole team.

Answering these questions and concerns is indicative of the role of the facilitator in making the CRAY system yield the feedback for which it was designed. Again, the focus for the facilitator is *always* on the process, not the content. If the facilitator is able to protect the integrity of the process, the content will flow from the team members. As they begin to see the results, questions and concerns will diminish.

When completing the Honesty Check, it is a good time for the facilitator to ask the group if it is aware of any aboutism in the team. If so, ask what leads people to engage in aboutism? Look for answers to the direct questions—without interpretation or commentary. Then, let it go and do the Honesty Check again each time.

As mentioned earlier, the CRAY system is not the only one which can be used to generate the performance feedback required of successful self-managed organizations. Which system used is not crucial; that there be a consistent and comprehensive system in place is. The use of such a feedback system is a crucial example of how the new human infrastructure becomes woven into the fabric of team-based organizations.

How to Receive Feedback

The CRAY system provides a structured feedback process. Part of what makes this process so necessary is the poor feedback skills found in most organizations. The rules and guidelines that structure the giving of feedback as people learn to hone their skills were discussed above. But learning to receive feedback is equally important. Developed by Dennis and Dianne LaMountain, the empowering notion that there is a definite role for receivers makes feedback more meaningful. What began as the LaMountains' groundbreaking program titled "How to Receive a Performance Appraisal" has been applied to empowerment and team-building structures nationally and internationally. Here, too, is another opportunity to build the new human infrastructure. The traditional model is for appraisals to be done *by* managers *to* employees. Even in receiving feedback, the new structures must support notions of responsibility, accountability, and true employee empowerment. Therefore, we end the chapter with a set of guidelines on how to receive feedback:

1. *Feedback is a gift.* Consider feedback a gift, requiring effort and commitment from the giver.

2. *Giving feedback requires risk.* Acknowledge the message and the messenger.

3. *Perception is reality.* You must accept the impact of your behavior as someone else's reality. You do not have to agree with it..

4. *Intent versus impact.* Be curious about your impact, not defensive about your intent.

5. *Look for the "germ of truth."* Adopt a "What can I learn from this feedback?" posture. Look for the developmental potential for you in the feedback. Ask questions for clarification and understanding, not to challenge, justify, or prove.

6. *Repeat the feedback.* Paraphrase to verify what you hear.

7. *Clarify for understanding.* Make sure you understand what is being said, versus assuming you know what they mean.

8. *Keep perspective.* Positive or improvement feedback relates to one aspect of your behavior, not your worth as a total person.

9. *Assume good intent.* Assume the giver is well intentioned, even if he or she has difficulty sharing the feedback.

10. *Separate consideration from action.* Take time to think about it. Consider all feedback.

11. *You are responsible for you.* You decide how much you can take in, at what rate, and what, if anything, you will do with the information.

12. *First impressions are valid.* Do not dismiss first impression feedback from newer people. It is their impression of you and represents some data you would otherwise not have.

14
Hazards of Teams

Misuse of the Process

The single largest threat to the team process is management. The same executives who can begin the process can subvert it. Teams can disempower people if the process is abused. When management goes about the transition to teams in bad faith, not only will it not work, but the experience will make the process of employee empowerment many times more difficult in the future. As the saying goes, "Once burned, twice shy." Employees have a long memory for management misfires and do not like being used as guinea pigs.

It has taken until this point in the book to fully describe the process of restructuring an organization to self-managed teams. The commitment of time, training, and effort has been elucidated. But getting the process from the page to real organizational life is a process fraught with challenges; if management's commitment is less than 100 percent, the hazards are more than likely to overshadow the benefits. Companies have begun the process only to see it flourish briefly, then fall into disarray. More often than not, this failure is the result of management's misuse of teams. Here are two examples from the experience of one of the authors (Darrel Ray) which illustrate the major management threats from misuse of the team-based system. The names of the corporations involved are not used, to protect them and the authors.

The first example comes from a division of one of America's largest companies. Here, management made three basic errors which destined it to abuse the team process from the start. First, management refused to work on team-building processes for itself. Few efforts at executive-team building were made—the managers never felt they should be a team themselves and never modeled team behavior. One manager said on several occasions: "This team stuff really works on the line, but we already are a team on the management level and don't need most of this stuff." That message was transferred to the balance of the organization as efficiently as any of the explicit training and official communications.

Second, management decided it could guide the process without a Steering Committee because the company had such a strong history of employee involvement. While it is true that the tradition of employee participation was embedded in this corporate culture, this in no way obviated the need for a specific group to drive the process. Without the Steering Committee to represent the various voices of the organization, some crucial information was always left to chance and left out.

Third, management was very slow to put a compensation system in place. When it finally was developed, like every other management action in the process, it was driven from the top down with no employee input. Collectively, these three errors made the failure of true teams inevitable, although it was not immediate.

In fact, management began the process well enough. For the first 18 months, productivity gains of 40 percent or more were seen. The early productivity success lulled the management into thinking it was on the right track. Closer to the truth is that there just had not been enough time for the flaws in the process to yield repercussions. But soon "management creep" set in. The pattern had been set from the outset, and management continued to direct the process, rather than implement. Management began trying to micromanage the process with little employee input. Results continued to climb for the next year. But—a harbinger of things to come—employee turnover also went to all-time highs.

This concern was raised to management in this second year, when author Darrel Ray was brought in as a consultant. Management had an explanation for the high turnover: the labor pool was poor, and while the pay scale was low, executives felt that the bonus system was adequate to keep good people. But as turnover began to rise, so too did predictable problems in quality control.

Management had a vast array of excuses for the problems it was beginning to face with respect to quality and turnover. Never was management able to face itself and identify itself as a major part of the problem. (In hindsight, the outcome might have been better if management had been confronted more forcefully and if a fully functional Steering Committee had been insisted on. It is such experiences that teach consultants to be tough on clients for the clients' own good, regardless of their reactions.)

From an outsider's point of view, the organization had a high degree of employee involvement, especially when compared to most other contemporary organizations. But on closer analysis, it was clear that all involvement was very closely managed. Many problems and issues were identified and resolved with the employee involvement program, but a high level of control from above left workers feeling less than empowered. As time passed, the teams began to wither. Employees became cynical. Their prevailing view: "We give them a 40 percent productivity gain and they want 40 percent more next year, without a dime more in pay!"

Over the course of four years, management took everything the teams gave and demanded even more without addressing the compensation problems. Management had never established communication opportunities through a Steering Committee or by allowing teams to succeed and fail on their own without micromanagement. The executives were operating without accurate information on what was happening to employees under the team-based structure. Although the job descriptions made it appear that they were offering jobs at market rate, in fact the demands of the job, along with the expected skill development, left the job underrated. As turnover increased, training costs for the high skills required increased dramatically. Management put extreme pressure on the teams to produce and began a "weeding out" process that was based on an individualized bonus system. The bonus system measured individual productivity with little or no emphasis on teamwork or quality. While management preached quality, it pushed the teams to speed up at the expense of customer satisfaction. Teams were encouraged to push people who took too much time with customers in order to put a greater emphasis on productivity. The net result was a drop in customer satisfaction and an increase in productivity.

Many of the customer-oriented employees began to leave, while production-oriented people got faster and faster. When management finally identified the low level of customer satisfaction, it tried once again to micromanage the process by decreasing pressure on productivity and focusing on quality. Production went down and quality did not improve as much as hoped. Examination of this company's four-year effort shows a clear pattern of management-driven employee empowerment. This level of empowerment is surely beyond that in many top-down and traditional companies. It is a better place to work than many, and has both good productivity and quality. What it does not have is high-performing, self-directed teams. The teams have fallen back to a level of development which is, at best, half of what they could achieve with full management commitment to empowerment. The results, in terms of customer satisfaction and productivity, have been purchased at a high price in stress and employee dissatisfaction, as the huge increase in turnover indicates.

Over the course of the four years there was some stirring for unionization. Of course, the company strongly discourages this, and may successfully hold off unionization. Nevertheless, the lack of employee involvement creates a need for management to micromanage; and it rarely meets employee needs. It is often not able to see or hear about problems until they are out of control. If a union were to come in, it could likely be a good thing for both the employees and the company, if handled correctly. The union would be able to enforce the missing employee involvement component of the transition to true teams. This company's commitment to participative management has always been strong. It does an admirable job of using the old participative management principles. But it does do a poor job of using self-management principles. Management simply cannot let go enough to let people plan, control, and do their own work.

The second example of management misuse of teams comes from a manufacturing company. This manufacturer had many of the problems described above, with some additional and instructive twists. Although the company was traditional, top-down, and bureaucratic, it had resolved to make its new plant a showcase, complete with self-directed teams from the day it first opened. With the help of an aggressive and insightful human resources manager, the process took off quite well. Everything worked like a charm for about eighteen months as this new plant became one of the most productive and profitable of its kind in the country. The employees did an outstanding job of producing, but during the development phase management did not come to a single training session. The local management's lack of knowledge of the process and commitment to it could only lead to management creep. As teams made mistakes or fell below production or quality goals, management would step in and micromanage. Executives were happy to let teams alone and do no micromanagement, as long as teams produced. But when production fell short, either due to lack of knowledge or training, management refused to teach them. In fact, management refused to put any significant money into training, other than what it paid its internal trainers. These trainers had little knowledge or skill in training or quality processes and could not fill the void left by management's ignorance and reluctance to involve itself in the team process.

An early sign of management's lack of commitment was the approach it took on state-funded training. When the plant first opened, the state had money available to train employees of new businesses which relocated in the state. The company took all available state funds without having to match funds. When the funds ran out, training stopped. Management in the first example was unwilling to relinquish control. In this case, management was unwilling to commit its own time or to commit sufficient company resources to training.

One of the strong forces which drove high productivity in the beginning was a progressive gainsharing program. In the first 18 months, when productivity gains were putting the new plant ahead of the existing ones, the program showed significant achievement. The fact that the plant was a new one and that it opened with teams in place allowed management a grace period. As there was no transition from some other system in the plant, employees were able to produce from day one in teams. The fact that teams were not getting adequate training or management attention was not as visible as it might have been in an existing environment.

Because of management's lack of attention to team details, proper adjustments were not made to the gainsharing system. No employee involvement was allowed in its design or redesign. The death knell came when the whole company had a bad year and decided to force a 10 percent takeback on all employees throughout the company. Even though this particular plant continued to have high productivity, the corporate mandate was followed.

Other things happened to further weaken the team approach. Shortly after the takeback, the plant manager was transferred and a highly resistant and authoritarian manager was put in his place. Needless to say, the teams virtually disappeared. The total lack of employee involvement in any phase of the ongoing team process led to the successful start-up going very sour. Employee satisfaction has been low for more than two years, and productivity and quality efforts are seen as management's problems, not employee issues. Efforts to get management at any level of the company to learn the principles of self-management have been futile. The two management champions of self-directed teams have left the company in frustration.

Management must decide from the outset either to fully support the team-based organization or remain in a different structure. These examples of less than total commitment to the process demonstrate how the process can wither and die. Just as one cannot be "a little bit pregnant," self-managed teams must be given *all* the human infrastructure sustenance they require. There will always be demands and difficulties—but if the teams are supported, there will be ways to deal with each challenge.

Bureaucratic Resistance

There are three special organizational realms which can impact self-direction in many companies, even where there is strong commitment at the top: human resources, finance, and labor relations. Each of these realms has major concerns with the team concept. And while they were originally developed as support activities for the business, they generally have taken on a very independent life of their own. These groups have entrenched territorial interests and often have put many self-serving policies in place which do anything but serve their internal customers. Rather, they have become bureaucracies which will always do one thing first: protect their turf from any erosion.

By nature, these management departments are conservative and risk-averse. They have a great deal of difficulty with global change because it directly impacts many of the systems they have spent years developing. CEOs and organizational heads often have more difficulty with one or more of these groups than with the rest of the organization combined in implementing the team concept. As one CEO put it: "They can find seventeen reasons to Sunday to avoid giving the teams what they need to function; then they want to blame the teams when things don't go right."

Where there are supportive managers in these areas, they have facilitated the team process, making it more effective and quicker to accomplish. When these internal bureaucracies are populated by unsupportive managers, they have impeded the process through inactivity, ineffectiveness, and even hostility.

Of these three areas, the most important is human resources. When this group understands and supports the process, it can greatly speed the development of the entire organization. At Bell Atlantic, for example, the strategy for moving to self-directed work teams was developed in the Human Resources Department, which has lent strong support throughout the implementation. Human resources must be in close contact with the teams and quick to name task force groups to examine human resource problems and develop solutions. Human resources will see need for changes in hiring, compensation, attendance, grievance, and leave policies, among many others. The conflict management and communication skills of human resource professionals will be valuable assets to the teams as they develop. Their systems understanding and policy development skills will be valuable to the Steering Committee. To sum up, if human resources can take the skills and talents it has and turn them toward the transition to true teams, the process will be greatly enhanced.

Finance is traditionally among the most conservative aspects of the corporate world. The team concept impacts many of the systems over which finance has had tight control. Purchasing, payroll, inventory control, financial reporting, capital improvements, and information systems all can be impacted by the implementation of teams. Strong, innovative leadership in this area can also create systems which enhance the effectiveness of the teams. Teams need reporting systems which give them information on their performance in a timely manner. This means access to financial data, inventory data, budgets, production figures, and information configurations no one has ever asked for—or even thought of yet. All this boils down to a need for change in the accounting and financial systems to make them both customer-friendly and team-friendly. Most reporting structures are focused on satisfying upper managers and corporate headquarters. In the future, these structures must be realigned to serve their internal customers so that they can serve customers better.

Labor relations is the third area with a strong impact on the team process. This can be among the most entrenched enclaves in any organization. By custom and tradition, labor relations personnel have been trained in some very negative approaches to employee relations—if not in their actual schooling, then in the practice of "union prevention," and other endeavors which attempt to control line employees' work life. They are paid to be wary, conservative. They have difficulty going beyond legal strictures into the goal-driven mentality. In conversations with labor relations representatives over the last decade, those who have admitted to being progressive also say they pay a dear price for it. If they support an innovative approach and it does not work, they often bear the brunt of the legal work. They see their job as a thankless one—one in which prevention of harm is their major concern. Like union officials, labor relations personnel are all too often involved in "putting out fires" rather than building bridges.

Just as bureaucratic resistance is possible, support and commitment is also a likely outcome from any and all of these organizational territories. If support is displayed, it should be nurtured, recognized, and appreciated. The way to deal most effectively with these three areas and the possible bureaucratic backlash they represent is education and involvement. Especially for those who will want to "close ranks," "circle the wagons," and take all manner of defensive action, education and involvement are the best offense.

What works for the teams will work for all parts of the organization, no matter how entrenched. All voices must be listened to and encouraged; then teams can succeed. These three areas are voices which have traditionally been listened to in deciding how the organization will run. They are represented by leaders who have had a say. They will still have something of value to say in a self-managed organization. As roles change—as who speaks, how they speak, and what they say change—everyone must be shown how their voices will be heard and their concerns addressed.

Compensation and Teams

One crucial area where voices are raised and concerns expressed is that of compensation. It is incumbent upon management in cooperation with labor and the Steering Committee to get to work on a new team-based compensation system as soon as planning for self-directed work teams begins. The process of changing the compensation system may take as long as three years, especially in a unionized organization where contract cycles must be respected.

Old, individualistic compensation systems will begin to drag the process of transformation down within a year to eighteen months after start-up. Unless management is prepared to implement the new system before that time, a dramatic retrenchment is predictable. When teams see the increase in quality and productivity resulting from their work, it does not take long for them to wonder when this will increase their bottom line, not just the organization's.

Teaming up is a group partnership where all parties must feel they benefit materially. Management can no longer keep the work force in the dark about financial issues and expect it to continue producing. People soon begin to feel manipulated and exploited by management, and the whole mistrust cycle begins again. Compensation is one of the cornerstones of teamwork, and compensation issues merit a much more extensive discussion than the purposes of this book allow. For two good book-length treatments of the subject, see the Bibliography, under "Compensation Issues."

Performance follows rewards, and most compensation systems reward exactly the wrong behaviors. If individual performance is rewarded, that is what will be given. For the team transition to succeed, compensation must reward cooperative behavior. If the compensation system is not redesigned to accomplish this, then the team concept will die within a year or two. The change to a team-based organization will not work unless team members are in some way evaluated on how well the team performs. Companies who continue with the old individual performance evaluations while trying to implement a team will inevitably fail.

The old compensation systems pit individuals against one another. People tend to think, "There is only a limited amount in the bonus pie and I intend to get my share or more by outperforming my coworker." The evidence is plentiful that traditional compensation systems *do not* enhance performance in the majority of employees. This is equally true of traditional profit-sharing systems. There is no evidence that profit sharing has any positive impact on behavior. The reward is too far removed from the behavior. General Motors had a profit-sharing system in place for decades with no appreciable effect on performance.

Saturn Corporation (GM's new company), on the other hand, has a very progressive team-based compensation system which has had obvious results.

There is no question that traditional systems also create internal conflict and competition. This saps the organization of much of its energy. It is ironic that the very system which is supposed to enhance performance is the root of many morale and performance problems in organizations. Traditional compensation systems are based on very flawed theories of human motivation and are generally poorly designed as well. Most systems have absolutely no compensation for group-related behaviors or for meeting team performance goals. Instead, the highest performer is given the highest raise, even if that person stepped on everyone else to get there.

Besides rewarding individuals at the expense of the group, most compensation systems reward longevity over performance. A five-year employee who performs far better than a ten-year employee will still earn less. This focus on criteria not related to performance is a costly error. If longevity is to be rewarded, there are better ways to reward it than simply giving a raise every year. The practice of rewarding seniority also has the effect of demoralizing the rest of the work force. When the senior workers are the best paid and are also the poorest role models for new employees, the compensation system actually undermines organizational effectiveness. People have no incentive for cooperating with their teams, and often actively undermine team efforts, until their compensation is clearly tied to the team's performance.

The companies discussed in this book as examples of team-based organizations have nontraditional compensation systems. No two are exactly alike, but all reward group cooperation first and individual performance second. It matters little how well one person performs if in the process he or she undermines the group. If one person performs at 100 percent while the rest of the group performs at 50 percent, the group will always be outproduced by a team which collectively performs at 80 percent. Group performance is the most important component. Leonard Bernstein needed the orchestra to succeed as a conductor. Great as Joe Montana is, he still required a superb team to win four Super Bowls. While star performers are good, in organizations, a consistently high-performing team is much more desirable. A team can serve a customer in ways that no individual can. The compensation system is the basis for consistent high team performance.

Here are brief views of the compensation systems of the three organizations whose transitions to teams we've been discussing throughout the book:

Over the years, Wolferman's has modified the compensation system to reward its emerging teams. Wolferman's has a sophisticated "team sharing" system which gives teams a payout against a preset "plan." There are three levels of "plan," with a different payout at each level. This system is homegrown but works well for Wolferman's.

Standard Motor Products has a more traditional gainsharing system which rewards teams for improvements against a three-year rolling average for such things as safety, quality, and productivity. In the first year under the new compensation system, most employees received around 7 to 10 percent in gainsharing above their base pay.

South Central Counseling has a system based on measures related directly to the bottom line. The result has been an organization which saved $60,000 on a $2 million budget the first year. The second year, the savings was $160,000. While other mental health centers were downsizing or reducing budgets, South Central was able to give a $2000 bonus to most full-time employees. The notion of any bonus, much less one as substantial as this, is astounding in social service agencies.

Examples are helpful, but like so much of this process, compensation must be organization-specific. Compensation redesign must be undertaken, and there must be people involved who know about team-based benefits. If the organization looks outside itself, the compensation consultant must be knowledgeable about nontraditional systems, especially gainsharing. A word of caution: The large compensation consulting firms seem to be very short of experience in nontraditional systems. They tend to have their own system based upon traditional notions of compensation. As in hiring all consultants, talk with other companies with whom they have worked. Be sure they know how to design group-based compensation systems.

Storming and Troubleshooting

Chapter 11 began by detailing the four stages teams experience. The most hazardous of the stages is the second, "storming." As each team develops it will go from the first stage, "forming," through a "storming" phase in which there is arguing and bickering. Power and control issues will become paramount, and teams may even have difficulty functioning. The team developers are critical during this period, since they are most in touch with the teams and can help them stay focused on goals and new skill development. Management has a hard time knowing how to behave. The temptation is for the upper levels to jump in and "solve the problems," but such intervention teaches a dangerous and destructive lesson to teams. They soon learn to become helpless, so that management will continue to intervene and rescue them and the teams will have someone else to blame for the next set of problems. Once teams fall into this "dependency trap," their death knell has been rung. Management must remain "out of the fray" and refrain from making decisions for the teams. Management needs to concentrate its efforts on facilitating and teaching systematic problem-solving skills and insisting on teams setting goals and objectives by which they are measured.

Just as individual teams go through storming, the entire organization will also experience this stage, with all its hazards. Six to twelve months into the team process, the organization will begin experiencing difficulties. Organizationwide power and control issues will be acted out in grievances, complaints, cries to go back to the old ways, reluctance to cross-train or learn new skills—all the signs of frustration brought on by dealing with a new way of working. It is important for management to have good diagnostic skills, or a reliable outside consultant who can give guidance in how to work through this period.

Below is a two-part troubleshooting guide to help in maintaining team strength through this period. Asking the questions on the checklist for a given team, or for the organization, will help in pinpointing specific actions to take. A list of more general guidelines follows the checklist.

Troubleshooting Checklist

Questions for Management or the Steering Committee to Ask Itself:

1. Have the cross-training plans been developed and implemented for every team?

2. Have the trainers or team developers implemented the mini-courses for the team roles?

3. Has training in quality tools begun? Are team developers expected to teach and reinforce these skills in regular team meetings and problem-solving sessions? What evidence is there that they are using these skills effectively as well as teaching them?

4. Has the Steering Committee created a viable method of communicating its decisions and discussions to the entire organization?

5. Is the management team functioning as a team? Has it had a feedback session in the last month? Are members of the management

team being honest with each other? Are the management team's goals visible to the entire organization and reviewed with the teams?

Questions for the Teams or Team Developers to Ask Themselves:

1. Has the team had a formal problem-solving session where problem-solving skills were used by a trained facilitator?

2. Are the team's charts, measures, and goals clearly established and are the charts up to date and visible to all on the team? Are they discussed at each team meeting?

3. Has the issue been brought up in the monthly team developer meeting to get ideas on how to develop the team past this problem or stage?

4. Is the team following and enforcing its own code of conduct?

5. Have the team developers been too involved or directive in the team meetings?

6. Has the team developer placed himself on the agenda of the meeting one to two times in the last month to conduct some kind of team-building activity or game, or teach a business principle?

7. Is the team leader, or other appropriate person, attending management meetings with the developer, or in her place?

8. Are new tasks being delegated to the team as well as teaching it how to do the task?

9. Has the team had a feedback meeting in the last month? Was the honesty check above 8? Is there ongoing aboutism in the team?

10. Are the team wheel roles being followed?

11. Is the cross-training plan being followed?

12. Is the cheerleader/recognizer finding ways to recognize team members?

13. Have developers led a brief discussion after the team meeting on how the meeting was conducted?

14. Are developers coaching the team leaders immediately after the meetings to help them improve their meeting skills?

Some Practical Guides to Stay the Course

- Use the system and the system will create the profits and prosperity desired. If something goes wrong, try first to find out what part of the system may be missing or misused.

- Top managers, keep in close touch with the Steering Committee, and hold them accountable for auditing and holding teams accountable.

- Work closely with the Steering Committee, team developers, and the teams to set clear and understandable goals for the organization.

- Train the team developers very well and expect them to be the leaders in the learning organization. A team developer who cannot train others in skills and business knowledge will weigh the system down.

- Begin work on a redesigned compensation system as soon as possible. Get expert guidance on this matter, since it is full of minefields. An antiquated compensation system will be the teams' worst enemy after about eighteen months. It is best to roll out compensation changes before too much time passes.

- Don't get hung up on perfection. No one knows what an organization will look like in three years. Waiting for the perfect time or conditions usually means never starting. The time to start is now, so that self-managed teams will be strong and vital masters of their fate, not easily buffeted by the winds of economic change.

- This book is only a beginning. It has the basics, but there is much more. Read constantly and expect all other managers and team developers to read. Professionals read and learn constantly; anything less leads to mediocre leadership.

There are many hazards along the road to self-direction. There will be backlashes against teams. Problems will largely be a result of violation of fundamental principles. It is possible to start learning from the mistakes of the past. Teams work! The future of teams will be in higher levels of sophistication in the new human infrastructure.

Overuse of the term *team* remains a hazard to the concept itself. So many companies use the term loosely, but really only have Level I work groups (leader centered/leader focused). Failing to clearly define the team process leads to misappropriation and misapplication of the concept. Only harm and ill will can come from this. Accuracy and integrity require that a team be called a team, and a work group a work group. If a company wants better work groups, there are many ways to improve group efficiency. But avoid calling them *teams*—they are not. Whatever structural choice an organization makes, it must be clear about its own definitions. The clearer the definition of teams the more effective they are likely to be.

The Second Transition

Once the team process is in place, there is an inevitable change in management—sooner or later. The time when this change occurs can be the most dangerous one for the team process. If forces unfamiliar with the team process are responsible for replacing the original manager, the team structure can be placed in real danger.

Most managers think themselves team players who know the team process. In practice, there are almost no managers who have the familiarity and knowledge required to continue the process after the originating manager has left. In the vast majority of cases, the manager at the vice president level who has been in charge of a transition is promoted after implementing the team process. The main fear of team members at this point is that corporate management will step in and promote someone, regardless of his or her knowledge or understanding of the new team process and new human infrastructure. Where promotions occur among candidates who are very familiar with the process, the transition to new management is successful. In the case of a manager who is not knowledgeable being promoted, it can take less than six months for chaos to break out. The team process and traditional systems mix like oil and water. The old and new human infrastructures are not compatible. Grave consequences will come to the team process if a poorly trained manager, especially one who is hostile or unwilling to learn, comes to head it.

Tony Leonardi was the founder of the team process at Wolferman's. When he received a promotion from Kansas City to the Sara Lee Bakery Headquarters in Chicago, the one candidate who was intimately familiar with the process, Jack Padovano, was promoted to vice president. The decision has proven to be a wise one, as Wolferman's results showed in Padovano's first 18 months. His proven track record with the Wolferman's marketing team made him very well qualified to lead the entire Wolferman's team. He had already proven his capability as a team developer as well as a team manager. Since his promotion to Leonardi's former position, the company has continued to show record profits as well as posting significant decreases in waste and accidents. Jack is the master team developer for Wolferman's, as well as its vice president.

There is a major difference between a manager who has read the books and one who has lived in the process. That should be a major consideration in making the selection. When a manager with little true knowledge of teams enters a position of critical authority over the team process, the result can be disaster. This person can disrupt the process extremely quickly while at the same time honestly believing they are only doing what is right. The change in style and thinking is so vast as to be unfathomable to the uninitiated, to those who have not lived through the process of making this transition. The new manager will not even have a clue that she or he is disrupting the system, while all the time believing the system is itself poorly organized.

Once the team system is in place, it is actually easier to manage than a more traditional system and certainly gets better results. But it must be respected as a whole system. The system does not work if its integrity is compromised by attempts to manage it in a traditional way.

15
Epilogue: The Future of Teams

If you have read this far you must be pretty serious about the process.

In trying to put down on paper years of experience with hundreds of teams, we still leave out more than we say. There are hundreds of details which can make or break a project. Our best efforts cannot begin to tell the many things which create a successful company built on empowered teams. This closing chapter tries to point out some key ingredients and ideas which will help you stay focused and move toward our vision of the future.

When we began working with the self-directed-team concept, it all seemed very simple. But with more experience it became more complex. What seemed like a simple group and interpersonal skills exercise became an entire system. There was no way to isolate any one team or group from the rest of the organization. Employee empowerment and self-direction is a holistic approach to corporate systems. We are giving an organ transplant to save the patient's life, but that requires major adjustments by the entire body.

From the point of view of the consultant, it is an undisputed fact that this system, when implemented correctly, yields unqualified results. Profits improve, grievances decline, quality increases, employees take pride in satisfying the customer and serving each other. From the organizational psychologist's viewpoint, the workplace can be envisioned as a learning environment where the skills of tomorrow are being learned today. It is a vision of joint commitment between labor and management to one another's well-being and prosperity, in a workplace where suspicion of one group by another is eliminated through unqualified sharing of information. This vision entails a workplace where mutual survival is assured through unheard of levels of cooperation; where there is a focus on mutually beneficial goals; an environment where shared information magnifies the power of everyone. It is a place where the web of communication and relationships allows influence and information to flow instantly to the most advantageous place for the organization; an environment in which prosperity can be achieved by everyone who is committed, though not guaranteed to anyone.

While we may never see an organization which has fully achieved this vision, many are approaching it. These organizations have their problems and successes. Like any pioneers, they show great resilience, as well as having their doubts at times. As organizations gain experience with self-directed teams, they often begin having positive effects on their environment. Suppliers are expected to work more closely and often directly with teams. As we will see later in this chapter, other institutions like a hospital, nursing homes, and a pharmacy were positively impacted when one small medical practice was reorganized as a team. Government systems will be impacted, as we have seen from the example of South Central Counseling in Nebraska; there, other regional centers and the state's Department of Social Services have elevated their own level of care and service in response to South Central's vast improvements.

While a single team does not tend to spread into an organization, a whole organization's team approach can spread, to a limited degree, into other systems. The teamed-up organization is like "good bacteria," spreading to other systems and making them healthier. In the future, we will see more and more positive influences of well-designed team systems. Organizations like the Aid Association for Lutherans Insurance, GM's Saturn, Wolferman's, and the Gaines dog food manufacturing operation have caused many in their industries to take notice and find ways to improve. The sooner a company begins, the better prepared it will be to lead into the future, rather than try and catch up.

The Future of Employee Empowerment

We would like to discuss here some issues which will impact the effectiveness of employee empowerment in the future, and to offer suggestions for action on several levels.

Education

Our educational system is a popular whipping boy for societal dilemmas. It is also a powerful tool for transformation. While self-directed teams are effective in the workplace, elements of the team concept work equally as well in school. Beginning in elementary school, children should be taught the skills of cooperative learning. Concepts like that of "learning cells," where pairs of students learn and prepare for tests together, have proven to be equal or superior to traditional individualized learning. Most experienced teachers will testify that students make the best teachers. We need an educational system that provides more opportunities for peer education.*

Research on such techniques goes back into the 1950s. They are not new. But they are neither reinforced by administrators, nor taught effectively in teacher education courses. Our cultural fixation on individual performance prevents us, as a nation, from teaching our children the art of cooperation. In teaching children to "get the grade," we miss the goal of learning and working together to excel. If more can be learned in teams or pairs, then individual grades should be deemphasized. Let us begin teaching our children how to work together early in life so that when they go to work they will work easily in teams. The value of this is seen every Friday and Saturday night when high school teams play, yet those same students who play so well as a team are rarely encouraged to learn together as a team. Teamwork is such an important part of our sports curriculum. Why is it not a part of the academic curriculum as well?

Working within the educational system—whether primary, secondary, or postsecondary—one finds intractable institutional resistance to the team concept, cooperative learning, and even employee empowerment. If the model is not practiced in our educational system, then the burden falls to employers to retrain or untrain employees so that they can become true team members. Our educational system does a grave injustice to the next generation of leadership. To be competitive, America will need leaders with far more sophisticated tools and interpersonal skills.

Higher Education in Management

It is appalling that, as late as 1990, most major management schools had no serious courses on employee empowerment and teamwork in the workplace. Management schools are generally twenty years behind

---

*For a professional educator's views on these topics, see M. L. Goldschmid, "The Learning Cell: An Instructional Innovation," *Learning and Development*, 1971, 2(5):1–6; B. Goldschmid and M. L. Goldschmid, "Peer Teaching in Higher Education: A Review," *Higher Education*, 1976, 5:9–33.

in teaching cooperative team-based skills. In *Fortune* 500 companies, it is possible to encounter dozens of would-be managers fresh out of MBA programs whose preparation for employee empowerment is virtually nonexistent. Consultants in team processes find that their biggest job is to help these MBA graduates unlearn much of what they learned about human motivation in graduate school. These new managers have read the right books and say the right words, but their behavior can be very disempowering. We need to create a graduate curriculum which trains these young professionals in how to empower people. The real message of management schools seems to be ambition at any cost. The goal taught seems to be: *Get on the fast track and stay there without regard to people skills.* This type of behavior has been strongly rewarded in corporate America in the past, but it does not fly in a self-directed team environment. To get the kind of commitment and productivity teams can offer, organizations must be careful about the types of new managers hired. If managers are expected from the start to show exceptional interpersonal and group skills, then most likely they will.

Meanwhile, most of today's business graduates have no clue about human motivation and group dynamics. They do not understand human systems, nor do they understand the basics of quality processes and problem solving. A consultant will often hear upper managers ask: "What are they teaching if they are not teaching these skills?" It is a source of great frustration to upper management when their management recruits have little knowledge of employee empowerment and poor interpersonal skills.

When one looks at the major graduate business programs, here is what one sees: academic territories, infighting, and highly individualistic approaches to teaching. The question must be asked: "How can this type of institution possibly prepare empowered managers?" Most graduate schools of management are the bulwark of old fashioned, top-down management by executive fiat. And the kinds of infighting and territorial battles seen in major graduate schools are poor models for anyone seeking to learn how to manage effectively. This is equally true of schools of engineering, medicine, and other institutions preparing professionals—the ranks of future managers.

Two Special Cases: Health Care and Government

Besides education, there are two other areas of our society having exceptional difficulty adapting to the new business environment and accepting concepts of employee empowerment. These are our health care system and government systems in general. Here, the public should sound the alarm. Education, health care, and government comprise a large portion of America's gross domestic product and command a large share of our resources. Major positive changes in each of these would have a multiplicative effect on much of the economy.

Health Care

In a small medical practice in Iola, Kansas, two physicians, Brian Wolfe and Glenn Singer, decided to structure their office as a self-directed team. With a small amount of education, strong commitment on the part of the owner-physicians, and six months of development, this small-town medical practice demonstrated large improvements. This transition in work structure began having major effects on other systems, including the local hospital, the pharmacy, and the nursing home. The physicians empowered their team to solve ongoing challenges faced by most medical offices: problems of phone coverage, interruptions of the front office, patient scheduling, and cooperation with hospitals, pharmacy, and nursing homes. They were able to work with these other entities to try new approaches which yielded immediate improvement for the doctors' own practice and also had strong positive effects in the other areas. After two years the team has solved previously intractable problems in record storage and retrieval, communications management, office versus nursing, and a host of issues around patient scheduling, billing, and payments.

The team now hires and disciplines its own members, provides performance feedback to everyone including the physicians, schedules its own workload and vacations, and establishes task groups which tackle problems with previously unheard of sophistication and speed. This office was already so busy that the physicians rarely took on new patients, so the motivation was not to expand business. Wolfe and Singer felt they could give better patient care if their employees were empowered. And in fact, patient care has improved dramatically according to anonymous surveys. The team process freed the physicians from much of the day-to-day office management and eliminated the need for a dedicated office manager. This is how Wolfe describes his current work environment:

> We do a better quality of medicine now. The patients feel we are doing better medicine too. The process has allowed us to solve problems we did not even know we had, like handoff problems between clerical and nursing staff, between clerical functions, and between the nurses and physicians. We eliminated 20 or more phone calls per day from the pharmacy and nursing home through

the team's ideas and are cooperating better with them than ever before. When we found out that medical offices needed to be in full compliance with OSHA standards, we put together a safety task force. With the task force, the team has been able to identify safety problems and OSHA issues we didn't know we had.

Glenn and I have eliminated two to three hours a week of administrative work which the team does now. It gives us some break time and allows us to serve the patients better. The reality is that with the team concept I don't put out fires anymore—the team does that. When they see an issue, they don't come complain to me, they do something about it. We have eliminated half to three-quarters of a position out of a staff of twelve, and are doing more work with better quality than ever before. Now, people are cross-trained well enough to do almost any job. If someone is sick or absent, the patient gets service that is just as good. The patient might never know we had a staffing shortage.

Now, the team looks at pricing and cost and tells us what adjustments should be made. We [the doctor-owners] used to do that. They actually do it better and save us time and money. The other day I had been thinking about a new way to computerize our patient scheduling. I brought it up in the team meeting and the team told me they had already studied the problem and had a recommendation to make. I did not even know they were aware of the problem!

Our accounts receivable went down; we cut our collection period by more than half. The team was largely responsible for that. Our profits have not changed, more because of market forces in health care. But if we had not changed to the team concept, it is likely that our profits would have taken a hit.

We realize that reorganizing a two-physician office is a far cry from teaming up a large hospital system, but the principles are the same. Where health care professionals are given authority and skills to serve the patient, the patient will be served much better. Health care is not a hopeless case, but it will require a new level of commitment to patient care and big changes in the roles of physicians, nurses, administrators, and other key players. While health care reform on a national level may be important, we believe that individual health care organizations can empower employees now, without waiting for national changes.

Government

We are least optimistic about government and education with respect to these important changes. From the viewpoint of one who has worked inside many governments and several educational institutions, as an employee, educator, or consultant, these two important parts of our society appear fundamentally disempowering to most of their employees. The web of bureaucracy and financial disincentives is so deep and strong as to make almost any effort on the part of a local manager look like career suicide. We have talked about education already; our attention turns toward government.

In his book *Liberation Management,* Tom Peters asserts that "most products and many services are actually receiving value for only .05 to 5 percent of the time they are in the value delivery systems of their companies. Reverse those figures and you have the phenomenon of 95 to 99.95 percent lost time. On average!"* In government, this is true in the extreme. The amount of value we receive for our tax dollars is pitifully small. It is easy to blame "lazy" government workers, almost any present or former government worker can speak of the incredibly inefficient and demoralizing system which forces civil service employees to "check their brains at the door" and use their creativity in the service of bureaucratic controls. Employees are beaten down and demotivated by a system which can subtly, but effectively, punish anyone for taking personal initiative. Bureaucratic government is the least trusting of all human systems. The system has checkers checking checkers piled three deep.

We have spoken of one courageous mental health director, Gary Henrie, who made major strides in providing efficient and effective service through employee empowerment at a government-funded and -regulated organization, South Central Counseling Center. It can be done. The question is not one of employee willingness or skill, but of institutional volition. The ultimate political will lies not in the administrator, the governor, or even the President of the United States; it lies with the legislative branch. Leadership of the executive branch is important, but it will change with each new administration. Only the legislature has the continuity to ensure that quality and employee empowerment initiatives have momentum from one administration to the next. In confirmation hearings, legislators should be clear about their commitment to quality and the continuation of process improvement initiatives from one administration to the next, without regard to party affiliation.

The key ingredients in the future will be a complete overhaul of the employee classification and compensation systems. The vast number of different employee classifications in most government systems has nothing to do with skills, competencies, or education. These systems are based upon 1950s notions of job classification. They prevent large numbers of employees from bringing their full talent and initiative to the process of serving citizens.

Author Darrel Ray once worked in an organization with only 120 employees which had 30 different classifications: one classification for

---

*Tom Peters, *Liberation Management,* Knopf, New York, 1992, p. 60.

every four people. Only four of the classifications called for an education-al level above high school. Many classifications only had one person. If that person was absent, the work did not get done. In terms of efficiency, this could not be better organized to waste taxpayer money. In our opin-ion, government classification and personnel systems are the most obstructionist anywhere. In the organization just mentioned, while large numbers of people had too little to do, a few were regularly overworked. Regulations prohibited one classification from doing the work of any other. The staff had a running joke: "How many maintenance people does it take to change a light bulb? Five: one to fill out the work order, one to approve the order, one to hold the light bulb, and two to turn the ladder."

Another anecdote from Ray's experience in the same organization:

> One day, much to my amusement, I walked into my office and saw five maintenance men standing around a ladder. I asked what was wrong; they replied they weren't sure they could change the ener-gy-saving light bulb in this receptacle with a regular bulb, since there were new government regulations out which specified energy-saving bulbs only. I watched them debate for 15 minutes on the con-sequences of putting in a less-efficient bulb. Eventually, they all departed, leaving the old bulb in the socket, where it stayed until a shipment of the new efficient bulbs arrived. When I asked how much these new bulbs cost, the maintenance man told me the gov-ernment paid about twice as much for them as for the regular bulbs but you could get them at Wal-Mart for only about 10 percent more.

What was the real cost of that light bulb? What would have happened if these were empowered employees? This is a system for wasting our resources, and only the legislators of this nation can really effect per-manent change.

Civil Service compensation systems are among the most antiquated in the Western world. There is rarely any direct relationship between productivity and pay. Pay is largely based on seniority and classifica-tion. Some kinds of pay for performance can, and will, work in gov-ernment; it is time to begin experimenting with new systems of com-pensation. Above all, management structures and regulations need to be seriously revised to create a teamwork-friendly environment in which to develop employee empowerment.

Much more emphasis needs to be placed on performance and skill, much less on seniority and classification. Government employee unions should be brought into the process from the very beginning, and given an important role in implementing employee empowerment systems. The taxpayers of this nation should not be asked to support an obviously inefficient system of government services. Government must be reinvented if this country is to remain in the forefront.

Government Policies and the Future

After World War II, Germany enacted a constitution which mandated very clear cooperative arrangements between labor and management. This forward thinking has served the German economic community very well. Labor and management do not view each other primarily as adversaries. The number of labor disputes is much lower than ours, yet the quality and standard of living is among the highest—and there is a higher percentage of union members than in the United States.

Labor laws in the United States are based upon the assumption that management and labor are adversarial. Legislation is designed to encourage animosity and strife. The legal system encourages an after-the-fact approach to labor problems, rather than encouraging parties to anticipate problems. Contract negotiations are the only time top management and labor actually talk together in many companies. There is no good reason for this approach. Our national laws should encourage, even mandate, forms of labor-management cooperation. Let us begin eliminating the adversarial approach and learn to work toward mutual goals which meet the needs of shareholders, workers, managers, and the community.

Legislation should address the needs of the labor force for retraining and the needs of management for skilled workers. The United States needs increased emphasis on trade schools and technical training in lieu of college for those 70 percent of students who will never go to college. Most German and Japanese children attain a two-year postsecondary equivalent education, as well as benefiting from a lifetime of continued training and retraining in the vocational education system or in company training programs. American unions and other employee groups could play a vital role in pushing for better opportunities in vocational education and retraining.

Unions often express the fear that they will be less necessary if self-directed work teams are widely implemented. The simple answer is: unless unions rethink their role in society they will find themselves having less and less impact, with or without true teams. If unions are to thrive, not just survive, they must see protection of the worker as only one part of their job. The more important role will be in fostering strong education and retraining systems. If unions want to be a vital economic player in today's economy they will find that the union which guarantees a highly trained, skilled, and motivated work force will be valued by ownership, management, and the community. A skilled and motivated work force is the best security for workers, whether or not they are represented by a union. America's historical hostility to labor is an albatross around our collective neck. Neither

Japan nor most of Europe has the aversion to unions and discussions with workers which America has shown for a hundred and thirty years. Contradictory work rules, political posturing, and traditional animosities hurt workers and managers.

Antitrust laws should be carefully restructured to allow easier cooperation between competitors where international competition provides adequate checks against monopolistic behavior. Tax laws should be revised to force corporations to tie top-management compensation directly to company performance. And national policy should encourage employee incentive programs which reward productivity.

National policy should make the worker a full partner in America's competitiveness. That means employee partnership at the highest levels of governance. When workers are represented as a full partner with ownership and management, the process of employee empowerment will be taken much more seriously. America's long romance with "shoot from the hip" management and "flavor of the month" fixes will come to an end when employees are seriously involved in the process at the highest levels.

Some of these suggestions are seen as radical in American management circles. Some managers have even called them communistic. They are neither. They are proven alternative methods of running free enterprise successfully. They are major departures from the sacred cows of management's past. American managers must realize that they cannot "go it alone" anymore. Effective, synergistic partnerships are essential for future survival. What better strategic partnership can there be than one with the very employees who work in our organizations. Our partnership with them should be our first and most important partnership. With them, anything is possible.

As we have said from the beginning, we believe our system of self-directed work teams is an effective method of creating this partnership. The twenty-first century will see technological developments far beyond today's. But it will be the human infrastructure upon which these advances will be built. The human infrastructure must be redesigned before a system for quality can take hold.

Much of what has been discussed in this book has been known in one form or another for over fifty years. The uniqueness is in its configuration and application, not in the knowledge itself. From Eric Trist's first studies in British coal mines in the late 1940s and 1950s, to the work of many researchers on groups in the 1960s and 1970s, this wisdom is not new. The challenge has been to put the intelligence to practical use in corporate and organizational settings. The jury is in and the verdict is unanimous: the team process works when it is applied appropriately.

Bibliography[†]

Team Development

An Ethnography of a Self-Directed Work Team in a Communications Company, Margaret Smith Sears, Ed.D., dissertation, University of Maryland, College Park, 1992.

*All Teams Are Not Created Equal: How Employee Empowerment Really Works, Lyman D. Ketchum and Eric Trist, Sage Publications, Thousand Oaks, CA, 1992.

Empowering Teams, Richard S. Wellings, William C. Byham, and Jeanne M. Wilson, Jossey-Bass, San Francisco, 1991.

The Adventures of a Self-Managing Team, Mark Kelly, Pfeiffer, San Diego, 1991.

Employee Involvement and Total Quality Management, Edward Lawler et al., Jossey-Bass, San Francisco, 1992.

Groups That Work (and Those That Don't): Creating Conditions for Effective Teamwork, J. Richard Hackman (ed.), Jossey-Bass, San Francisco, 1990.

How to LEAD Work Teams: Facilitation Skills, Fran Rees, Pfeiffer, San Diego, 1991.

The Schuster Report: The Proven Connection between People and Profits, Fredrick E. Schuster, Wiley, New York, 1986.

*Self-Directed Work Teams: The New American Challenge, Jack D. Orsburn et al., Irwin Professional Publishing, Burr Ridge, IL, 1990.

Succeeding as a Self-Directed Work Team: 20 Important Questions Answered, Bob Harper and Ann Harper, Croton-on-Hudson, 1989.

Self-Managing Teams: Creating and Maintaining Self-Managed Work Groups, Robert F. Hicks, Ph.D., and Diane Bone, Crisp Publications, 1990. Available from ODT, Inc., Amherst, MA.

Superior Work Teams: Building Quality and the Competitive Edge, Dennis C. Kinlaw, Pfeiffer, San Diego, 1991.

The Ten Minute Team: 10 Steps to Building High Performance Teams, Thomas Isgar, Seluera Press, Boulder, CO, 1989.

Team Building: Blueprints for Productivity and Satisfaction, W. Brendan Reddy and Kaleel Jamison (eds.), NTL Institute, 1988.

Teamwork: Involving People in Quality and Productivity Improvements, Charles A. Augrey II and Patricia K. Felkins, Qual. Resc., 1988.

[†]One asterisk indicates a highly recommended book; two asterisks indicate a good introductory book.

General Material on High Performance and Empowerment

Driving Fear Out of the Workplace, Kathleen D. Ryan and Daniel K. Oestreich, Jossey-Bass, San Francisco, 1991.

The Addictive Organization, Anne Wilson-Schaef and Diane Fassel, Harper & Row, San Francisco, 1988.

The Breakthrough Strategy: Using Short-Term Successes to Build the High Performance Organization, Robert H. Schaffer, Harper & Row, New York, 1988.

The Change Masters, Rosabeth Moss Kanter, Simon and Schuster, New York, 1983.

*The Empowered Manager: Positive Political Skills at Work, Peter Block, Jossey-Bass, San Francisco, 1987.

***The Goal: A Process of Ongoing Improvement*, Eliyahu M. Goldratt and Jeff Cox, North River Press, Great Barrington, MA, 1992.

High Involvement Management, Edward Lawler III, Jossey-Bass, San Francisco, 1988.

Influence: How and Why People Agree to Things, Robert Cialdini, Ph.D., Morrow, New York, 1984.

Liberation Management: Necessary Disorganization for the Nanosecond Nineties, Tom Peters, Knopf, New York, 1992.

The Race, Eliyahu M. Goldratt and Robert E. Fox, North River Press, Croton-on-Hudson, New York, 1986.

*One Way, John J. Nora, Plymouth Proclamation Press, Plymouth, MI, 1990.

Thriving on Chaos, Tom Peters, Harper & Row, New York, 1987.

The Ultimate Advantage, Edward Lawler III, Jossey-Bass, San Francisco, 1992.

***Zapp! The Human Lightning of Empowerment*, Wiliam C. Byham and Jeff Cox, Fawcett, New York, 1989.

Analyzing Performance and Problem-Solving

Analyzing Performance Problems: or You Really Oughta Wanna, Robert Mager and Peter Pipe, Lake Publishing, Belmont, CA, 1984.

Coaching for Improved Work Performance, Ferdinand F. Fournies, Van Nostrand Reinhold, New York, 1978.

Developing Managers through Behavior Modeling, James C. Robinson, Pfeiffer, San Diego, 1982.

Goal Analysis, Robert Mager, Lake Publishing, Belmont, CA, 1984.

*Maximum Performance Management: How to Manage and Compensate People to Meet World Competition, Joseph H. Boyett, Ph.D., and Henry P. Conn, Glenbridge Publishing, Lakewood, CO, 1988.

Solutions: A Guide to Better Problem Solving, Steven R. Phillips, Pfeiffer, San Diego, CA, 1987.

General Organizational Theory

The Fifth Discipline: The Art and Practice of the Learning Organization, Peter Senge, Doubleday, New York, 1990.

Corporate Cultures, Terrence E. Deal and Allen A. Kennedy, Addison-Wesley, Reading, MA, 1982.

The Ropes to Skip and the Ropes to Know, R. Richard Ritti and G. Ray Funkhouser, Wiley, New York, 1977.

Process Consultation: Its Role in Organization Development, Edgar H. Schein, Addison-Wesley, Reading, MA, 1969.

Process Consultation: Lessons for Managers and Consultants, vol. 2, Edgar H. Schein, Addison-Wesley, Reading, MA, 1987.

The Ultimate Advantage: Creating the High Involvement Organization, Edward E. Lawler III, Jossey-Bass, San Francisco, 1992.

Creativity and Problem Solving

Six Thinking Hats: An Essential Approach to Business Management from the Creator of Lateral Thinking, Edward De Bono, Little Brown, Boston, 1985.

Managing Differences, Daniel Dana, Ph.D., MTI Publications, 1989, distributed by ODT, Inc., Amherst, MA.

Quality Issues

The Deming Guide to Quality and Competitive Position, Gitlow and Gitlow, Prentice-Hall, Englewood Cliffs, NJ, 1987.

The Eternally Successful Organization, Philip B. Crosby, McGraw-Hill, New York, 1989.

Juran on Leadership for Quality: An Executive Handbook, J. M. Juran, The Free Press, New York, 1989.

Kaizen: The Key to Japan's Competitive Success, Masaaki Imai, McGraw-Hill, New York, 1986.

**Quality without Tears: The Art of Hassle-Free Management*, Philip B. Crosby, McGraw-Hill, New York, 1989.

Quality Is Free: The Art of Making Quality Free, Philip B. Crosby, McGraw-Hill, New York, 1989.

Service America: Doing Business in the New Economy, Karl Albrecht and Ron Zemke, Warner Books, New York, 1990.

Compensation Issues

Gainsharing & Productivity, Robert J. Doyle, American Management Association, New York, 1983.

Gainsharing, The New Path to Profits and Productivity, John Beacker, Gulf Publishing, Houston, TX, 1991.

Resources to Plan Activities to Help Teams Mature and Grow

Games Trainers Play, Edward E. Scannell and John W. Newstrom, McGraw-Hill, New York, 1983.

More Games Trainers Play, Edward E. Scannell and John W. Newstrom, McGraw-Hill, New York, 1983.

Still More Games Trainers Play, Edward E. Scannell and John W. Newstrom, McGraw-Hill, New York, 1991.

A Whack on the Side of the Head, Roger Von Oech, Ph.D., Warner Books, New York, 1990.

A Kick in the Seat of the Pants, Roger Von Oech, Ph.D., Warner Books, New York, 1986.

Index

About the Authors

DARREL RAY has been a pioneer in the development of self-directed work teams in union and non-union environments, and has consulted throughout the United States since 1978 on management development and self-directed work team building. A resident of Kansas City, Kansas, and a graduate of George Peabody College of Vanderbilt University, Dr. Ray holds a doctorate in counseling psychology.

HOWARD BRONSTEIN is president of ODT, Inc., an employee-owned consulting and publishing firm specializing in personal and organizational effectiveness through employee empowerment. Perhaps best known for its flagship program "How to Manage Your Boss," ODT serves *Fortune* 500 clients nationally from its headquarters in Amherst, Massachusetts.

CPSIA information can be obtained at www.ICGtesting.com
Printed in the USA
LVOW060246011112

305369LV00002B/7/A